Contents

Foreword   v
Lois Zachary

Preface to the Original Edition   ix

Preface   xix

The Author   xxxi

Part One: Adult Learning as Development

1   First Shards: The Search for Meaning as a Motive for Learning   3

2   Mentors, Myths, and Metamorphosis: Education as a Transformational Journey   17

3   Maps of Transformation: How Adults Change and Develop   43

Part Two: Learning as a Transformative Journey

4   The Deep and Savage Way: The Unsettling First Steps of an Educational Journey   89

5   The Dynamic of Transformation: How Learning Changes the Learner   125

6   Returning Home: Helping Adults Integrate New Insights   147

Part Three: Fostering Adult Learning

7   The Ecology of Adult Learning: Barriers and Incentives to Learning and Growth   181

8   The Yoda Factor: Guiding Adults Through
     Difficult Transitions   203
9   The Art of the Mentor: Limits and Possibilities   231
     Afterword   249
     Notes   263
     References   269
     Appendix   279
     Index   281

Foreword

In his classic work *Mentor*, Larry Daloz reminds us that "mentors are guides. They lead us along the journey of our lives. We trust them because they have been there before. They embody our hopes, cast light on the way ahead, interpret arcane signs, warn us of lurking dangers, and point out unexpected delights along the way" (p. 18). With these words I believe that Larry actually describes his own developmental journey. His rich and engaging narrative creates a mentoring hologram for us—a multidimensional laser blending of adult learning theory and practice—in which he indeed "casts light on the way ahead."

Larry Daloz knows the terrain of the adult development journey well. He has traveled many miles with adult learners, both as a teacher of adult educators and as an adult learning student and practitioner. In *Mentor*, we are privileged to travel alongside him on his personal odyssey of reflection and heartfelt yearning to understand the developmental journeys of adult learners. In effect, he becomes *our* mentor—and the consummate mentor at that—empowering us, offering up maps, and pointing out the signposts that illuminate our path through the book.

In *Mentor*, Larry makes us privy to deep and transforming conversations as he actively reflects on his own mentoring practice in a way that is both familiar and empowering to us as readers. Through a series of vignettes, we are drawn into his professional and often very profound developmental journey. His burning question, "What is my place in the growth of those I care for?" becomes our question as we search for an answer together.

I know of no one in the field who can pen a story the way Larry does. His prose is elegant, poetic, and almost magical. From the very beginning he invites us to join him, making his story our story. We are transported as he guides us through each story, and we forget for a moment that the story is part of a larger book canvas. As we walk with him, we wonder and reflect. He challenges us, supports us, and provides a vision of the possible. We share his angst, his perplexities, and his delights. He gives us maps to use as we listen to the many conversations and interactions that Larry has with himself and with his students.

You will delight in the stories. The dialogue is rich; the conversation, deep and intense. You will follow Emerald and Gladys with great anticipation, worry for Jean and Delores, and want to cheer Eric and Dave on as they each muddle through their midlife crises. You watch the relationship between Sandy and Grace (her mentor) shift as it unfolds over time.

Larry and I have known each other for over thirty years. We share a mutual passion around adult development and learning. When the first version of this book came out (under the title *Effective Teaching and Mentoring*), I was eager to read it and devoured it from start to finish. What he had to say really spoke to me because it was so thought-provoking and well grounded in reflective practice. Since that time I have reread both editions many times. Coffee stains, dog-eared pages, multicolored underlines, and sticky notes decorate the books' borders and make them stand out on my bookshelf.

Since its original publication, *Mentor* has been highly recognized as a definitive work in the field. It is widely referenced, often quoted, and regarded by many as the primary resource for understanding the dynamics and developmental pathways that lead to change in people's lives. Its publication has spawned a whole generation of research and inquiry, continuing to make a significant contribution to both adult learning and the practice of mentoring.

It is important to understand the context (what Larry calls "the circumstances, conditions, and contributing forces that affect how we connect, interact with, and learn from one another") in which *Mentor* came to be written. The context in which Larry's story is embedded is the 1980s, a time when we were just beginning to grapple with how to coherently apply what we were learning about the dynamics of adult learning. By that time we had come to the realization that most adult educators were practice-rich and theory-poor. Larry's contribution closed that gap and made theory approachable and practical. The theories he draws on lay the groundwork for much of current practice today. The genius of his work is the menu of options he offers us as he applies multiple maps—Loevinger, Perry, Fowler, Kohlberg, Kegan—to guide the journey of adult learners and the work of the adult educator.

The added value of Larry's Afterword in this new edition is pure gold—a gift of "wisdom about wisdom." His voice in the Afterword is spiritual and at times almost transcendent. This alone is worth the price of the book and clearly demonstrates why he has secured a place as a thought leader in the field of adult learning.

Lois Zachary

The Jossey-Bass
Higher and Adult Education Series

Preface to the Original Edition

Happily, it is no longer necessary to argue that colleges must pay special attention to adult learners. Plummeting enrollments of traditional-age students have made the case far more effectively than could those of us who have been in the trenches these long years. College after college has faced the choice: either reach out for these "new learners," as K. Patricia Cross (1971) called them over a dozen years ago, or hire an auctioneer. Partly as a consequence of this and partly because of broader technological, demographic, and social changes, the proportion of students above the age of twenty-five has billowed from barely a quarter to over 43 percent in the past decade alone. By the turn of the century, fully half of all students in higher education will be adult learners.

Although for younger students the campus is often the central focus of social and intellectual life, this is rarely the case with older learners who often return to school complete with jobs, spouses, children, well-developed roles in their communities, and extensive experience in both love and work. To adapt appropriately to this group, colleges have learned to offer classes in the evenings, to make degree requirements more flexible, and in some cases, to accredit off-campus courses and less formal learning experiences. Such modifications have been important, the changes necessary.

But one program's flexibility has become another's slovenliness. Along with these developments, though by no means solely because of them, have come charges of a decrease in quality, a diploma-mill mentality, grade inflation, and a general failure to achieve a definition of excellence derived from an earlier era. A fresh "educational crisis" is upon us, and words like *quality* and *excellence* buzz through media reports like flies after carrion.

Something must be done; everyone agrees about that. Critics differ only in the direction of their gaze.

For some, the quality that has fled and the excellence that is our proper legacy will be regained only when the liberal studies are returned to pride of place in the curriculum—and all those "merely applied" vocational subjects and technical studies are consigned to the shop whence they came before those meddling Progressives muddied the clarity of our Platonic vision. If only we could fill again our classrooms with ears eager to quiver at Shakespearean iambs or minds anxious to dance between Hegelian dilemmas, then we could truly call ourselves educated.

For others, education must have immediate utility. If college simply turns out graduates without salable skills, the taxpayer has no business supporting it, and the number of consumers who will squander on so impractical a dalliance the small fortune it takes nowadays is minuscule. Said my farmer neighbor recently, "Anyone dumb enough to want a Ph.D. these days ain't smart enough to get one."

Yet however vulnerable the argument between purist and pragmatist, it springs from a spurious dilemma. For quality and excellence are to be found neither in some mystical characteristic of the subject matter alone nor in the raw demands of the market but in the behavior and attitudes of the human beings who embody that tension—in the teacher and in the student. We know that the quality of learning is high when students show intellectual, emotional, and ethical growth; we know that teaching is excellent when it fosters such growth, when we have teachers who are willing to care—both *about* their subjects and *for* their students.

But it is one thing to say these things, another to do them. What do those fuzzy words *growth* and *care* really mean? How do we know them when we see them? What principles underlie excellence in advising and teaching? And how do we incorporate the elements of care into the design of our programs, the practice of our teaching, the everyday work of advising our students? The book in your hands is an effort to provide an answer to those questions in an engaging yet practical way. Using the central metaphor of a transformational journey, it combines a fresh look at the intuitive wisdom of the mentor with an informative introduction to foundational adult development theory. Lacing these with a series of vignettes and conversations with adult students, the book goes on to derive a number of principles for enriching instruction and revitalizing the advising process so that regardless of their age, the growth and development of students can take its place as the proper aim of education.

When I began teaching over twenty years ago, I quickly came to see that teaching was a good deal more than simply asking my students questions, telling them the answers, and asking the questions again. True, they had to acquire certain content, but over the years I felt with increasing urgency that if education were to make any real difference in their lives, my students had to learn how to think for themselves as well. That ability, it was obvious, did not necessarily come with the territory. But it was not until I became familiar with the idea of intellectual development—and later with the whole field of adult development theory—that I began to understand in specific and concrete ways the meaning of the word *growth*.

I first began to splice the principles I was learning into the design of a "process curriculum" for community college students. Later, as participant in a national project to apply current developmental findings to adult programs, I was able to carry out further research with a number of nontraditional students. This work convinced me of the potential that developmental theory holds for adult and continuing education. Shortly thereafter, I directed a project examining the impact of the liberal studies on the intellectual and ethical development of rural, adult learners. The results made it abundantly clear that higher education can bring about substantial changes in the lives of adults—changes I later came to understand as "transformative." But one finding stood out with particular clarity. Almost without exception, the students cited certain teachers or mentors as having been of particular importance in the changes they had made. A mentor myself in two different external degree programs, I resolved to look more closely at what good teachers and mentors actually do as they guide their charges along on their transformational journeys. With the help of a Mina Shaughnessy grant from the Fund for the Improvement of Postsecondary Education, I conducted a close look at a variety of mentor-protégé relationships over the course of several years. Out of that study, augmented now by some twenty years of direct experience in teaching and advising adult students, have emerged the principles and materials on which this work is based. The story of that study appears in the Appendix. I should note, however, that this book is primarily the story of one person's effort to see his students in a fresher, more promising way. I have tried to share with the reader what I have seen through those theoretical lenses that proved most helpful in my search, but I make no pretense of offering a comprehensive survey of current research. This is neither a textbook nor a technical manual. At the same time, it is my hope that in the pages that follow the reader will hear something familiar, something universal in the words of this tiny sample of the human family.

This book is directed to all those who seek a fuller understanding of the life changes accompanying adult learners as they go on to postsecondary education. But it does more than simply describe or dramatize those changes. It goes on to suggest how we can work more effectively with the new learners to enrich their educational experience and decrease the likelihood that they will drop out. Thus it has special value for student affairs practitioners trying to understand this new population, for graduate students in adult education, counselors and advisers helping adults returning to college, faculty facing the mature students in classes, academic administrators seeking a fresh view of their changing student body, adult and continuing educators working in all settings, adult students themselves, and finally, that growing band of practitioners who actually call themselves mentors and who are by definition committed to making an "education of care" really happen.

The primary purpose of this book is to offer new perspectives for understanding adult learners and to suggest in concrete and practical ways based on current developmental theory how we can work more effectively to improve the quality of their educational experience. At the heart of the work are the interviews and personal descriptions needed to ground the principles, concepts, and theories. For it is in the living tissue of conversations between real students and real teachers that we can best apprehend the meaning of developmental advising and instruction.

But while the perspectives may be new, teachers and learners have been going about their business in some form for nearly as long as they have been walking upright. Mentor figures appear prominently among the earliest written epics, *Gilgamesh* and *The Odyssey*. Not surprisingly, mentors abound in children's stories as well. For that reason, I have included material from the great myths as well as from children's literature. For each of us writes with his or her life the story of our species, and in those tales of transformation can be found the maps by which we guide our own lives—and the lives of those for whom we care.

Thus, while I have tried to include ample practical ideas and illustrations, the book is more than simply a how-to manual. It is an effort to encourage all of us in postsecondary education to assess our stance toward our students, to think afresh about the meaning of teaching and the part we all play in the ongoing evolution of life on this planet. Education, it asserts, is not a bunch of tricks or even a bundle of knowledge. Education is something we neither "give" nor "do" to our students. Rather, *it is a way we stand in relation to them.* The nature of that relationship is best grasped through the metaphor of a journey in which the teacher serves as guide. For that reason, the book itself is constructed as a voyage of discovery, beginning with the appearance of a few shards, questions about our mutual goals on this educational quest.

Arguing that development, continues throughout the life span and that education plays a central part in that process, the first chapter presents a vignette of a meeting between a student and myself at a roadhouse in midwinter Vermont. The conversation is about what is worth learning in our lives, and it sets the questions for the remainder of the book—questions about education, effective teaching, the teacher-student relationship, and our own search for meaning as teachers, mentors, and human beings.

Chapter Two introduces the idea of the mythic journey as a way of making sense of life's changes. Through legends and literature, it illustrates how humankind has used tales of transformational journeys to address the problem of growing both older and wiser. As master teachers, mentors are guides on such journeys, appearing in a variety of forms. Here, *The Divine Comedy* provides a model of the mentor-protégé relationship as it evolves during Dante's epic journey. The chapter includes a discussion of some principles of teaching embodied in the story and ends with a real-life journey tale.

Three detailed vignettes of conversations with adult students form the basis for Chapter Three. Each highlights a major current theory of adult development that is then described and serves as an overlay for analysis of the vignette. These theories are then used extensively throughout the remainder of the book as "maps" with which to understand the educational journey.

Chapter Four follows several teachers and their adult students on their respective journeys. As before, vignettes of actual conversations with students are interspersed with discussion of the significance of each particular experience. Initially, the journey involves a downward movement from simple "rights and wrongs" into the confusion of a multifaceted world in which authority no longer has the answers. It parallels the descent into Hell, the "deep and savage way."

It is in the "winter of our discontent" that transformation can most readily take place. Chapter Five, the central chapter, at the heart of both the journey and the book, discusses the meaning of the word *transformation* in light of developmental theory and shows how much change occurs through the confrontation of opposites, a dialectical resolution of tensions arising from the search for "the truth."

With the dissolution of former, simpler perspectives comes a need to reconstruct meaning in more complex and inclusive ways. In Chapter Six, the reader accompanies teachers and students as they grapple with new forms of "truth" and construct "reality" in new, more contextual and socially responsive ways. With this evolution, the mentor-student relationship also undergoes a change from the earlier hierarchical form to a more equal one—from "god" to "friend."

In Chapter Seven, we pull back again and look at what it is that helps or hinders personal growth. Using a lengthy case study, the chapter argues that people live in environments that alternately support and challenge development. To understand who changes and how, we must shift our focus to the *whole systems* in which people live.

How do teachers and advisers fit into all of this? Arguing that growth is best understood in the context of human relationships, Chapter Eight shows how mentors provide support, challenge, and vision for their protégés, suggesting numerous concrete ways in which teachers and advisers can strengthen their work with students. It includes a discussion of some of the pitfalls in mentoring relationships and concludes with a summary of the teacher's functions as catalyst for development.

Chapter Nine offers a final cautionary tale and discusses some of the limitations and dangers of the mentoring trade. It concludes with a summary of my own educational convictions: education as care and why mentors matter.

Although the book has emerged from the study of one-to-one relationships, it is ultimately about teaching and learning in any setting. For when the aim of education is understood to be the *development* of the whole person—rather than knowledge acquisition, for instance—the central element of good teaching becomes the provision of *care* rather than use of teaching skills or transmission of knowledge. And because care is so profoundly human an activity, it is fully within the reach of all of us. Do not be deceived that the setting and some of the episodes described in the book may appear at first to be impossibly distant from the everyday press of your own life and work. Whether you teach accounting to classes of three hundred or psychological anthropology to a seminar of six, whether you are semesterly swamped with a river of advisees or meet individually as tutor for a dozen, the material here is pertinent. For although students do indeed learn differently in groups than alone, and although it may seem that when we enter the lecture hall we are "teaching a class," always it is individuals who are learning. Each is bound to learn in a unique way. Recognizing this,

- We can listen to our students' stories, seeking to understand how their quest for education fits into the larger questions and movement of their lives;
- We can view ourselves as guides on our students' journeys, challenging them to their best, supporting them when they falter, casting light on the territory ahead;
- We can sense the whole lives of our students, recognizing how the aspirations, relationships, and values of their lives hold them in a web of forces enhancing or inhibiting their movement; and
- We can recognize the place our students have in our own lives, in our own attempts to care for ourselves as we care for others.

Developmental theory can help us to do these things. It can teach us to respect each student's uniqueness while we illuminate common questions about meaning in their lives—questions to which, regardless of subject matter, we all hold relevant answers. For the principles of an education of care are no more limited to a lone itinerant teacher in northern Vermont than are the questions that give rise to them. If we are willing to listen afresh to the words of our students, we can help them to make of their education an experience that will meet more than simply their needs to be either knowledgeable or rich. We can help them grow wiser. This book offers a way that we can begin to do that.

It sometimes seems that no one ever reads acknowledgments except the people one inadvertently left out. Still, I think I finally understand why authors write them. For the process of reaching back through the years that grew this book has been an unanticipated delight. I had forgotten how much I owe to so many. What a pleasure to remember!

To the students, of course, goes my deepest gratitude. Yours is the earth from which everything sprang, without which nothing could have grown. There is no naming all of you, but I want you to know that this book came from you, and for that I am grateful. May we never cease to hear one another.

To my fellow teachers and mentors who have so freely offered your words, experience, and wisdom and yet who go nameless, my thanks too. We are brothers and sisters in our work. I only hope this book can begin to repay the gift.

For the planting and care of the seeds, to my own teachers and mentors I also offer thanks. To Jill Mattuck Tarule, Rita Weathersby, John Griffith, Mary Belenky, Bob Kegan, and Zee Gamson, all of whom helped me not only to understand developmental theory but also to respect its place in the lives of real people, thanks. And thanks, too, to Alan Knox, who saw something in there moving and snatched a dying manuscript from the Jossey-Bassian flames, to Lynn Luckow, my editor and now friend, who conspired with Knox, to Ron Gross, whose outrageous enthusiasm kept me alive in the dark, and to the staff and outside readers at Jossey-Bass who spent so many hours poring over draft after draft of the manuscript, helping to produce a work that I have grudgingly come to acknowledge is notably improved. Pat Cross, who has encouraged me for years, has been more than gracious in her contributions. Fred Rudolph, recipient of the first tercentenary Yoda Award, has truly been a mentor's mentor. And finally I owe a special debt of gratitude to Bill Perry, who first suggested that I tape-record my meetings with students, whose work in its simplicity is so profound.

I'm not sure how one thanks the sunlight. I've a hunch that gratitude is not what it's about at all. But, my friends—Kate, Todd, and Judy Daloz, Cyrie Barnes, Bob Duggan, Alice Eichholz, Ella Farrow, Len Foote, Bill Mitchell, Joanna Noel, Sharon Parks, Lyn Sprogell—you read and listened, prodded, suffered, cajoled, and loved me long before dawn, I know that and I'm glad.

Finally, there are the gardeners, those who provided the setting and the concrete help to make it possible: Peter Smith and Myrna Miller, whose vision transformed higher education in Vermont (though it may not know it yet), Carol Stoel, Richard Hendrix, Alison Bernstein, and Leslie Hornig of FIPSE, who leave candles burning in the most unlikely places, and finally (especially!) to Louise Eldred, who listened to weeks of tapes, turning them one after another, painstakingly and brilliantly, into the printed word.

Glover, Vermont   Laurent A. Daloz
July 1986

Preface

I'm often asked how this book got started. What's its story? As with many tales, it's difficult to know just where to begin, much less whether it's worth telling. But this book had a hard birth, and its tale might be at least informative, perhaps even a minor inspiration to those who aspire to write.

I must have run into the name Mentor as a schoolboy reading some housebroken version of *The Odyssey*, but that remains in the shadows. I do know that the first time I linked the term *mentor* with education was when I was part of a small team founding the Community College of Vermont in the early 1970s. A model for us at the time, New York's Empire State College was a pioneer of nontraditional education. To distinguish them from conventional professors, the faculty were referred to as "mentors." At about the same time, Gail Sheehy's *Passages* and Daniel Levinson's *Seasons of a Man's Life* brought the term into the public eye. Mentors, it seemed, were an important part of the story of human development. People blessed with a mentor, they told us, do better in life. Meanwhile, corporations had begun to discover their importance in the work world.

But it was not until I was myself dubbed a "mentor" in Vermont's newly formed External Degree Program that I grew curious about the deeper meaning of the word. What did mentors *do* anyway? That's when I went back and reread *The Odyssey*, discovering to my delight that Mentor was in fact inhabited by Athena, the goddess of wisdom. I think that must be when I began my search for what Mentor had to teach me. It was the Old Ones, I began to realize, who knew what I needed to learn: Homer, Socrates, Dante. And before long, there I was meandering among the mists of myth and metamorphosis, in the firm grip of an ancient archetype. I found myself reading J.R.R. Tolkien, C. S. Lewis, and the Arthurian legends to my children. As it happened, *Star Wars* had burst onto the scene, and dinnertime with our children and their friends crackled with talk of Obi-Wan and Yoda, Gandalf and Merlin. By then I had begun pounding away on my trusty Smith Corona portable at the first drafts of a book about the mysteries of mentorship. When the Fund for the Improvement of Postsecondary Education announced a series of small grants for independent scholars—wasn't that what I was?—I leapt at the chance. I would study the mentor-protégé relationship in external degree programs for returning adult learners, I wrote in the proposal. On a whim, I called it "The Yoda Factor" and sent it in.

Some weeks later I got a letter back. "Sorry," it said, but no luck. Uncharacteristically, for I am quick to scuttle into a hole when rejected, I was sure there had been a mistake and wrote back requesting the readers' comments. When they came, I saw that two of the three had been very enthusiastic; one had rejected it out of hand. "That's what I get for trying to be cute," I thought, and the next year I sent the same proposal back, unchanged.

This time it hit, and for the next year I drove around Vermont interviewing students and their mentors about what they were learning and how they were changing. It was delicious work. The research brought me into contact with a range of scholars, many of whom provided me with enduring "mentoring moments," offering vital encouragement at just the right times. Ron Gross, who wrote widely and enthusiastically about independent scholars and the "new adult learner," told me, "If you want to make a mark, find something no one else knows about and become the expert." Jill Tarule and Mary Belenky, who were drafting what was to become an influential study of women's development, taught me everything I know about qualitative interviewing. Jim Fowler, Bob Kegan, and Sharon Parks served up models of human development that became the conceptual core of the book. All were writing the books that were to make them famous, and all had been influenced while at Harvard by Bill Perry, whose work in epistemological and ethical development among college students remains the most powerful intellectual gift I have ever received.

But as every student knows, it's one thing to do the research and quite another to write it up in a way that holds the truth and engages the reader. When Ernest Hemingway told interviewer George Plimpton that he had rewritten the ending to *A Farewell to Arms* thirty-nine times, Plimpton wondered what had stumped him. "Was there some problem there?" he asked. In classic form, Hemingway replied, "Getting the words right." Indeed.

I was discouraged over and over as I tried and failed to get the words right. But it seemed that each time I hit bottom, some little nudge would come from somewhere and I would be back at it rolling the boulders around—moving paragraphs here, inverting words there, combing draft after draft. At one of those points, over a glass of single malt as I recall, Bill Perry suggested that I tape my own conversations with students as well as the interviews. Research is rarely purely objective, we agreed, and it was important that the researcher be part of the story. Besides, it would make it a whole lot more interesting. I tried it and then began to write up the conversations in their context, placing them in their settings, adding the visual and other sensory cues that the tapes lacked. I remember thinking as I reread the first of them, "This may not be science, but it sure is a whole lot more fun!"

A year later I had a manuscript. I knew nothing about how to get published and began sending ream-sized packages out to publishers—seven of them altogether—without even a query letter. One after another they all came back: "Dear Mr. D. We enjoyed reading this, but it is not for us. Good luck. Etc. Etc." At that point, another mentor, my old college professor Fred Rudolph, suggested that I try his publisher. "Jossey-Bass? I'm afraid my book's not academic enough for them," I protested. "Well, why don't you give them a try anyway?" he said. "Here's the name of my editor."

A few weeks later the letter came back. "Dear Mr. D. We enjoyed reading this, but it is not for us. Good luck. Etc. Etc." It was a week before Christmas. My marriage had just broken up, I missed my children terribly, my life was a dog's breakfast, and my last hope for the book was gone. But there at the end of the letter, after one of those ugly etceteras, was a little note, a tiny thread dangling from the edge of the envelope. "Call me if . . . " No one had ever left such a thread, so I gave it a tug. "The words are all there," said Lynn Luckow on the other end of the phone, "but we just can't make the numbers work. No one is interested in reading about mentors. [Long pause]. Still, why don't you call Alan Knox? He's our series editor. He might have some ideas about where you could take this."

Alan Knox? I knew him as the author of the thickest book ever written on adult development and the current president of the major professional organization in the field. Why would he care about me? But when I had slogged through the holidays, I dialed his number. Through the line came a deep, warm voice: "Alan Knox here." I carefully spelled my name, but he knew me at once. Yes, he said, this was a fine time to talk. Something in me relaxed, and I began to listen. With exquisite kindness, he explained that there were simply not enough people in the role I had described to buy the book. If I could expand it to address the role of academic advising for adult learners in a developmental context, he told me, perhaps we could make something work. He went on to make a set of concrete suggestions for the still-unwritten final chapter and then offered to review it for me. "And if it doesn't work for Jossey-Bass," he added, "I have a couple of other ideas we can try." When we hung up, I collapsed into a chair where I sat sightless, as the tears came. I could never have imagined that the book that grew out of that moment would go on to receive two national awards for writing in adult education.

A lot has changed in the twenty-six years since the book took its place in its original incarnation (titled *Effective Teaching and Mentoring*), a shy newcomer perched on the edge of a library shelf. At that time there were only a handful of articles and one other book specifically about mentoring. Today mentoring books slither off both ends and the shelf sags under binders fat with newsletters, stacks of journal articles, and piles of slick magazines proclaiming mentors' virtues or sniffing at their defects. Doctorates by the dozen have probed its innards; reams of scholarly articles have analyzed every crease and cranny. Mentors have been discovered everywhere that people need help learning something. Ten-year-olds "mentor" first graders, hard-driving execs mentor earnest wannabes, master teachers mentor interns, senior nurses mentor aides, reformed street kids mentor youths at risk, dying old men mentor curious writers, and thick-skinned politicians mentor idealistic novices.

When I search the word *mentor,* Google tells me it just got 150 million hits on the word in a sixth of a second. God only knows how many it would turn up if it took its time! There are hundreds of Web sites, endless discussion threads, and list after list of quotes for your next speech on the topic. The term is used for everything from breast implants to condoms. The mind boggles; the hand reaches out for a sturdy desk to lean on.

Just as when a child learns the word *truck* and for a while everything is a truck, our society seems to be doing the same with mentoring. Fortunately, however, we are beginning to make some long-overdue distinctions—between mentoring and coaching, for instance, or mentors and sponsors. As we learn to peel these apart, I think, we will be better able to focus our attention on the *essence* of the role that this passionate and fertile relationship plays in the drama of human development.

Fortunately also, we have begun to understand the range and importance of the many contexts that affect the mentoring relationship. In the newest edition of her best-selling book *The Mentor's Guide,* Lois Zachary (2010) helpfully describes several different configurations in which mentoring can occur, including formal and informal mentoring, reverse mentoring, supervisory mentoring, group mentoring, and distance and virtual mentoring. Weave these with considerations of cultural, gender, generational, racial, and power differences, and we begin to realize how far we have come.

Then there's the microchip. Its impact on mentoring, not to mention the education world, never mind the nature of knowledge itself, has been incalculable—and it's just getting started! In the Preface to the 1999 edition of this book, as the shadow of electronic distance learning was darkening my desktop, I wrote with decidedly mixed feelings of the fantasy of "just-in-time learning" and the illusion of "multitasking." Recalling Robert Frost's scorn for "speed reading" two generations back, I wonder if it isn't the assigned task of elders to raise bushy eyebrows at what they view as the depredations of contemporary culture, a touch on the brakes of the careening juggernaut that some call "progress." But my daughter Kate, herself a writer and teacher, issues her own caution. "Dad," she scolded not long ago when I was replaying a tattered tape about the diabolical nature of the Kindle, "You can keep right on snarling at these things if you like, but we live in the future now. George Washington would have killed to have a cell phone. I happen to love the future, and you can either get with it or rot under a rock somewhere!"

She is right, of course, and it is increasingly clear that, among other things, the Internet has enabled a degree of remote yet *interactive* experience that daily challenges not only our ways of knowing but also our ways of relating to one another and thus our very understanding of what it means to be human.

I found myself recently in an e-zine discussion thread on the slippery topic of gender that at times resembled a pickup hockey game. Almost all the participants taking their slap shots hid behind monikers. Ducking the flying pucks, I noticed that I was one of the few who had used his real name. The players knew nothing of one another save that they agreed or thought the other stupid or insensitive. The anonymity of cyberspace enables a sometimes shocking degree of coarseness among people. And yet at the same time, it also makes possible a range of connections and a quite unexpected, if paradoxical, intimacy. People bully in cyberspace, but they also fall in love. In the end, as Palloff and Pratt argue in their compelling *Building Online Learning Communities* (2005), the key to effective electronic learning is the formation and nourishing of a sense of community. A new frontier for mentors is how best to promote such mentoring communities.

As I revised the first version of this book more than a dozen years ago, I was enjoined to address some of its shortcomings but to leave the stories alone. I did that, also updating the references, paring away (I hoped) some of my more sexist assumptions, and adding greater shading to the sometimes sparkly holiday card image of *Mentor.* In an early critique of the book, Stephen Brookfield gingerly remarked that I seemed to have cast myself as the hero, and what did I think about that? The original Mentor, I knew, may have been part divine, but he was no angel. He returns at the end of the epic and joins Odysseus, his father, and his son in a lurid massacre of dozens of would-be home-wreckers and their hapless handmaidens. Mentors are not all pure light, and as Sharon Parks likes to remind us, one may be as readily mentored into the mafia as the ministry. Still, mentoring is rightly regarded as intrinsically a moral enterprise. We undertake to "mentor" another presumably on the other person's behalf. So in the second edition I added a

story at the end that raised the question What right have we to ed-
ucate, to disturb another's universe, much less to "promote their
development"?

Another criticism over the years has been that the book places
undue emphasis on the one-to-one relationship rather than recognizing that development is enhanced by our entire environment—
by relationships of varying intensity with many different people,
by events predictable and unpredictable, by the media, by deep inner experience, and especially by the company we keep. Perhaps
we ought to think of a "mentoring environment" or of the role
of "mentoring communities" instead? This question was strengthened by our *Common Fire* study of lives committed to the common
good (Daloz, Keen, Keen, and Parks, 1996), and the current edition refers to that. But in the end I hope that what this book has to
contribute is simply a close look at the dynamics of the mentoring
relationship itself in its most archetypal form—that what happens
in the one-to-one relationship informs in fundamental ways what
happens in all learning experiences that lead to the growth and
development of the learner. In that regard, I have been deeply
gratified that the "challenge-support" grid that appears in Chapter Eight has proved useful to dozens of doctoral students seeking
a platform for understanding how mentors can promote the development of their students.

In this edition I have added this new Preface and the Afterword. In both, I hope I have said something useful about what I
have learned and come to believe over the past thirty years. Because, however, my life has swept me during that time from the
bony halls of eastern academia to the cool, green forests of the
Pacific Northwest, it has taught me new things, not all of which
would contribute to a full update of the references here. For that
I commend the reader to Lois Zachary's recent updates (2010),
as well as Allen and Eby's *Blackwell Handbook of Mentoring* (2010);
Ragins and Kram's *Handbook of Mentoring at Work* (2007); Empire
State College's superb journal, *All About Mentoring;* and Ginsberg
and Wlodkowski's *Diversity and Motivation* (2009).

Several years after the book was launched, I joined with Sharon
Parks and Cheryl and Jim Keen to undertake the research that was

to result in the publication of *Common Fire,* a study of the lives of over one hundred people who had committed themselves to work on behalf of the common good. What kinds of life experiences, we wondered, had cultivated such people, and what sustained them in the face of overwhelming complexity and moral ambiguity? Among the findings, two stood out: first, almost all described what we came to call "a transformative engagement with Otherness," and second, over three quarters told of the presence of a mentor or mentoring community in their lives. Obviously, the latter finding was satisfying, but so also was the former in that as educators we had come to appreciate how the power of conflicting and differing perspectives promotes cognitive development and leads to a larger sense of the common good. As people developed, it seemed, they grew more inclusive, more receptive to people different from themselves, more capable of making nuanced distinctions, yet more able also to connect the dots, to see things whole. Paradoxically, they grew more tolerant but more critical, more open-minded but tougher to fool. In short, they became fuller human beings more capable of dealing adequately with the growing complexity of their worlds. All this helped me better understand why it was so important for teachers and mentors to recognize the deep importance of their work. Mentorship was about a good deal more than simply getting people into good jobs; it was about helping them become better thinkers, more compassionate actors, and just possibly, wiser human beings.

As that book made its way into the world, with one more good professional chapter in our lives and the children safely tucked into college, Sharon and I headed to the Pacific Northwest to join with colleagues in founding the Whidbey Institute. Suddenly finding myself wandering amid forests that held almost mythic power in my New England imagination, I began soaking up everything I could about forest ecology, nurse logs, mycorrhizae, mosses, and lichens. Invariably what I was learning made its way into my writing and teaching. We are, after all, a part of nature, and a knowledge of how things grow in the beyond-human world has much to offer our understanding of how human beings grow as well. It was impossible to understand how the natural world works, I realized, without encountering the reality of interdependence. On every scale, from gravitons to galaxies, interdependence is at work. To recognize this, however, demands a profound transformation in our own ways of knowing. Truly grasping the radical interdependence of all things is itself a developmental achievement. Theory, they say, is biography writ large. We come to see the world through an imagination evolving over a lifetime. As our vision grows larger, so also grows the world. In the Afterword, I have endeavored to explore the implications of this realization for our own ongoing evolution as mentors.

I have responded to the invitation to issue a new edition because I believe that much is at stake today for the quality and practice of higher education. Pat Cross was right when she wrote in the original Foreword that "to Daloz it is inconceivable that an excellent education would not make a profound difference in a person." But I would add now that it is my conviction as well that if education does nothing more than make the trains go faster and the ovens burn hotter, it is not just failing but is actively contributing to the downfall of our society. To the Daloz writing now, education must make a profound and positive difference in the world as well. Committed, caring, ethically informed mentoring is a vital part of that, and it matters not just for our students' individual lives but also for the life and well-being of our planet and all its inhabitants. More than ever, we need mentors who work to promote their students' development from fundamentalistic, authority-bound, and tribal worldviews to critical, systemic, connected, and committed ways of knowing in a radically interdependent and profoundly endangered world.

I am sometimes accused of being a bit apocalyptic. But whether we choose to accept or deny it, the looming tsunami of climate change has cast its shadow of fear over our planet, and as Franklin Delano Roosevelt famously said, our greatest fear is fear itself. For when we are afraid, at best we stop thinking, and at worst we lose hope and turn cynical. We long for an authority who will comfort us with simple answers. We lunge after the reassurance of religious, economic, or social fundamentalisms; we lurch toward the company of those who share a familiar world; we recoil against those who don't. And in so doing, we fail our world and betray our future.

This is why our education must do more than address our rational minds alone, must be more than the transmission of knowledge. It must transform not only the contents of the mind but also its very structure. It must change the way we think—and not just the way we think but the very way we make meaning; and more yet, it must inspire us and give us hope in these dark and challenging times. Finally, education must change our minds, charge our hope, and transform our souls, for in the end, real mentors care about our souls. I would like to think that this is why the value of this book persists—that it reminds us that mentorship is finally about living and cultivating lives of depth, compassion, and wisdom for ourselves, our students, and the world.

Acknowledgments

I am staggered, as I look back, at the numbers of people who have been a part of this work over the years. Truly, nobody does it alone; we need each other, and what a joy it is to remember! In addition to all those whom I have thanked in the original Preface, I owe first gratitude to the students I have been privileged to work with since then, particularly at Lesley College, at Columbia Teachers College, and at the many mentoring retreats that Sharon Parks and I have led at the Whidbey Institute and around the country. They have continued to propel me along a steep learning curve. I am particularly grateful to my colleagues at Lesley whom I hold in a very special place after years of close and largely joyful work together: David Bennett, Mary Bettley, Charlie Clayman, Patsy Cobb, Judith Beth Cohen, John DeCuevas, George Flavin, Bard Hamlin, Lynn Kass, Anita Landa, Kate Marrone, Deb Piper, Olive Silva, Sarah Sutro, and Frank Trocco. In addition, as the book drew me into a wider world of discourse with people vastly more knowledgeable about my field than I had known in my tiny corner of Vermont, some of the critics and many of the defenders of developmental theory became valued colleagues, and some have completed their legacy and moved on. In particular, I thank Stephen Brookfield, Rosemary Caffarella, Carolyn Clark, Phyllis Cunningham, John Dirxx, Ellie Drago-Severson, Leona English, James Fowler, Morris Keeton, Malcolm Knowles, Victoria Marsick, Sharan Merriam, Jack Mezirow, Cheryl Smith, Kathleen Taylor, Libby Tisdell, and Lyle Yorks. I am also grateful to my former editor, Lynn Luckow, as well as David Brightman, Gale Erlandson, and Tom Finnegan at Jossey-Bass. And special thanks go to Sheryl Fullerton and my longtime colleague Lois Zachary, whose Foreword now graces this volume, for conspiring to bring this new edition into life.

My children, Kate and Todd, have now grown into full adulthood, loving well and living committed lives. I am blessed and grateful beyond telling for them, their loving spouses, and the dazzling little ones, Maeve and Hannah, they have given the world. They continue to hone me on a fine stone. And Sharon Daloz Parks, one of the "shafts of sunlight" whom I acknowledged in the earlier Preface, is long since a cherished spouse and treasured colleague; what we have continued to learn together has swept far beyond the scope of any mere curve.

Whidbey Island, Cascadia Bioregion   Laurent A. Parks Daloz
August 2012

*To my granddaughters, Maeve
and Hannah:*

*May they and all their generation
be blessed with the wisdom of
good mentors.*

The Author

Laurent A. Parks Daloz served as mentor to adult students for many years while on the faculty of the Norwich University Adult Degree Program, the Johnson College External Degree Program, and the Lesley College Intensive Residency Option. Larry received his A.B. degree in American history and literature from Williams College, his M.A.T. in English, and his Ed.D. in educational planning from Harvard University. He was a Peace Corps volunteer in Nepal, a curriculum consultant in West Virginia, a teacher in Hawaii, and an educational planner in New Guinea before settling in Vermont, where he helped to found the nontraditional community college system. Thereafter, he served for many years as teacher and adviser to adult learners. In 1982, he received a Mina Shaughnessy fellowship, enabling him to reflect on the implications of his experience. The result was this book.

Subsequently he joined Sharon Parks in both marriage and professional colleagueship. Along with Cheryl and James Keen, they conducted a study of the formation of people committed to the common good. The result was *Common Fire: Leading Lives of Commitment in a Complex World.* Currently, he is a Senior Fellow of the Whidbey Institute on Whidbey Island in the Cascadia bioregion. There, where he continues to serve as a mentor, he cofounded the "Powers of Leadership Seasonal Retreat Cycle" and works with others to bring about a greater sense of our interdependence with the natural world, our relationship with Spirit, and our commitment to both sustainability and justice in a shared human future. He also serves as a speaker and consultant. He is particularly interested now in the developmental challenges facing men in the twenty-first century.

He holds honorary degrees from the University of New Hampshire and De Paul University and is the author of numerous chapters, articles, and reports, some of which have appeared in *Change* magazine, the *Chronicle of Higher Education, Adult Education Quarterly,* the *Journal of Continuing Higher Education, Lifelong Learning, Religion and American Life,* and other journals.

Part One

Adult Learning as Development

First Shards
The Search for Meaning as a Motive for Learning

What is education? I should suppose that education was the curriculum one had to run through in order to catch up with oneself.
—SØREN KIERKEGAARD, *FEAR AND TREMBLING*

We are all adult learners. Most of us have learned a good deal more out of school than in it. We have learned from our families, our work, our friends. We have learned from problems resolved and tasks achieved, but also from mistakes confronted and illusions unmasked. Intentionally or not, we have learned from the dilemmas our lives hand us daily.

Some of what we have learned is trivial; some has changed our lives forever. Much of the time, learning is a joy, especially when it meets a clearly felt need, takes us toward some destination, or helps us make sense of something formerly obscure. But sometimes it brings pain, and we struggle mightily not to see the obvious. There are few among us who have not wondered at such times why it was that the more we learned the less we knew, where our lives were taking us, and whether it was all worth it.

Our students are no different. Most have sacrificed a good deal to return to school. Education is important for them, not simply because they see it as a ticket to a better life but because in some

3

more profound sense, they hope it helps them make sense of lives whose fabric of meaning has grown frayed. For a multitude of reasons, they seldom lead with this revelation; some have yet to realize it. Fewer still see the erosion of meaning in their lives as a normal process, part of a lifetime of growing up. Yet both recent research and timeless insight have made it clear that our lives do not simply level off after the age of eighteen (Knox, 1977; Cross, 1981; Heath, 1991; Merriam and Caffarella, 1991; Tennant and Pogson, 1995). We continue to grow and change. What was once trivial can turn suddenly monumental, and what earlier appeared essential now seems unimportant. Women who for years sacrificed themselves for their families suddenly declare "It's Mom's turn" and replace the cookware on the kitchen table with textbooks; and men who were locked into the upward struggle for money and prestige may all at once turn inward, wondering what it all means.

A good education can help people understand these changes; indeed, it may play a part in bringing them about. A good education tends to our deepest longings, enriches them, nourishes the questions from which grow the tentative answers that, in turn, sow fresh questions about what really matters. As teachers, we do vital work in the lives of our growing students. This book is an attempt to portray students and teachers at work, to demonstrate how we can discuss important matters together so that our students can regain the courage, insight, and passion they need to move ahead in their lives more fully, to weave and reweave the fabric of meaning more richly and strongly.

As I began writing this book, I struggled with the tension between writing a "scholarly" work on the one hand and something with broader appeal on the other. Gradually I came to see that what I wanted most was to tell a good story, to engender good conversation. I have tried to do that, and because I am writing about what I do, I have attempted to remain a visible storyteller. For me, being a teacher is more art than science. I am uneasy with claims to an "objectivity" that I doubt exists. Perhaps that is why I have found the metaphor of a journey to be particularly useful for understanding what my students and I are going through. For although journeys differ for each of us, like education, they do have direction, they have a common syntax, and we can mark our progress by the passing signposts. In their form itself lies their meaning. Thus, although some of what happens between teacher and student has about it the quality of magic, by casting our two protagonists as pilgrim and guide we can learn much about that dark and fertile art. The question for us as teachers is not whether but *how* we influence our students. It is a question about a relationship: *Where are our students going, and who are we for them in their journey?*

This question underlies most of the book. In this chapter, I try to illustrate why it became so important for me and why I believe it to be central for all of us who are struggling to construct an education of care. So, let me invite you along on a short journey to eavesdrop on a conversation between Emerald and me. She was one of twenty returning adult students I was working with as mentor for an external degree program several years back. My job was to guide them along the misty and often confusing pathways through higher education. I would help people decide what they wanted to learn, explain the program requirements, and work with them to select courses or design independent studies that would take them to their goal. Once under way, it was my job to provide moral and academic support, which often involved conversations like this one.

When the Thunder Comes

The ski trails on the side of Mt. Mansfield were etched white against the blue of the horizon as the car glided around the corner, a bit fast for the icy conditions. It was one of those perfect winter days, utterly clear but still below zero in midmorning. Glittering flakes of frozen air drifted in the sunlight as a carful of skiers heading for the mountain passed me in the opposite direction, eager no doubt to play in the fresh powder of yesterday's storm. Days like today are the stuff of postcards, I thought to myself, everything in its Sunday best. Yet there's something glossy and unreal about the countryside in winter. People who live here know what's under the snow, and one needn't drive far off the main roads to see the trailers and the shacks, the shattered doors and the torn polyethylene covering windows, to know that *Vermont Life* is a magazine intended mostly for export.

I turned north outside of Hardwick and headed into the heart of the Northeast Kingdom, where I live and work. So named some years ago by Sen. George Aiken in recognition of the three northeastern counties' determined insularity, the region is Vermont's poorest and probably harbors most of what's left of a way of life earlier called Yankee, now outdated and overromanticized. The barn, once our predominant architecture, has been largely replaced by the trailer, topped—as soon as the owner can afford it—by a roof pitched against the cold.

The road and the frozen river danced together as I glided past overgrown pastures scored from time to time with the tracks of snowmobiles. Just beyond a half-buried garage sale sign—the tip of our underground economy's iceberg—the Come & Eat roadhouse peered over the stacks of snow. I slowed down and pulled into the newly scraped lot beside a huge semi loaded with pulp.

The steam swirled around me as I swung through the door, struck by the blast of warm air redolent of coffee and bacon fat, gravy and canned string beans. The place was nearly empty save for a couple of men layered in chocolate rags, huddled over coffee cups and cigarettes. They must belong to the truck, I thought, as I looked for Emerald. I spotted her nestled in the next-to-last booth, nodded, and peeled off my parka as I made my way to join her.

Widowed after a brief marriage some years ago, Emerald returned to her hometown; she has worked here ever since as a bookkeeper in her brother's small sawmill. Now in her mid-thirties, she dresses softly and with incongruous class, bats her eyelids with accomplishment. Seemingly shy, she scarcely opens her mouth in group meetings; even outside, she volunteers little. Yet when she does speak, she does so with near-perfect certainty, ending her sentences in the air as if to say, "Isn't it obvious?"

A year ago she graduated from the local community college and entered the external degree program to study for a degree in business management. The program requirements were broad and flexible, allowing her to take courses at a number of different institutions but specifying a certain number of liberal studies as well. The task of the mentor was to help her design a program that met both her needs and the program's expectations. Like many adults, Emerald began her studies with courses directly relevant to her work: accounting, office management, computers. As her adviser, I chose not to resist that, for older students are generally much clearer about what they're doing in college than their younger counterparts, and it doesn't do to thwart their firm intentions—at least not at first. But the time came for Emerald to plan her program more comprehensively. We had arranged this meeting to discuss it.

From a folder on the seat beside her, Emerald removed a neatly typed sheet of paper and slid it across the table toward me. The brief narrative noted that her objective was to attain a degree in business management; her long-term goal was to become a CPA. Beneath the narrative was written:

> Liberal arts will be useful to offset patterns of rigidness prevalent in my main objective: achieving a balance in education. I realize that all numbers and heavy concentration in one single area with no balancing influence is apt to lead to undesirable personality maladjustments and mental introversion. Liberal arts is and has been my mode of relaxation.

Then came a list of the studies she planned to undertake during the next six semesters. Her intention was to study two at a time—a full load when combined with a normal workday. The list was fascinating. Next term, she planned to combine budgeting with the Old Testament, then data processing and archeology, business law and poetry, insurance and dance. Balance, indeed, I thought to myself as I scanned the list. The dichotomy was relentless, but I could discern no pattern beyond that. Why those subjects? Why that order? It baffled and fascinated me at once. What did this woman want for herself? Or, I wondered, is this for herself at all? Then I noticed her one liberal study course thus far—a course on death and dying she took last term. How could I have forgotten? Something about her mouth as she described her widowhood during an earlier meeting had prompted me to suggest that she take it. I decided to begin there.

"So. How was that death and dying course?"

"Oh, fine," she replied, sealing the statement with a tight smile, inviting more but offering nothing. She's going to make me work, I thought. Off balance already, but the game begun, I played another card.

"'Fine'? How do you mean that? What was good about it?"

"Oh, we learned a lot of useful stuff." Silent again, but there was an opening.

"Like?"

"Oh, you know. If somebody dies on the job, what you have to do. How morgues work, you know. We had an interesting trip to the morgue."

How morgues work? That escaped me. This fragile, tough widow whose lip trembles at a seven-year-old memory, takes a death and dying course and learns nothing but how morgues work? I tried to mask my disbelief and moved to check out what seemed obvious.

"Besides that—besides the trip and the practical stuff—did you get anything out of the course of *value* to you?" Palms toward her, I underlined "value" with empty hands. I wanted her to know that I knew, without either of us having to acknowledge it.

"Of value?" She caught my eye for an instant, then looked down at her own hands, half-folded in her lap. "Oh, some personal stuff." She paused a moment, then looked back up. Her eyes were moist, but she wouldn't give in. "Some people in the course had a lot of grieving to do." Then quickly, "But I just don't agree with that. I mean you have to move ahead. That's what I believe. You can't look back. I guess I learned that from my father. You have to put the past behind you and move ahead."

She held my eye doggedly while she spoke, testing herself. In the end, she passed. She was not about to give me that much, and I was not at all sure I wanted it. Besides, we each knew enough for now. We backed down.

"'Move ahead,'" I said as I leaned back. "What's that mean for you? Where are you headed?"

Her face broke into a smile and she turned, looking out the frosted window. Then, after a moment, "Oh, be more myself, I guess."

"How's that?"

"Oh, you know, not getting jerked around so much by other people, not always worrying about what they think of me."

I smiled at the familiarity of her sentiment. "Is there something wrong with that?" The question was clearly loaded, and she responded with a fire I hadn't seen before.

"Would you believe my brother had a fit when he saw that stuff?" she burst out, pointing to the degree plan. "He thinks I shouldn't study anything but what I need to run his stupid business!"

So she was on to her own tricks: even as she felt the heat of her brother's expectations, she resented them. Clearly, there was an Emerald inside this woman who wanted to be her own person. That puzzling dichotomy, that struggle over the meaning of "value"—was it the echo of an inner conversation between an old and a new Emerald? It often seemed that the educational worth of a given subject was inversely related to its apparent usefulness. Perhaps the new Emerald was crying out for something that would allow her to escape from the ordinary, practical "realities" of a life grown absurd.

Suddenly the waitress was above us, wanting to know what we wanted. We ordered coffee and smiled her away; I lounged back into the corner of the booth, wondering whether to go with Emerald's emotions or pursue my hunch. Plates clattered in the kitchen. I decided on the latter.

"Look, Emerald, just suppose you could have all the money and all the time you needed to learn about anything in the world you wanted. No need to learn a job skill, no need to be practical. Just to go after a burning curiosity. What would you want to learn?"

"Religion."

It came back so quickly I was thrown again. But it was perfect.

"Ah, so that's what the Old Testament next fall is about?"

"Yes." (Isn't it obvious?)

"Well, what... what, exactly, does religion mean for you? I mean, it seems so far from accounting and numbers and all that."

"Yes. That's what I like about it. It's so different from what I do all day long. I like to come home and do something completely different."

That made sense to me. After a long day in the left brain, we need to change sides. But somehow something wasn't quite right yet. I was beginning to get a sense of what the two parts were, of where they rested, but what linked those "completely different" studies? And where was Emerald in all this? I still needed a connection.

"What is it about the Old Testament or archeology—or death and dying—that is so different from accounting?" I tossed in that last, fingers crossed. But maybe she would connect it for us.

"Well," she replied, flicking glances at me like a chickadee, cautious but not at all frightened, "I want to learn how it all began."

"And you feel you can learn the answers by studying those subjects?" I was not at all sure where she was going with this. She was beyond the point of thinking she could find the meaning of life by looking it up in the dictionary. Yet she did seem to think The Answers were out there, that if she could just study enough, read the right books, get the right information, she would find them. Was that what she wanted?

"Well, archeology will give a kind of scientific answer, and the Old Testament course will give religion...." She broke off and looked at me with a question. "Does that make sense?" Evidently it didn't quite, to her.

I replied that I understood her uncertainty, but I still needed to clarify something. Was this quest no more than a counterpoint to accounting? I floundered for the question, then blurted it out.

"So there you sit, in your stuffy little office day after day with your numbers—your pluses and your minuses, your rights and your wrongs, your world of certainties—and suddenly you find yourself staring out the window at a cloud and asking, 'Is this all there is?' Is that what your quest is about?"

Her smile this time seemed almost a relief to her. She reined it in quickly, but the acknowledgment was there—as though it had all been a guessing game and I finally got it.

"What do you really want to know?" I asked her softly. And she began to talk.

"Well, like I said, I want to know how it all began. I mean I got interested in this and started reading, and I want to know about how the earth originated and I want to know what were the beginnings of Man. All I had to go by was Adam and Eve, and I don't buy that. I thought the logical way to attack it was to go through religion; then I find out that religion only goes back to 3000 B.C. Darwin goes back a couple million B.C., and I wonder what's going on all this time. Surely Neanderthal man must have some thoughts about what's going on, sitting out there in the cave looking at the stars at night; something must be going through his mind, definitely. And when the thunder comes, he knows he didn't do it."

"That's a religious question," I said. "'Who am I under these stars?'" But she went on, unhearing.

"—And the most difficult problem is, we have no concrete

evidence. I mean nobody walks up to us and tells us point-blank, 'Well, I can tell you. I was there.' It's kind of difficult."

"Why do you want to know all that, Emerald? What difference does it make?"

"It probably doesn't make any difference. It's a good way to keep me busy." Then, as if dissatisfied with her own diffidence, she frowned and added, "It helps my understanding of the world around me, and I think that's pretty important." She went on to muse about how simple it would be to be an animal.

"How come," she asked, "the animals are so successful and we're so unsuccessful? We're the ones with brains." Emerald looked across at me, her face a question. Yet something told me she didn't want an answer—at least not from me. I nodded, holding her eye. She looked down again, shook her head softly. "It seems everything is in chaos."

I waited a moment for us both. "What's to be done about it? Is your quest somehow a way out of it?"

She was silent for a long time, studying her own fingers on the empty coffee cup. "To find out," she said finally, passion sheathed in velvet, "or even touch on what the differences, what the hinge is, what the chaos hinges on."

I think we must have looked like lovers at that moment, leaning toward each other, eyes on something invisible between us, oblivious. But just then there was a loud bump and a screech as the door swung open and a huge checkered man burst through the steam and greeted the other two inhabitants of our world. "God-*damn,* ain't it some cold out there?"

We both leaned back; the clock caught my eye, and I signaled the waitress. I had several more people to see before dark. As we awaited our change, I spoke of my own journey toward a way of being that I didn't understand. I did so, not sure what my words would mean to her but wanting her to know that I too needed and valued the part of me that wouldn't come out even. Then we arranged for another meeting, put on our parkas, and plunged into the dazzling cold. She gave me a quick wave, slipped into her car, and purred off to the south. Turning out of the parking lot, I noticed a bank of clouds to the west. "At least it should warm up," I thought, and headed north.

❖

As I drove, my mind kept returning to the conversation with Emerald. I was intrigued with how she used language—that extraordinary concreteness: a course in the Old Testament would "give religion," archeology would "give a kind of scientific answer," "Religion only goes back to 3000 B.C. Darwin goes back a couple million...." There was a coarseness about how she packaged the ideas in their words, yet a marvelous poetry in her vision: "And when the thunder comes, he knows he didn't do it." Did that tangibility have something to do with her intellectual growth, or was it simply her personality? Would education blunt her intrinsic sensibility? How could I honor her curiosity without harming her innocence?

And what did "growth" mean for her anyway? "Not getting jerked around so much by other people, not always worrying about what they think of me," she said. Was that just selfishness, or was this thrust toward independence part of a larger pattern in her life? Did her returning to school cause this new concern, or was it the result? Clearly it was placing a strain on her relationship with her brother. How was it affecting her two children, her friends? What was cause and what effect in the game of hide-and-seek between Emerald and her world?

Then there was that astonishing drive for some sort of deeper meaning to her life. Was this a question she had always harbored and only now allowed to surface? Or did school have something to do with stirring it up? I wasn't sure how I felt about that. On the one hand, it seemed a positive thing for people to ask serious questions of their lives; on the other, it could be deeply disturbing for some to lose the sources of meaning that had sustained them for so long. Friends may be lost, and marriages suffer. Who was I to tamper with their inner lives? I was no psychiatrist; I wasn't trained in these things. Yet all I had done was to ask her about what she was learning and offer her my best version of an honest response. Was Emerald simply going through the kind of crisis of certainty that most of us have gone through as we continue our education, or was it something more?

Running Low

The clouds had already slipped beneath the sun as I pulled into Ed's place, a ragged farmhouse connected to the barn by a ramshackle chain of sheds. Ed still owned the land the house was on but had auctioned off the rest two years ago when his farm went under, a victim of economic forces he refused to understand.

I was appropriately sympathetic when he first told me the story, but it brought me up short when he added that in a way he was glad it had happened. He had long since grown tired of farming.

"I needed the change," he said. "Farming hasn't much to do, you know, with growing things any more. Mostly it's fixing goddamn busted machinery. If I'da wanted to be a mechanic I'da been one."

Besides, he had begun drinking and only recently dried out with the help of the local AA chapter. Now his wife was supporting the family, and he did odd jobs while he studied psychology. "I really want to work with people," he told me, "in the time I got left." Where he'd find that work was anybody's guess. But there was an urgency behind his words that hinted of more than a desire for vocational training. In his early fifties, he felt time was running out. Where was he headed? Would his educational voyage take him where he wanted to go? Did he know what a terrible chance he was taking? And what was my part in that journey?

I parked beside his old Ford tractor, hauled my briefcase out of the back seat, and headed for the shed where the kitchen would be. As I saw Ed's shadowy form through the frost on the storm door and reached for the frozen latch, the questions still burned.

Ed, Emerald, and thousands like them are part of a major revolution in higher education, one that has seen the proportion of older students in classrooms double within a single generation. Spurred by declining enrollments among traditional-age students and by a growing recognition that many adults want to continue their education but lack the means, a number of colleges began to design special programs during the 1970s to accommodate the new student. Because most adults had jobs, courses were offered at night or on weekends, and degree requirements became more flexible; classes were longer and less frequent. Because the majority were parents, part-time study became more available and financing more appropriate. And because the age range of this new group was considerably greater than that of traditional students, new assumptions were made about how best to teach and support them. After all, the conventional curriculum had evolved in response to the relatively innocent and distinctly different needs of late adolescents. People like Emerald bore a breadth of experience and depth of emotional capacity largely unavailable to traditional college-age students. To attempt to teach a thirty-five-year-old widow in the same way one would an eighteen-year-old halfback did not make good sense.

It is this last matter that has most intrigued me over the years. First as teacher and administrator in a community college, later as external degree program mentor and researcher, I was struck again and again with the awesome differences among adult learners and have long sought a better way of understanding them. Why is it that at only twenty-eight Susan seems so much more able to handle complex ideas than Arthur, a retired businessman, even though her knowledge and experience are so much less? Is it background, gender, friends, intelligence (whatever that means)? Or could it be age? Is Arthur simply over the hill? Do our minds, like our bodies, just deteriorate over time? Why do so many women return to school in their mid-thirties, so many men in their forties? What is happening in their lives or in our society that creates such a pattern? What are the special concerns of these groups that might give us a better basis for designing curricula? Is there any way to reconcile these students' pragmatic needs for specific, job-related knowledge with their deeper needs for more comprehensive understanding of their worlds?

I think I first began to entertain the notion that the metaphor of a journey might offer a useful framework during a conversation with Ellen, one of my first students. She was telling me about her experience of returning to school after a thirty-year absence.

"It's like a river," she said, drawing a line across the table between us. "It's like I'm back there and want to get over here, and the only way I can do it is to cross the river. So I say, 'OK,' take a deep breath, and go. And I make it over here. And that's where you are; you are alive. Sometimes I get mixed up about the journey across the river; sometimes I think it's the worst experience of my life; other times I think it's the most fantastic experience... but you know, when you get over here, you leave something—you have to—and sometimes I wish I was that person back there, but I can't be and I don't want to be. I mean I can't ever be that person again. Once you cross that river, the innocence is gone."

I was to hear the journey metaphor often after that, as I began asking people what it was like for them to *re-turn* to school. It was an extraordinarily useful way for people to get a handle on their experience, to name the feelings that too frequently kept them awake nights. Because journeys have destinations, it gave a sense of movement and purpose to what often seemed without meaning, helped them understand that confusion, uncertainty, and fear may be a necessary—even valuable—part of educational growth. And it helped me grasp the differences among them more readily. In a way, some had simply traveled more than others; some seemed never to have left home, while others had gone centuries away. But if my students were travelers, then who was I as teacher? If education was most about the growth of the learner, what was my part?

I was beginning to realize that teaching is, finally, a special kind of relationship, a caring stance in the moving context of our students' lives. Of course it involves knowledge; of course the teacher has to know *something*, but what we know is of value only as we are able to form it such that our students can make use of it for their own evolving ways of knowing. I was keenly aware that for every student I was a unique person. Each saw me differently, and I needed to be different for each. Our students are always in motion, I was coming to realize, and our task is to honor that motion, to understand how each student sees education and teachers differently at different times. The job, it seemed, was not so much to individualize instruction as to *enrich education* so each student could take from it what he or she most needed at the time.

But occasionally the questions seemed overwhelming. What was that loss of innocence that Ellen described so eloquently? How did my own journey mesh with hers? If we were all in motion, what did timing have to do with the art of teaching? Is there some way of understanding this more clearly, so we can ask sharper questions, offer better suggestions, provide richer support?

This book is at best an interim report, an attempt to sketch some beginning answers to the questions lurking behind the storm door at Ed's house. As they burned their way into my awareness, I found the outlines dimly swimming somewhere in the space between me and nearly every film or novel I encountered, every story I read to my children, every conversation with my students. They began to fuse into a single, deeper question: *What is my place in the growth of those I care for? As* I held the question, not surprisingly I began to discover shards all about me—answers that have been with us since the beginning of time.

In the next chapter, we look more closely at the metaphor of adult learning as a transformational journey, and especially at how Mentor serves as a guide for the journey.

Chapter Two

Mentors, Myths, and Metamorphosis
Education as a Transformational Journey

Not the least shyness, now, Telemakhos. You came across the open sea for this—to find out where the great earth hides your father and what the doom was that he came upon. . . .

Reason and heart will give you words, Telemakhos; and a spirit will counsel others. I should say the gods were never indifferent to your life.
—MENTOR, IN *THE ODYSSEY*

If mentors did not exist, we would have to invent them. Indeed, we do so from childhood on. They come in an array of forms, from the grandmotherly fairy godmother to the elfin Yoda to the classic bearded Merlin. Myths, fairy tales, fantasy, and children's stories abound with mentor figures: the spider woman in Native American lore, Gandalf in Tolkien, Charlotte in *Charlotte's Web*, Utnapishtim in the Gilgamesh epic, Shazam in Captain Marvel comics, the little old lady in *Babar*, Tiresias in Greek legend, the Skin Horse in *The Velveteen Rabbit*. They proceed from a place in us as deep as our dreams. Carl Jung tells us that the archetype, which may be of either sex or both, represents "knowledge, reflection, insight, wisdom, cleverness, and intuition." The figure appears in a situation where "insight, understanding, good advice,

17

determination, planning, etc. are needed but cannot be mustered on one's own," often arriving in the nick of time to help the traveler along the journey (Jung, 1958, p. 71).

Whether as close as the classroom or as distant as myth, mentors are creations of our imagination, designed to fill a psychic space somewhere between lover and parent. Not surprisingly, they are suffused with magic and play a key part in our transformation, reminding us that we can indeed survive the terror of the coming journey and undergo the transformation by moving through, not around, our fear. Mentors give us the magic that allows us to enter the darkness: a talisman to protect us from evil spells, a gem of wise advice, a map, and sometimes simply courage. But always the mentor appears near the outset of the journey as a helper, equipping us in some way for what is to come, a midwife to our dreams, a "keeper of the promise" (Parks, 1986).

We begin this chapter with a look at some ways in which the term *mentor* has been used recently. Although mentors have always been around, in the years since Gail Sheehy popularized the term (in *Passages,* 1976) mentors have become increasingly visible. Success, we are told—whether in industry or academia—is a lot slipperier without a mentor to show us the ropes. A flood of books and articles now proclaim mentors' virtues and defects (Speizer, 1981; Merriam, 1983; Gray, 1989; Bey and Holmes, 1992; Cohen, 1995; Luna and Cullen, 1997; Waters, 1998). And who has not read *Tuesdays with Morrie* (Albom, 1997), that bittersweet journal of a young man and his dying mentor?

Yet relatively little work has been done on the deeper, metaphorical and archetypal context of the word.[1] As we will see in a moment, it is of more than passing interest that the original Mentor was inhabited by Athena. Clearly, the mentor is concerned with transmission of wisdom. How, then, do mentors transmit wisdom? Most often, it seems, they take us on a journey. In this aspect of their work, *mentors are guides.* They lead us along the journey of our lives. We trust them because they have been there before. They embody our hopes, cast light on the way ahead, interpret arcane signs, warn us of lurking dangers, and point out unexpected delights along the way. There is a certain luminosity about them, and they often pose as magicians in tales of transformation, for *magic* is a word given to what we cannot see—and we can rarely see across the gulf. As teachers of adults, we have much to learn from the mythology of the mentor.[2]

To understand the mentor as guide, however, it is necessary to go back and look more closely at the journey itself. To do that, we consider the importance of "story" as a way of making sense of life's changes, focusing especially on a particular kind of story: the journey tale. We then follow one illustrious mentor and his charge on their journey through Inferno together, deriving from this great tale of transformation some beginning principles of mentorship. Finally, as we consider how the principles of mentorship might apply to the real-life concerns of teacher and student, we listen in on a conversation with Eric, an engineer hearing some unanticipated voices while on his way up the corporate ladder and into midlife. To conclude, the chapter suggests that combining developmental theory and the journey metaphor offers a useful lens through which to view students like Emerald, Ed, and Eric.

Embedded in the chapter are a number of questions we might ask of ourselves as teachers or advisers. What changes do I want to see in my students? What kind of responsibility do I accept for them? How do my students see me, and what do they want from me? How do I respond to their hopes, their fear? Can I learn this, or is it just so much magic?

But before we speak too much of magicians and mentors, teachers, healers and guides, I want to make it clear as sunlight that there is nothing here that does not meet the eye willing to see or the ear ready to hear. Magic, as all true wizards know, is available to anyone willing to stand in the right place. Most magicians are simply people who have refined, more than the rest of us have, the art of understanding how the world works. They know where lie the fault lines, clefts, and barely visible seams in what we call "real." In working their magic, they simply ruffle the line between imagination and reality, for they know that the greatest illusion is to believe we have no illusions. One need not meet students in wintry diners, or quiver with love of the Bach flute sonatas, to make good use of the principles here. I have known fine mentors who lecture to classes of two hundred and never set foot off a campus. What distinguishes them has little to do with student load, or publications, or even popularity. Nor do they necessarily wear beards, outrageous outfits, or hearts on their sleeves.

What makes the difference is their willingness to care—about what they teach and whom. They know they exist as teachers only because of their students; they know they are part of a transaction, a relationship.

Mentors

The original Mentor appears in *The Odyssey* as an old and trusted friend of Odysseus. He is appointed to look after the estate and, more to the point, Odysseus's son, Telemakhos. It is in Mentor's form that Athena, goddess of wisdom, speaks at critical times throughout the epic. Thus, Mentor is both male and female, mortal and immortal—an androgynous demigod, half here, half there. Wisdom personified.

In the story itself, Mentor serves as a guide to young Telemakhos in his search for reunion with his father. Mentor urges the boy on his quest, finds a ship, accompanies him on the first leg, and then departs, returning again at the end of the tale to assist father, son, and grandfather as they recapture their heritage and consolidate their return home. His part in the story is instructive, for he is a classic transitional figure, helping the youth achieve his manhood and confirm his identity in an adult world while helping the father complete his life's work.

Mentors, it seems, have something to do with growing up, with developing identity. In an excellent, qualitative study of the mentor-protégé relationship, researcher David Zucker (1982, p. iv) says with thinly veiled delight that "the most unexpected result [of the study] was that the structure of the mentor-protégé relationship... closely parallels the structure of the mentoring myth contained in Homer's *Odyssey*." While we may share his joy in discovering the power of mythology to elucidate human relationships, we ought not be too surprised. For most myths the sample is, after all, rather large.

In a detailed, longitudinal study of the lives of forty men, psychologist Daniel Levinson (1978) found that many of his subjects were guided and supported during their early adult years by older men, whom he dubbed "mentors." Indeed, it was his research that informed Gail Sheehy's popularization of the term in *Passages*. Interestingly, his later work on women's development (Levinson, 1996) shows a much less pronounced influence of mentors. On the other hand, Hughes and Wolf (1997) have compiled a rich trove of stories detailing the role that mentors play in the growth and healing of younger women. Lois Zachary (1999) has created an engaging and practical "toolkit" for training mentors, and Norman Cohen (1995) gives us the most systematic analysis yet of the specifics of the relationship.

Moreover, there is much evidence, especially in the business world, of the importance of a mentor for both men's and women's advancement in the organization (Kanter, 1977; Hennig and Jardim, 1977; Roche, 1979; Missirian, 1982; Phillips-Jones, 1982; Kram, 1986, Marsick, 1987; Murray, 1991; Shea, 1994). Similar work has been carried out in academia, especially regarding women entering the professoriat (Hall and Sandler, 1983; Maack and Passet, 1994; Wunsch, 1994; Mullen, 1997).[3] The gist of the research is that mentors are especially important at the beginning of people's careers or at crucial turning points in their professional lives. The mentor seems to manifest for protégés someone who has accomplished the goals to which they now aspire, offering encouragement and concrete help. In our own study of lives committed to the common good (Daloz, Keen, Keen, and Parks, 1996), mentors or mentoring communities were significant factors in more than three-quarters of our sample, exerting a powerful influence in shaping the particular form of each person's commitment.

The term *mentor* has been used sporadically in higher education for years, but it first caught my ear when used formally by Empire State College, one of the nation's first colleges created exclusively for older students (Schlossberg, Lynch, and Chickering, 1989). Although mentors obviously continue to serve young people, the term has since come into much wider use as a neologism meaning "teacher of adults" (Cohen, 1995). Mentors generally have a wider role than do conventional faculty advisers. They may or may not teach classes, but they are inevitably engaged in one-to-one instruction[4] and are consequently more concerned than regular teachers with the individual learning needs and styles of their students (Thomas, Murrell, and Chickering, 1982; Hiemstra and Sisco, 1990; Galbraith and Cohen, 1995).

Understandably, within the academy itself mentors are found most frequently among faculty and sports coaches. But unless there is some formalized process for assigning or recognizing mentorships

(Brown and DeCoster, 1982; Wunsch, 1994), the process remains largely invisible—a German instructor spends extra lab time with a particularly promising student, or a biology professor and student begin to share problems of child care. More visible in this role may be the student counseling staff, who (because their work is not to transmit specific content) are frequently more concerned with promoting the development of the student. But the range of possibilities is perhaps widest in those programs that view the learning environment as extending beyond the campus. External degree and cooperative education programs, for instance, frequently give formal recognition to supervisors and experts in the "outside world" who may often move into mentor status with their students. It is important for programs to recognize the potential of such people.

It is also important for institutions to acknowledge the centrality of the advising process, an activity that overburdened teachers almost inevitably view as a chore. Yet this is often the only point at which the instructor actually speaks individually with students, and it is certainly the only time he or she is called upon to view a student's progress in a context broader than that of a single course. Even where teacher-student contact lacks the intensity or personal quality normally associated with mentorship, students can be powerfully affected by their teachers. Many of us carry memories of an influential teacher who may scarcely know we existed, yet who said something at just the right time in our lives to snap a whole world into focus. To a certain extent, of course, the timing of such "mentoring moments" is a mystery. Neither teacher nor student can know when they will occur. But to the degree that as teachers we are aware of the shifting pattern of questions stirring the intellectual test tubes of our students' minds, we are in a better position to drop in just the right catalyst at the propitious moment to bring about the transformation that together we seek.

In the end, mentors have no more meaning without students than answers have without questions. Just what are those questions? Here, Sam Keen writes of his mentor's advice:

Once, in a dry time, Howard Thurman asked me: "What do you want, Sam? What are your dreams?" He had previously warned me about the proper order of . . . priorities. "The first question an

individual must ask is, *What is my journey?* Only then is it safe to ask
the second question: *Who will go with me?* If you get the questions
out of order, you will get in trouble" [1983, p. 172].

The first business of a guide is to listen to the dreams of the
pilgrim. How are our students moving? What do they want for
themselves? How do they tell their own stories?

Stories

We begin with stories. Children love stories. Within the narrative
structure lies one of the most basic ways through which we make
sense of our experience. But stories are important for adults as
well, for in the great tales lies the syntax of our lives, the form by
which we make meaning of life's changes. A good story transforms
our vision of the possible and provides us with a map for the
journey ahead. So we should not be surprised to discover that
many major developmental theorists draw heavily on literature in
their work. As James Fowler, a developmentalist theologian, notes,
"Theorists of adult development have begun to play the role in our
society that storytellers and mythmakers once played in primitive
and classical cultures" (1984, p. 15). By suggesting the directions
of growth throughout the life span, developmental psychologists
are offering us "master stories" against which to hold our own lives'
tales for comparison, and perhaps revision.

It is a basic premise of this book, as of much current developmental theory, that *development* is more than simply change. The
word implies direction. Moreover, development seems to happen
not in a gradual and linear way but in distinct and recognizable
leaps—in a series of spiraling plateaus rather than a smooth slope.
Each plateau rests upon and represents a qualitative improvement
over the previous one. It is good, I believe, to develop, and as teachers we cannot escape our part in this development. A ten-year-old
does not simply know more than a four-year-old; she *thinks* differently. She can order things in sequence; her younger brother
doesn't even try. She can classify objects into logical groups; her
brother couldn't care less. Perhaps most important, she can tell
(and appreciate) coherent stories because she has developed a

sense of linear time; her brother remains adrift in a labile and essentially timeless world. As such, she has gained the power to array her fears, her wants, and her triumphs in some sort of order, while her brother is still subject to them all—buffeted by and almost wholly dependent upon his immediate experience.

Is she, then, "better" than he for being at a later stage of development? Of course not. We can only be who we are at the time (and it's hard enough to do that well!). Yet because she has a capacity to construct a more elaborate interior "map" of the world, she is less likely than he to become lost if she finds herself in a strange place. She can rely more on herself and less on grown-ups to solve her problems. Because she can move beyond her immediate impulses and understand the motives of others more clearly than he, she is more able to anticipate their needs and thus serve her own. By virtue of her greater development, she is less subject to the demands of her environment and is consequently both freer and more powerful than he. In this sense, there are times when it is indeed "better" to think like a ten-year-old than a four-year-old.

I watched with fascination as my children, two years apart, moved through what Selma Fraiberg calls the magic years, struggling with profound fears of the unknown, of darkness, of powerful figures threatening to annihilate them. Their greatest weapon, as they grew, was their increasing ability to give fears a context by placing them in time. They did this by hearing, acting out, and telling stories, for in a psychological sense a story is simply our fears and triumphs given form in the context of time. Thus, when he was a preschooler, Todd, with the help of a Spider Man figure, could battle with the Incredible Hulk, physically battering that hunk of green cheesecake while emotionally reassuring himself that he had the power to overcome his fears. Over time, with his father's exuberant storytelling, to say nothing of his culture's current penchant for escape fantasy, Todd learned to construct evermore-elaborate scenarios with his little plastic Darth Vader and Luke Skywalker figures—while Kate, a reader, could take yet a further step by consuming book after book. For children and grownups alike, stories allow us to control and form the inchoate, to give our lives meaning.

We are told that Zen masters often respond to the pleas of their students for answers by telling stories. Indeed, the tradition is honored among most great teachers, from Lao-tzu, Plato, and Jesus to the Hassidim, Kierkegaard, and T. S. Eliot. The reason is not just that these teachers want to keep things simple; they also know that insights always shine brightest for those who have them, that *truth* is a word we give to a pattern that makes sense to us, and that by offering a story teachers provide a common structure on which each of us can order his or her own experience. Great teachers know that to provide an answer is to confuse ends with means—a bit like flying a group of hikers to the top of the mountain when one person's reason for the trip is to learn to climb, another's to collect wild flowers, and another's simply to enjoy the day. A good story is a kind of hologram of the life of an individual, a culture, or a whole species. Each of us hears in it, with ears conditioned by our own history, what we most need at the time to understand.

Yet not just any story will do. Su Wen, the Chinese tell us, was a great physician. He could heal any of a thousand illnesses with a single needle by placing it in the right way in the right place in the right person at the right time. That's high art. The good storyteller does the same.

In his book *Ascent of the Mountain, Flight of the Dove* (1971), Michael Novak talks of the importance of "story" this way. In those moments when the world falls apart, when we lose a sense of meaning, stories can reconnect things for us, place our fears in context, help us see new forms of meaning. They do so by offering a way out, not simply in the characters or the setting but in the very syntax of the tale itself, a syntax that seems almost universal. This seems obvious enough, but the point is that stories are not simply random recitations of events. They have an order in time, and to have meaning the order must go from somewhere to somewhere. It must lead the reader through some sort of journey. Like human development, stories demand a sense of direction to be good.

The Journey

By no means do all stories actually tell of a journey, yet most do involve some degree of movement through space as well as time, and in many of these a common pattern reveals itself. The journey tale begins with an old world, generally simple and uncomplicated, more often than not home. The Garden of Eden is a prototype.

The middle portion, beginning with departure from home, is characterized by confusion, adventure, great highs and lows, struggle, uncertainty. The ways of the old world no longer hold, and the hero's task is to find a way through this strange middle land, generally in search of something lying at its heart. Christ's anguish in Gethsemane forms the dramatic counterpart to Eden in this sense. At the deepest point, the nadir of the descent, a transformation occurs, and the traveler moves out of the darkness toward a new world that often bears an ironic resemblance to the old. It is not the same, of course; it only looks that way. But the resemblance is no accident.

This mythic movement from an old, familiar land into the darkness of the nether world and back home transformed (see diagram below) has been traced by Joseph Campbell from hundreds of myths and legends across numerous cultures and times. Calling it the "monomyth," he describes the heroic quest this way:

> The standard path of the mythological adventure of the hero is a magnification of the formula represented in the rites of passage—separation-initiation-return—which might be named the nuclear unit of the monomyth.
>
> The hero ventures forth from the world of common day into a region of supernatural wonder; fabulous forces are there encountered and a decisive victory is won; the hero comes back from this mysterious adventure with the power to bestow boons on his fellowman [1949, p. 30].

Along the way, a number of critical incidents may take place. The traveler may "refuse the call," preferring to stay at home after

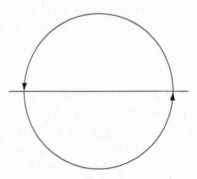

all; a mentor figure may appear to offer supernatural aid; a set of challenges must be met and overcome; an apotheosis occurs by which the traveler is transformed and empowered to return with a "boon" for his people; demons pursue him, but with help he escapes and becomes master of two worlds with a new freedom to live. The hero has been born again (Campbell, 1949).

The astute reader notes Campbell's language. Since most of the cultures from which he drew his information were patriarchal (including his own), his heroes are almost exclusively male; separation from "home" is essential to the journey. Contemporary critics (Bakan, 1966; Choderow, 1978; Gilligan, 1982; Belenky, Clinchy, Goldberger, and Tarule, 1986; Parks, 1989) have raised serious questions about whether separation has the same developmental meaning for women as for men, suggesting that the female journey may instead emphasize connection and care rather than isolation and hierarchy. We continue to recognize this in later chapters. For now, it is enough to note that the task facing both sexes is to reframe and understand in a radically new way the meaning of the world they once knew. This does not mean that the old world has been abandoned; rather, it has been incorporated into a broader awareness of its place. It is *seen* in a new way. The journey does not take away our old experiences, as we often fear before we embark. It simply gives them new meaning. This is the significance of the paradoxical Zen saying:

Before practice, there is the mountain;
During practice, there is no mountain;
After practice, there is the mountain.

Nothing is different, yet all is transformed. It is *seen* differently. In this change of perspective, in the transformation of meaning lies the meaning of transformation (Mezirow, 1978, 1991; Mezirow and Associates, 1990; Cranton, 1994; Kremer, 1997; Elias, 1997). Our old life is still there, but its meaning has profoundly changed because we have left home, seen it from afar, and been transformed by that vision. You can't go home again—or rather, the home to which you return is not the one you left.

The irony is that you also can't get there from here. That is, for this sort of mythic transformation to occur, we have to get lost.

By definition, there are no paths through the wilderness and no ways home save through it.

In one of the most richly imaginative of modern journey tales, *The Lord of the Rings* trilogy, Sam and Frodo, the central characters, are taking a brief break during their terrible journey into the Dark Empire of Mordor. Sam, lover of stories, is speculating with Frodo about whether their own tale will ever become part of the legends of their people.

"I wonder what sort of a tale we've fallen into?" he asks.

"I wonder," Frodo replies. "But I don't know. And that's the way of a real tale. Take any one that you're fond of. You may know, or guess, what kind of a tale it is, happy-ending or sad-ending, but the people in it don't know. And you don't want them to" (Tolkien, 1965, pp. 407–408).

For each of us, tangled inside our own stories, the endings are hidden. Yet most of us spend the better part of our lives trying to assure ourselves that our tales are already told, even if not yet lived, and that they have a happy ending. The discovery that this might not be so can, in itself, lead to profound transformation. But the appearance of someone who has already taken the journey can bring a sigh of relief to the best of us. This is where mentors come in. They have been there before; we greet them with awe and, above all, hope.

So it was with Dante, whose *Divine Comedy* is surely the most brilliant and richly detailed account of a transformational journey ever written. It is the story of his descent through Hell and Heavenward through Purgatory accompanied by the Roman poet Virgil, a classic mentor. In their friendship is a prototype of the mentor-protégé relationship. Join us for a closer look.

The Deep and Savage Way

The central theme of the tale is Dante's quest for Truth, represented by his journey through Hell to Heaven in search of union with his love, Beatrice. The tale begins at midlife, a fitting time for asking ultimate questions.

"Midway through the journey of life," begins the epic, Dante finds himself lost in a dark wood, terrified and fleeing in desperation from wild animals. He has lost all hope, when Virgil appears, coming toward him through the gloom. Assuring Dante that he is

an envoy from Beatrice, who awaits him near the end of his journey, Virgil leads the pilgrim through Hell on the paradoxically
downward journey toward the light.

Virgil knows the territory. He is Mentor Supreme, alternately
protecting his charge from threat, urging him on, explaining the
mysteries, pointing the way, leaving him alone, translating arcane
codes, calming marauding beasts, clearing away obstacles, and
encouraging—always encouraging.

At one point in the descent through Hell, the old man takes
the younger in his arms like a child and plummets down a rocky
embankment to escape a flock of vengeful spirits; at another, he
snaps at Dante for becoming too absorbed in conversation with
frauds and falsifiers. And finally, in his greatest single act of instruction, Virgil bids the pilgrim gaze directly upon the Emperor
of the Woeful Kingdom himself:

> When we had gone on so far that my Master thought it good to
> show me the creature who was once so fair, he took himself from
> before me and made me stop, saying: "Lo, Dis, and the place where
> thou must arm thyself with fortitude."
>
> How chilled and faint I turned then, do not ask, reader, for
> I do not write it, since all words would fail. I did not die and I did
> not remain alive; think now for thyself, if thou has any wit, what
> I became, denied both death and life [1961, p. 43].

Knowing that explanations in the pit of Hell are generally su-
perfluous, Virgil has the good sense to add nothing at the moment.
He has brought Dante to the brink of being and nothingness, bid-
den him look, and retired. The experience is transformative, for it
marks a momentous boundary, not simply between life and death
but between what Dante knows and what he cannot conceive. It
is a transformation precisely because it goes beyond both life *and*
death, making possible the unimaginable.

Then, telling Dante to grasp him around the neck, Virgil swings
down the very haunches of the Beast, leading him beneath Satan's
feet out a long pathway, back and upward toward Purgatory just
as the morning stars are fading. The first leg of their journey has
been completed.

As they walk up the seven-story mountain of Purgatory, the
relationship between the two men grows softer. In Hell, Virgil

bore clear authority and seemed virtually invincible. In this Middle Kingdom, both he and his protégé stand out less sharply from each other and from their surroundings. Here they are among peers, and despite Dante's continued respect for his guide, their relationship reflects this sense of growing equality. The sounds here are muted, the light less stark, and one has the sense that while earlier the pair walked in single file down narrow pathways, here they more often stroll upward side by side. Whereas formerly they were sightseers, largely detached from their surroundings, now they are participants engaging more fully with the inhabitants of the land as well as with each other.

At the very summit of the mountain is the garden of Eden, completely surrounded by a wall of flame. As they stand before the fire, unable to see through, the archangel's voice booms out: "There is no way further unless first the fire's sting is felt; enter into it and be not deaf to the singing from beyond." Heaven can only be attained by returning to Eden. But to do that, one must first pass through the flames of purification and transformation.

Standing before the wall of fire, the poet is entertaining second thoughts:

> When he saw me remain standing stubborn, being troubled a little, he said: "Look now, my son, between Beatrice and thee is this wall. ... " So, my stubbornness softened, I turned to the wise leader, hearing the name that ever springs up in my mind; at which he shook his head and said: "What, are we to stay on this side?" Then smiled as one does at a child that is won with an apple. Then he put himself into the fire before me. . . .
>
> As soon as I was in it, I would have cast myself into boiling glass to cool me, so beyond measure was the burning there, and my sweet father, to comfort me, kept talking of Beatrice as he went, saying: "I seem to see her eyes already." Guiding us was a voice that sang beyond, and giving all our heed to it, we came forth where the ascent began. "Venite, benedicti patris mei" [come, ye blessed of my father] sounded within a light that was there, such that it overcame me and I could not look at it. "The sun departs," it continued, "and evening comes; do not stop, but hasten your steps before the west grows dark" [1961, p. 353].

And so they are through the fire. By the time Virgil takes his leave shortly afterward, Dante is ready for the next leap, his momentum beyond question. The proximity of the light draws him on, and Virgil's prodding is no longer necessary. At the brink of Heaven, the mentor offers his blessing, explaining that he can lead no further and instructing his charge to await the appearance of Beatrice. His task is complete. "Free, upright, and whole is thy will and it were a fault not to act on its bidding; therefore over thyself I crown and mitre thee."

Turning to his guide for support, Dante finds him gone. His pathway now leads beyond the vision of his mentor.

Here, in this extraordinary tale, is embedded all the richness of the mentor-protégé relationship as it moves from a beginning rescue to a downward journey toward transformation and through to a growing equality as the pair separate. What makes this such a powerful and enduring model? What does it have to offer us as teachers and advisers?

Virgil as Mentor

Virgil begins by *engendering trust, issuing a challenge, providing encouragement,* and *offering a vision* for the journey. In so doing, he helps to transmute Dante's fear of abandonment into the call of adventure. Throughout the journey, he alternately supports and challenges his protégé to keep moving, to sustain his quest.

By way of engendering trust, Virgil reminds Dante that Beatrice sent him. He is thus an emissary of the light, a channel for truth, much as Mentor is a vehicle for Athena's wisdom. It is interesting to note that in these and other epics, a female figure is often closer to "the source" than men are. Both Dante and Odysseus are journeying toward the feminine, as though unification with the female constitutes wholeness for them. For a female hero, one might surmise, the converse would be the case: the journey toward wholeness would lead toward the masculine. But perhaps because our cultural mythologies offer so few tales of female heroes, or perhaps because—as I suspect—gender roles are more complex than this, one is hard pressed to find mythic tales that illustrate this. Still, there are innumerable stories of women who have found male mentors to be helpful in a male-dominated work setting.

In any case, it is noteworthy that both Virgil and Mentor are half-way creatures, residents of both this world and the next. As such, they are ideal guides for those in transition, human enough to understand this world, immortal enough to lead the way to the next. Yet they are only the embodiment of wisdom, never the source. This is a particularly important distinction, one too often forgotten by overly dependent travelers and easily flattered guides. No human beings can be a *source,* and for either mentor or protégé to believe as much is to lead the journey dangerously astray or abort it altogether.[5]

Notice that the mentor appears near the beginning of the journey when the pilgrim is most afraid and uncertain. Understandably, Virgil's power is considerable at this point, for there are good reasons why authority is important early in the journey. When we feel out of control, as Dante did, we need to believe that others are in it. We need something solid to hold to until we regain our balance. Returning to school after years away can be a deeply unsettling experience for many adults. Competent though they may be in their work or homes, they find themselves suddenly at the mercy of teachers sometimes younger than they and in danger of ridicule from fellow students who could be their own children.

Surrounded by forces that seem greater than ourselves, we are understandably anxious about those who wield power. Do they use it for us or against us? This is why mentors are sometimes feared at the outset or simply not recognized. And it is why, if they are known, they are welcomed with what may later seem a surfeit of adulation. As Campbell observes, they are seen as "intercessors with The Powers" and as such must be carefully courted. Teachers of adults do well to recognize the anxiety experienced by many beginning students. It is often masked as bravado or scorn. But underneath there often lies deep uncertainty—about the ability to succeed "late in life," about losing face before other students or teachers half their age, about working in sometimes starkly unfamiliar realms. Knowing this for the fear it is, we can act to relieve it gently rather than attempting to overcome or deny it.

Not only was Virgil's timing good, but he was experienced. He had been there before. He knew the dangers and many of the enemies lying ahead. He could explain to Dante the meaning of his encounters and steer him clear of threats. Students often speak this way of their advisers: "She explained all the forms and bureaucratic detail to me," or "He kept me on track so I knew I wouldn't get in trouble." In postsecondary education, the mentor holds the keys to membership in that other world of "the educated" (a world that holds a good many more mysteries than those of us who are on this side of the threshold readily remember). Like Virgil, the academic adviser is a translator not simply of the arcane ways of academia but of the very words themselves: *credits, distribution requirements, liberal studies.* We tend to forget that as do members of any specialized field, we cloak ourselves with mystery in the service of our mastery.

In addition to explaining the damned to Dante, Virgil also explains Dante to the damned—when they are not too preoccupied by rivers of boiling blood and similar infernal delights to notice. From this unique position between worlds, the academic mentor frequently finds it necessary to interpret to colleagues the special circumstances of a particular student's life, explaining, for instance, why Sheila's caring for three sick children and a dying aunt somehow took precedence over timely completion of a term paper describing the esthetic properties of a tenaculum.

For Dante, Virgil was a model poet. On the basis of their common craft, Dante was able to trust his mentor and was drawn toward him. For many students, the teacher serves as a concrete manifestation of what they wish to become. The attraction may be specific ("I'd like to have that kind of a job myself ") or general ("He seems to have a freedom I admire"). For others, especially women, a female mentor may seem to maintain an alluring balance between responsibilities of home and career (Erkut and Mokros, 1981; Collins, 1983; Wunsch, 1994). But all mentors serve some sort of higher tradition. As keepers of the educational fires, as the most accessible exemplars of what it means to "be educated," mentors embody answers to such questions as "How does she know so much?" "How can I become like that?" and "What am I supposed to know?" Viewed from sufficient distance, it all looks like magic, and we ought not be too surprised if we are treated like magicians.

As the journey progresses, Virgil offers great support and encouragement to his protégé, shoring up Dante's courage again and again. When asked to describe the good mentor, students point to this more than to any other aspect. "He was incredibly supportive, and I really felt liberated by that." "Even if she disagreed, I always knew she would help me get it right because she went out of her way to see my point of view." "Without his encouragement, I never would have made it." Unfortunately, this nurturant aspect of the mentor's job is often shortchanged. Many men, especially, see this as "mere babysitting," essentially unrelated to the real business of teaching. "By the time they are at this level they ought to be able to take care of themselves," goes the argument; "it's not my job to hold their hands." Yet if we are serious in asserting that education is most successful if students grow, that it is intellectual develop-ment we are about rather than simply knowledge acquisition, then the evidence is strong that emotional engagement must be a part of the learning process. Two hallmarks that distinguish the good mentor from the mediocre teacher are recognition that passion is central to learning and the capacity to provide emotional support when it is needed (Brookfield, 1990).

At the same time, Virgil is no mere patsy. Along with the rest of his breed, he sets intricate tests and challenges along the way and does not hesitate to express disapproval of Dante's behavior if necessary. Thus mentors also "teach" in a conventional sense, offering new information, giving advice, testing, and frequently stimulating their students to take issue with them. "I disagreed with a lot of what she said, and I still do," said one student. "But I have to admit she really made me think." The result is to unveil new perspectives. Blinded by fear, Dante literally comes to see the world afresh. "He really opened my eyes," said one student of her teacher. Followers may be unable to discern where their guides are leading them, but if the journey is a good one then they learn, as Don Juan says of Castaneda, to *see* in a new way.

Finally, it is time for Virgil to leave. At some point, the men-tor always departs, generally before the journey is over. The trip belongs, after all, to the traveler, not the guide—and the men-tor has her own promises to keep. Once the transformation has been accomplished by the student and accepted by the mentor, the departure may be smooth and caring. Sadly, such cases are fre-quently an exception, and many relationships end in indifference or hostility (Levinson and others, 1978). Still, if the journey takes its full course, the traveler has her own momentum. The power that seemed at the outset so overwhelming moves inward, and the student becomes her own teacher. If the mentor is also capable of letting go of this power so that the relationship can be genuinely reciprocal, the odds favor a lasting friendship. The paradox is that at the outset few students can imagine the relationship evolving to friendship. The idea of equality is literally incomprehensible. Yet afterward, it seems the only possibility. Describing such an ending, one student said of her mentor, "Yes, we're friends now, but there's still that respect; I'll always respect her. You know, I feel that we are now much more like colleagues than we were." The idea of "respect" has allowed her to hold both the earlier hierarchical form and her new equality at once. She can continue to honor her teacher while cherishing a new friend. Said another student:

> I used to think that I wanted more than anything else to be like Barbara; I wanted, almost, to *be* her. But I'm not, of course. I think I'm more myself now than I ever was... except that I'm not the person I used to be. Does that make sense? I think that's why we can be friends.

That *but* is telling, for it marks a fresh boundary between someone who once sought her identity through immersion with another and a person who now knows that she must be her own author. Because she came to see herself anew, she could reconstrue the relationship as well, and do so more maturely and equally.

Occasionally, both partners are fortunate enough to sustain the connection through its maturity. Of dozens of formal mentoring relationships, I count only a small handful in my own life that have done so. Ella, a participant in some of my early developmental research, was one such person, and she wrote this about her experience at the time:

> My first impression of Larry was of an almost-god standing above and apart from those of us in the [learning group], yet somehow tantalizingly reachable if we chose the right road to where he was standing.... [Our relationship] progressed through the emotionally charged and draining phases of growth, rebellion, and separation into a tenuous state of autonomy fueled by my desire to prove both to myself and to him that I was finally "educated" enough to go it alone, thank you very much.... Luckily Larry said and did the right things at the right times to both push and pull me through the process until some sort of level was reached between us.

That's a rare accolade, and I continue to treasure it (along with Ella's friendship). It was she, more than anyone else, who taught me about what is best in our work. We hear more from her before the book is out. Both of us are now off on our own paths, but they cross and cross again, and when they do, we find that we are learning similar things from our lives. The old hierarchical roles were shed back there somewhere, and in place of the earlier enchantment is a simple friendship—a whole new kind of magic. This kind of growth of relationship, from one resting on the authority of the teacher to one rooted in mutual reciprocity, is a key indicator of transformative learning.

So much for the violins. Long before this moment is reached (if it ever is) lie long hours of work—students struggling to understand difficult material and integrate it into complicated lives, mentors attempting to enter the thought frames of their students and help them pry loose their old assumptions on the fulcrum of a new idea. In the conversation that follows, meet Eric, an engineer in his mid-thirties who has gone about as far as he can go, unless he changes direction. He has returned to school to do that, but with the help of Milt, a true mentor, Eric discovers that something more than his direction must change. In reading, try to sense the movement of Eric's life. In what ways does his journey parallel Dante's? What does his metaphor about trenches suggest about *how he conceives of his journey*? Finally, consider how both Milt and I provide for Eric a *vision* ahead, *encouragement*, and *challenge* as we guide him into his own deep and savage way.

Into the Trenches

The walls are bare, beige, almost baleful; the table and chairs fit together perfectly with engineered elegance. Through the glass partition behind Eric, I can see people moving about the office space in utter silence: businesslike, correct, and very, very careful. We have met in the conference room of the small electronics firm where Eric works as an engineer to discuss his project for the adult development seminar that I am teaching.

"I'm still not sure what you want in this presentation," he says. A touch of impatience edges his voice. "Do you want me to go through the book and just give out Levinson's ideas? Hell, I can do that; I'm great at charts and that."

I don't answer right away. There seems to be an "or" coming, and I want to hear what it is. He holds his glance for a second and, not seeing an answer, leaps ahead.

"Or . . . or do you want me to criticize him, or . . . I mean, I can do that too if you want, but I haven't studied much psychology and I'm not sure I can. . . . " He falters.

"Sure, Eric. That would be good," I reply. "We've got three hours, and I'll need some time for an introduction, and we'll want to discuss what you've presented, so I'd say you should put together roughly a two- to two-and-a-half-hour talk. Try to help us understand Levinson's theory, but you should also try to help us engage with it. Get us thinking about where it does or doesn't make sense in our own lives."

The "we" is deliberately ambiguous. I've been trying to encourage Eric to connect the work with what is happening in his own life, but with only limited success. He's extremely skittish about his inner life and has no intention of "pouring his guts out," as he puts it. At least not in public.

"Yeah, I guess I can do some criticism of it too," he says with an amiable but belligerent grin. "That shouldn't be too hard."

The belligerence, I think to myself, hides a good deal of fear about handling this sort of material. Much of what he has studied until now has been related to engineering and business—courses, he says, that make sense. Now that he's being asked to deal with more fluid content, he's uneasy.

"Just remember," I remind him, "that this is only one of a whole handful of theories that we are looking at. None has 'the truth'; each is sort of like a slice of an orange—what you see depends on how you cut it. You don't have to worry about being 'correct' in the same way you might with calculus. What you need to do first is be clear about what Levinson is saying. Explain that to the class. Then, when you criticize, look at what kind of sample he used, what his assumptions are, and think about whether your own experience fits or not—or better, where it fits and where it doesn't."

Eric nods. He has heard all this before, but it is understandably still hard for him. Just over a year ago, fresh in the program, he and I sat in this very room and discussed his study plan. "I just want that piece of paper," he said back in that meeting, spiking me with a smile, at once friendly and dead serious. "I'll level with you. I've been in my current position long enough. I look around at some of the ding-a-lings that run this place and I know damned well I can do better. But they've got that piece of paper and I don't. So just tell me what I've got to do."

Everything about Eric said precision, from his neatly trimmed hair to his perfectly kept looseleaf notebook with every document and form in its place. For a long time after I met Eric, I would feel inordinately bumbling—sure I would trip over my briefcase, spill coffee on his registration form. Arriving five minutes late would find me trembling with guilt, angry at myself for leaving myself open to the judgment of his engineered intellect. Indeed, it was an application to which he freely turned his mind, sharply criticizing a current course at the community college as too "unstructured." "Why don't they get someone to teach that stuff who knows what she's doing?" he complained.

But in the months that followed, we warmed up considerably with each other. For all of his cross-grained irascibility, I found his candor refreshing. There was something deeper, driving that honesty. Eric knew something about himself that didn't square with the man he showed at work. One day, curious about Eric's urgency to get ahead, I asked him about it.

"Look," he said, "I've been spinning my wheels at this job for ten years, and I just don't want to keep spinning any more. I'm good at what I do, damned good." He fixed me with that competent look again and then turned to stare at the wall, as if trying to see through it, outside. "But I want to get doing what I *want* to do."

"What's that?"

"That's the trouble," came the reply, evenly. "I don't really know. The only place I really feel good is when I'm out in the woods. Or fishing." And for the next half hour, Eric talked about his love for the outdoors, his skill as a bow hunter, his fascination with natural history, and his very considerable knowledge of local fish and game.

"Why don't you study that?"

"Hell," he shot back, "Nobody pays you to do what you want to do."

"They do me."

"Sure. That's different. You've got all that education. You think I can afford to do that when I don't even have a degree? Besides," he added with a grin, "I couldn't live on what you're making." I laughed—somewhat bitterly I'm afraid—and agreed with him.

"Look," he said with a tinge of desperation, "I'm starting to feel a lot of pressure. Not just in my work but in other areas as well. It's like I've got this biological clock inside me that's just ticking away. And I figure I've wasted all this time in my life, and I don't want to waste the second half of my life. I've lived almost thirty-five years and I figure I'll live to be maybe seventy. Then, boom, that's it."

It was clear that there was a good deal more going on in this engineer's mind than little turning wheels and a quest for a piece of paper. So over the following weeks, we explored a number of possible areas of study for Eric other than simply more engineering. Although a complete shift to environmental studies was one such possibility, we both decided that it would be too drastic. As it turned out, during this time Eric pressed for, and received, a promotion to a managerial position. As a result, he chose to focus his studies on industrial management.

"More and more now, I'm working with people," he told me. "I need to learn more about what makes people tick." So that was how we ended up here, talking about Daniel Levinson.

"You know, reading this stuff is different from reading a math book," Eric is saying. "You have to pick and choose what's important." I grunt agreement and he goes on. "It's like this organizational behavior tutorial I'm doing with Milt right now. We read a lot of case studies, and at first I kept looking for the right answer, the right way you're supposed to come out on each case. But as soon as I'd say what I thought, Milt would come out with another whole point of view I hadn't thought of. I'm beginning to get the idea that... " (as he says this, he grins knowingly at me) "... I'm beginning to realize that there's no single right answer. You have to try to put them all together and come up with the best approach."

Predictably, my own grin answers his, and I respond with mock confusion, "But Eric, I thought you didn't like Milt. You said he was nothing but a wishy-washy college professor."

"That's right!" he bursts out. "He was. But now he's changed. Must have been my influence," he adds with conscious irony, and we laugh together. I remember that first study. Both Eric and Dave (whose story appears in the next chapter) needed to study accounting, and I brought them together with Milt, a business instructor, in the hope that a strong bond would form among the three. It did, and although Eric listened with open skepticism to Dave's praise for liberal studies and fought Milt's discursive teaching style, it was fascinating to see how he was drawn back to Milt now, how the very same experience he once thought too filled with "bullshit" and devoid of real content was becoming transformed into an experience he recalled with real respect.

"The thing about Milt," he continues, "is that he really helps you see that there's a lot of different points of view and that you have to try to make up your own mind for yourself about these things. There's no simple right or wrong answer when it comes down to dealing with people. Like, first there's the floor manager, then there's the boss, and then there's the production workers, and the union and all. I mean in their own way, they're all right. Or wrong," he adds, chuckling.

He goes on to talk about Milt and how shaken he has been by Milt's losing grapple with cancer. "He's come to mean an awful lot to me. You know, at first, he didn't even want to take me on. He said he would only do it as a favor to you. But since then we've gotten pretty close. He's shared a lot of things with me about his life that I don't even want to talk about." Eric stops and looks at his notebook, carefully framing it between his hands. "In a way, maybe it's just as well he is dying. Maybe I won't have a chance to see his warts."

We are both silent a long time, avoiding each other's eyes.

"Yeah," I say finally, "he's a rare man. He just won't let his . . . his condition get to him, will he?" Eric, who has been staring at the pale wall again, talks, almost to himself.

"You know, it's funny. This fall, during hunting season—I almost always get my deer the first day—this fall I ran into a deer. It was a big buck, twelve-pointer. He stopped right in front of me. Not ten feet away. And we just looked at each other. Neither of us moved a muscle. We just stood there . . . for a minute, two minutes, I don't know. Finally, he just turned and walked into the bushes. I never even lifted my bow. It's crazy. I don't know what's happening to me. Sometimes I'll put a fish back even though it's big enough to keep."

We're both silent again. Eric stares straight ahead, unmoving. At last I ask, "What's it about?"

"You know, sometimes in your class I feel pretty dumb. When Susan and you get going about Jung and Freud and all those names I don't even know, I feel kind of shallow. Well, maybe so. Maybe I am shallow." He looks directly at me now, but there's no challenge there. Simple declaration. "But I've got deep trenches."

I smile, moved by his honesty and eloquence. We both take a deep breath and straighten our chairs. "We'd better finish up," he says, glancing at his digital watch; "I've got to get back."

We discuss his presentation for a few minutes more and then pick up to leave. He opens the door for me as I go out, and I remark that I hope I won't get a ticket for parking in an executive parking space. "I hope it wasn't yours," I say, "now that you're a fat cat."

"Hell, you'd never catch me parking in one of those places," he replies, the familiar grin back.

"Oh? Why not?"

"You wouldn't believe this place," he snorts. "It's like a bunch of goddamn baboons. They all scrap for the parking place closest to the boss. A regular pecking order. Same thing in meetings. Number three man has to sit next to number two man; number two man has to sit next to number one man. It's a crock." Then he sticks out his hand, grinning broadly. "Thanks." I return the handshake but drive off feeling vaguely empty. In another place, another time, I'd have hugged him just then.

Clearly, Eric was growing, although at the time I was not sure how. Not surprisingly, the more I learn of developmental theory, the more complicated the picture becomes, and with every new developmental scheme there follows a period of seeing through the eyes of this researcher or that theorist. To a considerable extent, as I write now, I continue to see different people through different lenses depending on which perspective seems to illuminate the most. But over time, I am beginning to see some common threads, to develop a clearer vision of what happens when adults return to pick up an educational journey abandoned long before. Grasping developmental theory is more akin, I have discovered, to learning a language than it is to acquiring a new body of knowledge. More than the particular vocabulary, it's the syntax that matters; it's a way of seeing beneath the surface to the structures of growth. This is why the journey seems to work so readily as a metaphor for development. It gives us a model for grasping underlying structure in motion, of understanding deeply the meaning of metamorphosis as *the evolution of form.*

There is a tendency, on first encountering developmental theory, to think of stages as though they were a sequence of Procrustean operating tables onto which researchers clamp their subjects, lopping limbs with ghoulish abandon. But even though research demands such precision—and some writing does seem to emphasize the tables more than the people—for teachers this is not only unhelpful and inappropriate; it is an inhumane way to think about the movement of our lives. It is the people, not the stages, the moving picture and not the snapshots, that should command our attention. This is particularly important in education because few teachers or mentors ever see a student through an entire journey. Rather, we accompany students along some legs of some of their journeys; if we are to play our part well, we need to view their movement with a broader eye, to see whence they have come and whither they are headed. We'll need two or three good maps.

In the next chapter, we eavesdrop on three more conversations. Each illuminates a different facet of the growing adult. And each provides an opportunity to view growth through a different lens. At the end of the chapter, we return to Eric and look at him again through all three lenses at once.

Chapter Three

Maps of Transformation
How Adults Change and Develop

In order to understand anything well,
you need at least three good theories.
—WILLIAM PERRY

It has never been any secret that we change as we age. The only question is how. Cultures vary greatly in their answers to the question, ranging from those traditional societies in which age is synonymous with wisdom to our own high-tech belief that to grow old is to become less valuable. (When was the last time we had an American president we would characterize primarily as wise?) It is an appropriate paradox, then, that ours should be the culture that generates the most careful analysis of the question: What happens as we age? Perhaps precisely because of today's cacophonous change, we seek reassurance that our lives do not, in fact, run downhill from the beginning, like some maverick alarm clock. We need to know that life is more than what our mechanistic metaphors would suggest.

Ed must have been wondering, too, as I approached his door that frozen December afternoon carrying my papers and questions. Was his life simply winding down—or, for that matter, was mine? Was his return to education just a desperate attempt to forestall the inevitable, or might it promise a genuine rebirth? And what did that mean, exactly, "rebirth"?

In this chapter, the reader is invited to join conversations with three people: Dave, a man struggling at midlife with questions about what is important in his life; Sandy, at thirty-three feeling the stirrings of a ripening independence; and Monique, a young woman caught in a conceptual world too narrow for her new aspirations. We examine each conversation through the eyes of a different developmental theorist. Finally, we review Eric, whose story appeared in the preceding chapter, through all three lenses.

Although the differences among the three theories are important, all provide useful and overlapping perspectives. They all counter the implicit metaphor of the unwinding clock, which pervades so much of our conversation about aging. Instead, they suggest more profound and mythic metaphors: the seasons, an upward-spiraling helix, a journey. There is nothing supernatural about the number three, but genies, witches, and other beings who take pity on us probably have a good reason for giving us three wishes, three guesses, three tasks, rather than two or four. There is some powerful challenge in that number.

Developmental perspectives of this sort help to improve the quality of education in a number of ways. For administrators, knowledge of the real-life dilemmas faced by students like Dave can provide valuable arguments for enhanced use of liberal studies to help adult students confront the existential questions of their lives and consequently enrich the depth of their learning (Gamson, 1984; Schlossberg, Lynch, and Chickering, 1989; Merriam and Caffarella, 1991). Knowledge of the particular life issues of different age groups can sharpen marketing techniques (Aslanian and Brickell, 1980; Merriam and Clark, 1991). Perhaps most important, these developmental theories raise into clear view the question "What is education for?" thus offering an alternative to the self-centered and frequently directionless relativism that has recently become such a bête noir among contemporary critics (Kegan, 1994).

Meanwhile, in the classroom, as teachers come to recognize the motion of a person like Emerald, they can supplant their understandable but probably inappropriate frustration with more compassionate understanding of the range of ways in which their students make meaning, and devise methods to help their students see new choices. They can begin to design activities, exercises, and assignments that challenge their students differentially, in accordance with developmental needs. They can discover the educational power of controversial perspectives seriously debated, of placing theoretical constructs in a historical or cultural context, of flicking just the right question to just the right student at just the right time.

Finally, a ready set of developmental concepts can help counselors or professors, in their role as advisers, sense the unique movement of each of their advisees and work accordingly. They might, for instance, encourage older students needing to confirm a lifetime of experience to undertake projects with younger people, exchanging their accumulated wisdom for insights through the eyes of a younger generation; midlife women might discover themselves anew through women's literature; young adults seeking identity might study family history or read biographical material. As we learn to see people in the context of their potential for growth, the possibilities for enriching their educational experience expand rapidly. As learners come to incorporate more complex and diverse information into their intellectual vision, they tend to seek more of the same. When the process is occurring smoothly, it seems to progress almost by itself. This, indeed, is what John Dewey had in mind when he suggested that educational value ought to be measured by "the extent in which it creates a desire for continued growth" (1916, p. 62).

Concern about the meaning and experience of growth was hardly new to me, of course, when I read Dewey. In a sense, it had been with me all my life—at least since that day when I lay on my back as a child, watched a tiny cloud far above me dissolve with infinite grace into the blue, and felt terrible sadness. It was important to me to know that we *grow* as we age—not just bigger but in some way *better*. Later, as a high school teacher, I saw it happen with my own students, and then with participants in encounter groups and teacher training workshops, and finally with my own children. I knew people could make important changes, and I called this growth, but still I lacked a way to understand what I was seeing. It was clear that people were moving, but from where, to where? I needed a map.

Asked to imagine a map of America, most of us conjure up a vision of a multicolored United States—pink Massachusetts, yellow

Texas, green Florida. But as every cartographer knows, a political map is only one of dozens of possible maps. A geographic map might ignore state lines entirely, emphasizing mountain ranges, rivers, and lakes. A historical map might draw boundaries in sharply different places than our more familiar contemporary one. A demographic or weather map would look different in still other ways. What goes onto a map clearly depends on what interests the cartographer; the map we choose depends on what we wish to know.

The same goes for theories of human development. Although developmentalists, like cartographers, may assert at times that their maps are value-free or strictly descriptive, they make choices in constructing their schemes to highlight some elements and ignore others. Those choices inevitably affect the traveler who is using the map. In selecting one map over another, the traveler does not simply take a different path; she may be led to a new destination. Thus, when in 1977 Carol Gilligan offered women an alternative map to the prevailing ones, suggesting that optimal development need not mean ever-increasing separateness, she caused many women— and men as well—to reconsider the importance of striving toward a stance of detachment and abstract principle and to value instead those parts of themselves calling for connectedness and relationship. The very existence of a map stirs the traveler in our bones, and the places on that map color our dreams.

Yet good maps also offer choice; they are not mere formulas. And although developmental theories do imply direction, none insists that the journey can be taken in only one way, or indeed that it be completed at all. Just as a map frames the setting for a journey, so does a developmental theory offer a context for growth. It indicates landmarks, points out dangers, and suggests possible routes and destinations, but it leaves the walking to us.

One of most influential of the early maps is that offered by Daniel Levinson and his associates in *The Seasons of a Man's Life* (1978). I choose it here partly because it is they who first saw clearly how mentors help us through crucial times in our lives, partly because the study sheds penetrating light on what is going on in the lives of many men as they return to higher education, and partly because it is simply a well-written and insightful book.

As a member of the family of developmental studies that have come to be known as psychosocial or phase theories, the work is mainly concerned with the question "What happens to people psychologically as they grow older?" It is closely related to the earlier thinking of Carl Jung and Charlotte Bühler as well the research of the authors' contemporaries: Bernice Neugarten, Robert Havighurst, and Roger Gould. What unites this family is that each of these writers sought to understand common tasks that people confront as they face the problems associated with aging. The theories are thus chronologically and culturally determined to a significant extent. In any event, few of Levinson's colleagues locked life changes into specific ages as tightly as he did. Most have found considerably more room for variation according to gender, age cohort, life task, or ethnic and economic status (Knox, 1977; Tennant and Pogson, 1995).

A second map, offered in Robert Kegan's *The Evolving Self* (1982), represents another major branch of developmental theory, often called stage theory.[1] Jean Piaget is generally accorded fatherhood of this family through his contribution of the idea that we pass through distinct and qualitatively different stages in how we construct our childhood experience. This notion gained greater sophistication, as applied to adults, in the work of Jane Loevinger, Lawrence Kohlberg, and Gilligan, each of whom suggested that as we develop, we move first from a "preconventional" stance, in which our own personal survival is paramount, into a "conventional" orientation, in which our main concern is to fit into and be accepted by society, and later (if our development continues) into a "postconventional" position, in which we derive our decisions from broader considerations than personal survival or a wish to conform.

This family of theory is powerful because it asserts that growth involves more than becoming a well-adjusted member of society (moving from the first to the second level). It also means coming to see one's own culture from a critical stance and establishing loyalties that go beyond one's immediate community (moving from the second to the third level). Without question, Kegan's 1982 book provides the most carefully honed elaboration of stage theory available. His subsequent book, *In Over Our Heads* (1994), takes the work deeper, placing a more finely tuned version of the theory in dialogue with such very real "demands of modern life" as marriage, work, diversity, healing, and adult learning. A challenging, thoughtful work, it offers an enormously valuable map to understanding both our own lives and those of our students.[2]

Most stage theorists focus their attention on a kind of growth that does not inevitably come with age. They are less concerned with the process of becoming older than they are with the question of growing wiser. That is, Piaget noticed that some children seem to be able to comprehend the world more adequately than others, and he saw that the difference has less to do with static "intelligence" than with dynamic "development." The stage theorists extend this observation throughout the life span. Some adults seem to "understand" a complex world in a more complex way than others do. Rather than see intelligence as a fixed condition, developmentalists suggest that we all have the potential to evolve toward increasingly integrated and differentiated ways of making sense of the world. Thus, though two forty-two-year-old men may share common tasks in relation to their culture, they may interpret that experience quite differently, depending on the framework of the particular stage they are moving through. Because later stages are by definition more conceptually inclusive and discriminating— are better in some sense than earlier ones—this family of theory brings with it both exciting prospects and considerable dangers.

Drawing on some twenty years of listening closely to Harvard students talk about what they were learning during their four college years, William Perry sketched a third map, one he calls a "scheme of intellectual and ethical development." In certain ways it is the most useful and engaging of the three. Its value is that Perry describes just the sorts of change that liberal educators hope to see come about in their students, and he does so in a way that intuitively makes sense to anyone who has struggled to understand why some people seem so determined to see a shifting and multicolored world as though it were a black-and-white snapshot. As such, it offers us a beautifully articulated slow-motion film of the journey from naïve and simplistic thinking to complex and relativistic reasoning. Such movement need not necessarily happen as a result of formal education, but it seems evident that a good education increases the likelihood of it happening and thereby fosters growth in a number of ways.

It is time now to look more closely at how the theories can help us see and hear our students more clearly. Each of the conversations in this chapter highlights a particular question: What is important? Who am I? and What is right? But I hope it is clear, by the time we return to Eric, that no single vantage point or theory can reveal the extraordinary richness of the human territory. Rather, it is from the interplay of many perspectives that the teacher can best know how to be, for whom, and when.

We begin with Dave, at forty-three struggling to understand why his priorities have begun to shift under his feet. In listening, consider how the liberal studies courses he took mesh with the turmoil of his midlife transition. Notice how he describes the direction of change in how he sees himself and thinks about what is "true." And take note of how these changes affect those around him.

Through the Hourglass

He looks tired. I nudge the tape recorder closer to his bowed head, hoping to be unobtrusive. It's unlike Dave to mumble, and I find myself straining to catch his words. He still speaks in the same, somewhat inflated, yet disarming style, and the passion is still there, but it is subdued in a way that astonishes me. He speaks to the floor, to himself:

> A very, very dramatic change that I witness inside myself. No longer am I boisterous—you know, take an initial, active part. Not interested in that at all. Very quiet mannerisms as compared to very loud, robust type. I have an extremely hard time making decisions that I never had before, even though there used to be a lot of wrong ones. Now I don't make any if I don't have to. I wait as long as possible and think about it. That's what stands out for me.

We are sitting in the community college office where I've asked him to come for an informal, follow-up interview. Dave and I have known each other since we met eight years ago. He stood out then, a tall, handsome man in his mid-thirties, radiating confidence, a gunslinger of the construction industry. Owner of a highly successful small business, he fathered three sons, was Little League coach, and a respected member of the church community. He had gone about as far as he could, learning on his own, and wanted to "get more formal-type learning." With the kids mostly out of the way now, he could. On the basis of an unusually high award of experiential credit, Dave entered the external degree program and became my student. At almost exactly the same time, to the

consternation of his wife and friends, he sold his business and began work for a large industrial firm. He felt a need, he said, to "try
something with more of a challenge."

Not long afterward, he was selected to participate in a study
of adult development and gave us two intensive interviews, a year
apart. In the first interview, he spoke of returning to education as
a way of "filling voids" in himself. Once he attained the knowledge
he sought, he told us, he would achieve his goal: "peace of mind."

A year later, though still undaunted in his quest, Dave had
begun to entertain doubts. For the first time, he spoke of an "internal" self that seemed to be asking unsolicited questions: *Why
change careers? Why go back to school? Why am I feeling these feelings?*

> Internally I've been in combustion. I've been—I've got an internal
> upheaval, OK? Crazy thoughts, a lot of questions to be answered.
> Outwardly, I've been very, very energetic, trying something
> different.... I've always been in control of my external self. I
> thought about what I was going to say; my appearance was always
> right for the situation; I made sure the proper tools were always at
> hand... and suddenly, uncontrollably, the internal Dave Hyssop
> began to take ahold of his life. And all of a sudden the tools of the
> external weren't important; they didn't do the job, they didn't bring
> me any of that peace of mind I've mentioned so many times. It was
> the internal Dave that had control of me.... It kept reaching out
> and taking ahold of my life and shaking the hell out of me, OK?
> and saying, "No, you don't need this business, you don't need these
> tools, you don't need this appearance anymore. That's not what life
> is about.

I ask him about that now. How does he see his movement over
the years since that conversation? How might he describe it? He
looks at me sideways, wry grin baring a straight row of teeth; his
eyes reflect our brotherhood. We both know the territory.

"I'd still sketch it with my old hourglass theory," he says, squint-
ing out now through the dusty window of the old office building to
the brick facade of a tenement hotel across the street. "You know,
there's a coming into life so easily in the big bottom bubble....
I remember in my thirties being very self-satisfied with where
I was going, and tremendous energy, confidence in myself, and
feeling of success...."

His voice trails off; there's a long silence for both of us. Finally, I ask, "When did it start? I mean, when did you enter the neck of the hourglass?" More silence. Slowly, he turns to me, then back to the window.

"The hourglass? Oh, I guess, I'd say... I've been in there maybe five years."

"So you were about thirty-eight?"

"Thirty-eight. Yeah. And getting into the neck, I suddenly realized for the first time what an individual I was. I didn't need a lot of things that I depended on before. I began to question a lot of things that I was always taught to believe in or that always seemed to be right. I remember for a long time in there, just questioning everything."

We talk then for some time about what it's like "in there," for me as well as for him. He speaks of the internal struggle, between an "old self" that always seemed to be in control and a "new Dave" who seems to be more passive. Yet though his former self was more decisive, it was also less genuine, obsessed with "tangible things" at the cost of the "general concern for humanity" growing in importance now. "I was a bastard!" he says of himself. "A real bastard." And I begin to realize that when Dave calls himself passive he simply means that he no longer feels such a need to control his outside circumstances. He is drawing back, making way for the emergence of a more internal self, a self he calls more real.

"Did your education have anything to do with all this?" I ask, not sure I want to hear the answer.

He looks at me, a twinkle in his eye, jaw set. "Well, I'm very disillusioned about it right now. I was extremely disappointed in what I thought my education would do for me in terms of where I was in life when I began, some of my objectives, I mean. It's not going to do much for me in terms of employment or money, and [long pause] I'm not even sure I like myself anymore."

Somehow I had expected this, perhaps because I've heard it often enough; yet I hear a "but" coming. I nod and keep my mouth shut. After another long pause, it comes.

"The one thing it did for me is make me realize how little I know, how little learning I did have, and how much there is to learn and understand. You know, I read a lot more than I ever did before—all kinds of things interest me. I'm an entirely new person now, and I'm having trouble living with myself. Other people too—my wife and my kids." He smiles to himself. "The other day she said she wished I'd never gone to college."

"What did she mean by that?"

"Well, I'm not the strong man in the family anymore. She wanted me to tell Ted, our youngest, to mow the lawn, and when I asked him, he said he wanted to work on the basketball court first. So I said, 'Fine, but the lawn's got to be mowed.' I got home that night and the lawn was mowed—no big deal. Now my other kids, I'd beat their ass if it wasn't mowed right then and there. I was a bastard, I tell you. My wife got used to living with that."

We talk on about how much strain there is on our relationships when we go through changes ourselves, how hard it is on marriages, on friendships. And he speaks of his own changes as a journey. I ask him what he feels he is moving toward.

"I'm beginning to see the whole world as being relative," he replies. "It's like, like . . ." searching for the words, ". . . time means nothing to me anymore. Like Einstein, you know; it's only a measurement of space. It's got nothing to do with beginnings or endings." He falls silent a moment, then grins and shakes his head. "Man, you can go any way you want. You know, all of us, we get thinking about our thinking and we immediately start to judge our thinking—why we're thinking that way or if it's all right to think that way. And, you know, you suddenly realize that in your mind you can think about anything you want to think about. You're a self-entity, irregardless of what you were before or what you're going to be tomorrow."

"Sounds like you've been traveling."

"Oh yeah," he says, grinning broadly at me now, the old Dave back. "I've traveled a long, long ways. You know, my education was like a catalyst when I think about it. I always enjoyed that word: *catalyst*. I always thought it was fantastic ever since I took a science course in junior high—a catalyst, you know? Something that starts something, helps something burn brighter, or you know, gives something more energy. Yeah, that's what I think my education was, a catalyst."

"Can you describe that a little more? A catalyst?"

"I think it brought to the surface things that were probably always inside me," he replies, sending a chill down educational spines at least as far back as Plato. "Maybe I lived a kind of phony life before; you know, it wasn't the real me. My education, how I studied, working with other adult learners, that was a catalyst. You know, look in the mirror and be truthful with myself. At least I'm being truthful with myself because that's the real me. My education brought out those things; it provided me with the confidence and the freedom to see things as they are, truthful about everything, not hide and act other than the way it actually is."

The power of his words leaves me drained. It's almost as though we have changed places—he now the active one, I sitting passive, in awe before the new Dave. We talk on a bit, and he speaks of his need to make new connections with the world. His frustration now is that he has left the old world behind but is having trouble finding a place in the new one. "You know," he says as we stand up, "no man is an island. And I'm an island. I guess it's time to make some connections."

Watching his lanky form disappear down the hallway, I realize that he has not so much lost connections as redefined them. He still has his friends, his family. They might well be the same as they have always been. But the image he holds of them no longer fills his inner spaces the way it used to. The spaces themselves have grown, and he's feeling the gaps.

Levinson

Dave's hourglass is a fitting metaphor for the midlife transition described in *The Seasons of a Man's Life*. Levinson and his associates divide men's lives into four major eras. Like a stairway, they ascend through time, the risers representing periods of consolidation with relatively little change, the steps indicating disruption and what Levinson calls structure changing (see Figure 3.1).

Levinson pays particular attention to the middle two eras of the life span, the years from about seventeen to sixty. The defining task of the late teens and early twenties is to move into the adult world and become accepted on its terms. For men in our culture, this means getting a job, establishing a household, and developing a sense of competence. During the twenties, says Levinson, men devote their energy to exploration and tentative commitment. Many of those he studied began to form a "dream" of how and

Figure 3.1. Levinson's Developmental Periods.

65	(Late Adulthood)
LATE ADULT TRANSITION	
60	
Culmination of Middle Adulthood	
55	
Age 50 Transition	(Middle Adulthood)
50 Entering Middle Adulthood	
45	
MID-LIFE TRANSITION	
40	
Settling Down	
33	
Age 30 Transition	
28	(Early Adulthood)
Entering the Adult World	
20	
EARLY ADULT TRANSITION	
7	(Childhood and Adolescence)

Source: Chart from Daniel J. Levinson et al., *The Seasons of a Man's Life,* Copyright © 1978 by Daniel J. Levinson. Reprinted by permission of Alfred A. Knoph, Inc., Co. and Sterling Lord Literistic, Inc.

who they wanted to become—a kind of projected script for their lives. Often they would find a mentor who embodied that dream and who could help them move toward it.

Mentors, in Levinson's ground-breaking research, are closely linked with the dream. They are living proof that it can be attained, and they usually help their protégés toward it. Appearing most frequently during one's twenties and thirties, mentors tend to be a half-generation older and remain in the role from three to ten years. Because much developmental research has looked at men and women in the workplace, it is perhaps not surprising that mentors are more commonly associated with the working world, with building competence and career rather than with developing the awareness and emotional maturity more appropriate to caring for oneself and others. Levinson's subsequent study of the lives of women (1996) confirms this. Mentors appear far less prominently in the lives of the women in his sample than they did in the earlier work, and when they do appear as teachers they play "a remarkably limited part in these life stories" (p. 237). Moreover, those relationships that developed in the working world were primarily with men and lacked the kind of intuitive identification that can occur when mentor and protégé are of the same gender. We can only hope that as more women enter positions of power, this will change.

As the figure suggests, our lives move rhythmically back and forth through periods of building, breaking, building, breaking, and building again, as we grow older and accommodate to the changing circumstances of our lives. The building period of the twenties ends with the midcourse correction that Gail Sheehy called "Catch 30." It is a time when we ask, "Is this *really* what I want?" Sometimes we discover that when we thought we were asking the same question years before, we were actually asking, "What *should* I be doing?" In effect, we grow more serious about our lives, hearing an inner voice that urges us to make our commitments, "for soon it will be too late to turn back." Depending on the answer, this breaking period may be relatively mild or tumultuous, but typically it involves the act of self-assessment: "Is this what I want?"

This transitional time bridges our thirtieth birthday and comes to an end with the beginning of the settling-down time, around age thirty-three. Now we begin to act on the commitments we have come to, spending the next five or six years building again—establishing a business, settling into a job, raising a family.

Then, beginning in the late thirties and extending into the early forties, comes the notorious midlife transition. It represents the elbow joint of our lives, squarely in the middle, separating spring and summer from fall and winter. The most dramatic transition, it prompts many men to reappraise life, not simply against our dream as we did years before but against our whole life span, cast with growing sharpness against the backdrop of our death. The neglected parts of ourselves call out more loudly to be heard, and for many a longing for wholeness begins to replace the ideal of perfection. It is during this time, says Levinson, that we address more fully the polarities that lie within us, like scales seeking equilibrium.

What tends to throw us off balance is our impulse to hold onto one end of the scales. By midlife, they may be so unevenly laden that only a major jolt can right them again. Such a jolt has the twin possibilities of either deadening our systems entirely—sending us down the remainder of our lives in slow despair—or refreshing us and pointing the way toward something like wisdom. Writing about this possibility, Carl Jung termed it *individuation*, the process by which we differentiate our selves (yet again) from our surrounding culture in a way that leads not to isolation but paradoxically to a greater sense of membership in the whole. Levinson "operationalizes" the term by suggesting that individuation happens as we redress imbalances along four polarities. Although he discusses them in detail in the context of the midlife transition, he makes it plain that the stuff of each polarity is always with us, and each transition requires tinkering with our little imbalances. To the extent that we maintain a reasonable equilibrium through early transitions, our midlife crisis remains relatively placid. The more fully we can engage with the tumult of one crisis, the more fully we grow in our ability to cope effectively with the next. Like paying off parking tickets, regular glove compartment cleaning keeps the Big Fine down.

The tension between being at once both *young* and *old* is the first and most apparent polarity. To address it, we must first acknowledge that we have changed since we last looked. Since the change is inevitable and since at all ages we contain within ourselves some aspects of both youth and age, the important question is "In what ways am I older and in what ways young?" To retune the balance each time, we need to draw out those parts we call young and old and label them afresh. "The task in every transition," Levinson reminds us, "is to create a new Young/Old integration appropriate to that time of life" (Levinson and others, 1978, p. 212).

A similar process of introspection and redefinition is at work with the other polarities: creation-destruction, in which we come to acknowledge our capacity for evil; masculine-feminine, in which we question a sexuality formed by earlier needs; and attachment-separation, in which we reassess the boundary between ourselves and others.

Different cultures tend to value one end of each polarity more than another. In American society, for instance, youth, masculinity, creativity, and separateness are almost universally more weighted than their counterparts. To right the balance, then—to "develop" in Levinson's terms—implies that we must swim upstream against our culture. We need support for such action, and in this respect it is interesting to note that mentor figures are frequently androgynous (Mentor or Tiresias), ageless (numerous Eastern bodhisattvas), or both helpful and destructive (Merlin). They embody the polarities and thus make it safe for us to move into our own.

By the mid-forties, Levinson writes, we begin to move out of our midlife wilderness and build a new "life structure" for the second half of our lives. It is time for the realignments that took place during the last transition to settle in and give more lasting meaning to our relationships, work, and spiritual commitments. There was great variability among the men studied at this period of life. Consolidating the gains of a lifetime, some entered more deeply and richly into their lives than ever before; others seemed simply to be marking time until retirement; and still others seemed to find it a time of great pain, of "constriction and decline."

Although Levinson delineates several further phases, the work loses much of its power after this period, in part because the research grows thinner but also, I suspect, because the authors have outreached their own experience and simply lost their passion. In any event, those portions of the life span that they illuminate most thoroughly stand out with great vividness and provide guides and pilgrims alike with a valuable map.

There is, however, one important caveat. Levinson studied men. Since the majority of returning adult students are women, this poses an obvious problem. The very narrowness of the book casts a particularly sharp light on the lives of many of my white, middle-class male students, but it has proven an inadequate map to the lives of those outside its beam, particularly women. The subsequent work, *Seasons of a Woman's Life*, on which Levinson and his spouse collaborated, attempts with mixed success to address this shortcoming. For both cultural and biological reasons, women's life paths are different (Baruch, Barnett, and Rivers, 1983; Josselson, 1987). Our culture's expectation that they take time out as mothers wreaks havoc with the neat, linear male trajectory. How a woman decides to juggle her "family responsibilities" has major ramifications for when she returns to school (Bernard, 1981; Evans, 1985; Merriam and Clark, 1991). For another thing, long overdue research is increasingly demonstrating that women define themselves in relation to others differently than men do, placing more emphasis on connectedness, less on separateness (Choderow, 1978; Dinnerstein, 1976; Gilligan, 1982; Baker-Miller, 1976; Rubin, 1983; Klein, 1985; Benjamin, 1988; Goldberger, Tarule, Clinchy, and Belenky, 1996). This fundamental difference holds major implications for education, implications that are only now being spelled out in a call for a "connected education" to counteract what some consider undue emphasis on detachment as a prerequisite to "rational thought" (Belenky, Clinchy, Goldberger, and Tarule, 1986; Weiler, 1988; Harris, 1991; Maher and Tetrault, 1994).

Midlife and Liberal Studies

But Dave too seems to be feeling the effects of too much separation. Let's return to him and consider what we see through Levinson's overlay.

It should be apparent that Dave was squarely in the midst of a rousing midlife transition. The hourglass metaphor was a unique and effective way to make sense of what he was feeling as he moved from the confidence, self-satisfaction, and tremendous energy of his early thirties into the neck of the hourglass—a time he traces to his late thirties, when he sold his business and returned to school. Though he physically remained at home, in a metaphorical sense he had left. His friendships fell away; he spent more time with studies and work, less with his family and community. In a real sense, he found himself wandering alone in a wilderness of questions, dancing, as he put it, in a twilight zone.

It was during this time that the sea change he describes as a shift from active to passive occurred. Although there are hints in his description of Levinson's male-female shift, the change seems more profound than this, more encompassing. Dave links the changes in a number of aspects of his life: from interest in tangible things to the intangible ones, from material to humanitarian considerations, from external to internal concerns, and from being in control to being out of it. He describes an old self who was a "bastard" and a new Dave whom he's not sure he likes but who is at least much more real, meaning no longer obsessed with appearances. Although he acknowledges that he is not as satisfied as he once was, he is more content now than he has ever been. Superficial happiness is no longer the goal of his life. Dave is clearly hearing new voices in himself and is listening with rapt, if sometimes uneasy, attention.

Transformations rarely, if ever, come about abruptly. Rather, they slip into place piece by piece until they become suddenly visible, often to others first and only later to ourselves. Yet it is possible sometimes to see key moments that seem central to the change. In Dave's case, the discovery that "in your mind you can think about anything you want to think about" is such a moment. Able now to think about thinking (a capacity Piaget considered of critical importance for the later stages of intellectual development), Dave realizes perhaps for the first time that *what he thinks can be separate from who he is*—that he can *have* his ideas rather than simply *be* them. This new capacity is both liberating and frightening, because although he is free to have his own thoughts he can no longer hide behind the old beliefs. All at once, the givens of his life—patriotism, the work ethic, his boyhood religion—come up for scrutiny. With confirmation that "the whole world is relative" comes a new kind of responsibility. Dave's reluctance to act impulsively, or even decisively, is grounded in this discovery.

What is the place of education in all of this? After all, with or without his further education, Dave would confront his midlife transition. What difference does a theory like Levinson's make in how we work with adult learners? At times, the connections between Dave's transition and his education appear so organic that it is senseless to try to tease them apart. Yet it seems clear that his educational experience changed the quality of his transition in significant ways. A course in anthropology helped him gain distance from his own values, to see his own conditioning freshly; a psychology course encouraged his capacity for self-examination; an aesthetics course put him in touch with universals in human experience; conversations with his mentor helped him name what was happening and gave him permission to do it. However familiar, his own term *catalyst* has a fresh power as he uses it to describe what his education was for him: something that starts something, helps it burn brighter, gives it more energy. So although the inevitable midlife transition brought on the questions, his education gave them a broader context, legitimized them, and allowed him to draw on far wider experience for answers.

"I learned it was OK to ask those questions," he told me later. "Everyone else was going through those changes too. It was those liberal studies that really pulled me through, no doubt about it. Funny. When you told me I ought to take so many of them, I can remember thinking, 'Now, what the hell do I need those for?' I guess you must have known something, eh?"

Did I? There certainly was no formula. Dave's particular track was utterly his own. Yet because his life had led him to ask fundamental questions of meaning, studies that welcomed such questions without answering them would clearly hold promise. But how to connect the student with the study? As Dave's remark implies, this is often a good deal clearer to teachers than students. The teacher's art lies in helping to bring those questions to the surface: in giving them legitimacy and giving the student permission to go about answering them.

A quite different set of questions confronts Sandy, at thirty-three working hard to replace her old roles as daughter, mother, and wife with a new relationship to her family—one that includes herself as an independent person. As she talks, listen to her description of where she is coming from and where she is headed. Note the function of her studies in that movement, and try to see how she is redefining the boundary between herself and others.

Joining the World

Although it is only three in the afternoon, what little light the day has to offer is fading fast as I shut off the engine, hoping it will start again in the subzero cold. I step over a frozen snowbank and stiffen against the sound of branches crackling overhead. To my relief, Sandy opens the door quickly and gestures to the kitchen table, where I sit, a bit too far for comfort from the compact wood-stove against the far wall.

"That's where I do most of my work," she says, smiling toward the table with gentle irony. "Coffee?"

We make small talk for several minutes, and then feeling the press of the growing darkness outside, I remind her that I have stopped by to listen to her talk about what it is like for her, at the age of thirty-three, to be back in school studying again after twelve years.

She explains that she spent much of the time after acting school trying to find work, to prove to herself that she could be a successful actress. She also married and bore a child. At her husband's urging, she began to think about resuming her education. Staying at home seemed stifling to her; she felt an intense desire to "participate in the world." The program in which she recently enrolled seemed right. She liked its flexible structure, liked being treated as a unique human being, felt that "it was time," she says, laughing somewhat self-consciously, "to prove to myself that I wasn't dumb."

"Has it worked?" I ask, drawn to her laughter.

"Well," she pauses, catching a breath, hearing it as a serious question, "yes, I think so. I mean, I'm finding out that I have my own thinking process and I have my own way of learning and that I have my own way of understanding myself and learning how to deal with things in life. I'm finding what that is now. I think that I had previously... I hadn't developed that side of myself at all. I feel like that the way I guided myself through life was to go back to my family and say, 'Tell me what to do. Am I OK?' you know, rather than seeing, looking, understanding how *I* operate and finding out how *I want* to think and *I want* to deal with myself and how *I want* to treat other people from my own perspective and my own point of view."

I'm struck, as I listen, by the contrast in her voice, dark and somehow burdened as she speaks of that earlier self who turned so often to her family and to others for guidance, hardening to a kind of driven urgency as she tells of her new self, underlining *want,* nailing it home, setting each word of "my own point of view" up on end for display.

"And I feel like that it's just happening. I'm starting to see who I want to be, and it's really—it's getting away from my family and getting away from all that security. I was really cowering late in my twenties and realizing I had to find a way out or I was going to get smothered by it." Her voice drops, and she looks down at her hands, laughing softly, wryly. "And I don't know if I'd like that."

"Away from all that security?" I ask, curious about the tension in her words.

"Well," she replies, "my last study was about family systems, and I know my family has a definite system of how it operates to keep its members secure. There's a loyalty in families that gets so ingrown and so protective that its members all stop growing. And I've had to find out what my philosophy is and how I want to live as a separate person. It's all in letting myself think and feeling secure enough to think."

She goes on to describe her experience with feminism, her struggle to understand it not simply as a women's issue but as a source of power for both women and men. It has changed her relationship not only with her husband but also with her family, separating her from them in still another way.

The language of movement suffuses her speech. At one point, I ask her whether some of the changes she describes have been easy for her.

"No, but it's been forward moving; it's been exciting; it's been ... more and more I feel that I'm being pulled with a current. I'm connected now with where I'm going, and I wasn't before."

"Where's the current going?" I ask.

"Well, I guess that what I *want* is to feel that I am ... to know that I am independent. And that I am responsible for myself emotionally and intellectually, and that I stand alone." She is choosing her words carefully now and rounds off that word *alone* like a sculptor her clay. "That I can support myself, support myself and my kids if I have to, that I'm not at the mercy of greater forces, that I've got some control, and that I've got a vehicle to express myself—you know, to participate in the world rather than isolating myself and putting it down. That's what I want: I want to be a *legitimate member of the world.*"

She laughs at this, disarming the considerable power of her speech, but I can feel the chill on the back of my neck. Perhaps she senses it too, and we both fall silent for a moment. On cue, the phone rings, and I take a deep breath.

The conversation goes on for some time after that, illuminating corners like a flashlight in the attic. Sandy's sense of motion is striking, the more so as she chooses to describe her adviser as a guide, moving ahead under some mysterious force, leading the way on a voyage she cannot take alone. Her use of the journey metaphor is quite explicit. She sees herself moving toward a clearer sense of independence, a self defined more by her own actions than others' expectations, away from security that no longer protects so much as constrains. Far off, too dim to make out, there might be an edge to the horizon of independence and self-rule—a kind of reblurring of distinctions, a new sort of legitimate dependence. But it is dark out there, and she can't be sure. For now the struggle is to feel responsible for the shape her life has taken, for what she does in her life, for *herself*. Never again will she allow someone else to do that for her.

How best to understand this drive toward independence so powerfully described by Sandy? It is a movement familiar enough to those of us in traditional higher education, accustomed to watching our late-adolescent students using the newfound world of college to bridge away from their families into the world of full adulthood. But are we then to understand Sandy as somehow "retarded"? Simply because she followed a different schedule from her more conventional sisters seems scarcely reason to think of her as an aberration. Isn't there some better way to characterize Sandy's movement than out of step? Besides, what does it mean to be a full adult? Are we to believe that all adults think and function as autonomously as Sandy? Ten-year-olds value independence too; is this the same thing? Levinson's work and the findings of those who have studied women's lives in a similar, age-linked fashion tell us much, but these psychosocial theories seem to stay on the outside, to cast light mainly on the boundary of the person and his or her culture. To see more deeply inside, we need to turn to the stage theorists.

Although the stage theorists share the recognition that development continues throughout the life span and does so in a series of plateaus rather than a smooth progression, they differ from the phase theorists in their assertion that each successive stage represents a qualitative *advance* over a previous one. As we grow older, they would suggest, we may or may not grow wiser. Their stages are an effort to describe what happens if we do.

Wiser is clearly a loaded word. I know of no leading stage theorist, except Erikson, who uses it formally. Most are much more careful, following the lead of the biologists and general systems theorists who have inspired much of their thinking, speaking of development as a sequential series of adaptations to the interaction between the organism and its environment. For *wisdom* they might substitute something like "increased differentiation and integration of the cognitive structures." In effect, we grow through engaging with the world, changing and being changed by it. We become ever more discriminating in our ability to see the world on its own terms, or as others see it, and ever more able to make sense of it despite its growing complexity—able to make sense of it in ways that both retain our own sense of meaning and yet respect its diversity.

Kegan

One of the clearest thinkers in this field is Robert Kegan, like many developmentalists a former literature scholar turned psychologist. In *The Evolving Self,* he describes with charm and eloquence his vision of the meaning of growth. Although clearly derived from the work of Kohlberg and Piaget, Kegan's model avoids the sometimes boxy quality of the earlier theories, substituting for the ladder metaphor an upward-spiraling helix.

Beginning stages (Kegan prefers to call them *balances,* a term that better catches the dynamic nature of development) are characterized by impulsiveness and self-centeredness; these yield to a more "other-centered" stance, in which interpersonal relationships and mutuality are paramount. This in turn gives way to the birth of a new and more separate self, from which finally evolves an "interindividual balance" in which the tension between "self" and "other" reaches a new synthesis. From this position one is able to maintain a clear sense of self and yet merge with others, dissolving and reforming one's separateness when appropriate. If this sounds a bit abstract, yet vaguely wise, this is the case with most stage theories. Their highest stages tend to fade into the mist—or is it light?

In any case, it seems necessary that this be so, for their creators can only see so far beyond themselves, and as a critic once observed, doesn't one reach a point when all this is irrelevant? After all, the exemplars of these "advanced" stages—Martin Luther King, Jr., Mohandas Gandhi, Mother Theresa—were not, to my knowledge, developmental scholars.

Several things are worth noting about Kegan's map (see Figure 3.2). First, what is important for our purposes here is not the particular balances so much as the overall direction of movement. That is, as we cycle through these levels, we go through times when we are preoccupied primarily with our relations with "the other" and times when we are mainly concerned with our "self," apart from the other. In an important sense, our lives can be understood as a series of transformations of how we see ourselves in relation to others, how we negotiate the twin claims of what David Bakan has called agency and communion (Bakan, 1966). Thus, the early-stage "impulsive" child is unable to distinguish his own impulses and wants from those of anyone else. We *are* our impulses, says Kegan; we don't *have* them. It is very difficult, as any parent knows, for a four-year-old to see through any eyes but his own. The "imperial" ten-year-old, however, knows what motivates her younger brother because she is more able than he to get outside of herself. She understands the importance of reciprocity (and the power of bribes) in a way he cannot. More self-possessed than her brother, she *has* her impulses; what she can see less clearly are her needs.

With movement into the interpersonal balance, however, we open up in a whole new way as we seek to redefine ourselves through others, often as teenagers but frequently later in life as well. This is the time of falling in love ("I am *nothing* without you"), of conforming to the ways of the tribe, and of transforming the earlier mutual back-scratching morality into a more communal group ethic of trust. A more fitting paean to interpersonal virtues than the Boy Scout law would be hard to find: trustworthy, loyal, helpful, friendly, courteous, kind, obedient, cheerful, thrifty, brave, clean, and reverent. Now we *have* our needs, but we *are* our relationships.

With the swing back and upward toward what Kegan calls the institutional balance, we "zip up" in a sense, drawing our boundaries more clearly, struggling (often against the inner and outer

Figure 3.2. Kegan's "Helix of Evolutionary Truces."

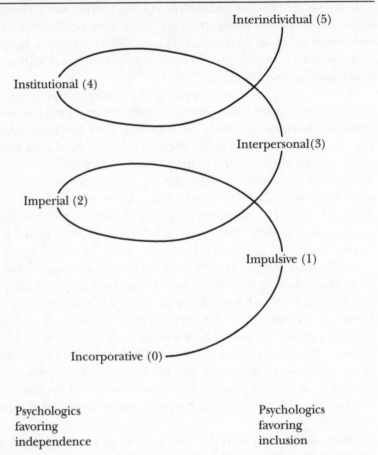

Interindividual (5)

Institutional (4)

Interpersonal (3)

Imperial (2)

Impulsive (1)

Incorporative (0)

Psychologics
favoring
independence

Psychologics
favoring
inclusion

Source: Chart reprinted by permission of the publisher from *The Evolving Self* by Robert Kegan, Cambridge, Mass.: Harvard University Press, Copyright © 1982 by the President and Fellows of Harvard College.

voices of our culture) to define ourselves in terms less borrowed from others than earned of our own effort. Loving becomes more an act of will than of self-denial; responsibility is redefined to include oneself; loyalty to the tribe is based less on friendships than respect for abstract principles; and guilt replaces shame as a form of social control. Finally, we swing back in a new yielding to something greater than ourselves, dissolving our boundaries once again as we work to let go of a self that may have grown too narrow. We reach out again to others in an effort to heal the wounds of too much separateness with a new compassion and often a new spirituality. Each transformation, each move involves a swinging outward, away from the familiar world into the strange, a leaning into uncertainty, a risk. Often we experience this move as a kind of impulsion toward our own opposite, our dark side, and we go at times unwillingly.

More than any other stage theorist, Kegan respects the motion in our lives; he has focused the chapters of his book not on the stages but on the quality of the transitions between them, emphasizing how our movement involves both a reaching out and a letting go. Development is not a self-contained process that takes place inexorably. How readily we grow, he says—indeed, whether we grow at all—has a great deal to do with the nature of the world in which we transact our lives' business. To understand human development, we must understand the environment's part, how it confirms us, contradicts us, and provides continuity. Of this we see more later as we look closely at how mentors function, at crucial parts of the "holding environment" (Winnicott, 1965) within and because of which we grow.

Most returning adult learners are moving through Kegan's interpersonal balance toward the institutional stance. Without benefit of developmental theory, Malcolm Knowles made a career of describing this shift among adult students. Among those changes he described as "dimensions of maturation" are moves from dependence to autonomy, passivity to activity, subjectivity to objectivity, and selfishness to altruism (Knowles, 1970). Each of these corresponds to Kegan's "three/four" shift.

Because stage changes take years to accomplish, we generally see our students only during sections of their passages. Our task is not to peg them into particular stages but rather to see them in their movement and to help them understand what may lie ahead. Consider Sandy again.

Clearly, her story tells of transition out from the interpersonal security of her family that defined her for years, toward the more mature security of a self-conscious and deliberately construed identity. Her tale reverberates with the voices in numerous feminist writings about the struggle to define a new self apart from the reflections of a male-dominated society in which her place was to keep her place. Increasingly, adult educators and students of human development detail the uniqueness of women's developmental pathways. Josselson's *Finding Herself* (1987) remains a classic, while Taylor and Marienau (1995) have compiled an invaluable summary of current research on learning environments for reentry women.

So the appeal *and importance* of feminism to Sandy should come as no surprise, since the movement is a powerful cry for an ideology of self-affirmation to enlarge the personalized world of face-to-face contact with family and friends. It calls us to identify also with people we do not know, thus defining a new and broader sense of our place in the world.

But beyond this, Sandy's frequent return to the theme of separation, of emergence from embeddedness in her family's expectations, of a sense of breathing again after being essentially smothered, is striking in its evocation of liberation. There can be no doubt that she is moving into Kegan's period of self-authorship; feeling her oats; reveling in the new promise of independence, of control, of participation in the world. This is the time when people think of career rather than simply job; goals and a sense of achievement take on a new power; a feeling of purposefulness and the capacity to achieve what one sets out to do make themselves felt more strongly than ever. Those who return to school at this time tend to see the value of education not as a means simply of gaining new status (a concern more strongly felt at earlier stages) but as a way to achieve career goals or sometimes as a way to expand and develop that precious new inner self that they are beginning to discover and value so highly.

All of these are movement out, as the inner self comes more clearly into view. At the same time, recall that separation for women at this point may have a different quality than for men

(Miller, 1976; Gilligan, 1982). Sandy may not be splitting herself off from her family so much as attempting to redefine her relationship to include *herself* as one of those deserving of care. We will return to this when we meet Sandy later in the book.

Ahead for Sandy lie a new career, new friends, and perhaps a new basis for friendship. Her marriage may experience strain as she redefines the terms of relationship, taking her own needs into account in a new way. Her mentor might do well to stand back and watch carefully before moving too precipitously, because Sandy needs her head. Her question is about who she wants to become, and she must answer that by herself.

This shift toward what Sharon Parks (1986) calls greater "inner-dependence" is the most common transformation among women returning to higher education. Like Sandy, many women do well in high school and are headed for college when they fall in love and marry instead. Their husbands are encouraged by society to complete the break with family and begin to confirm their worth in the outside world, but the women remain inside the home, caring first for the husband and later for the children, enmeshed in a web of relationships that often (though not inevitably) continues the earlier patterns of dependency and self-sacrifice that characterize the interpersonal balance.

For such women, return to school—triggered perhaps by the children's departure from the home, or the dissolution (impending or accomplished) of a marriage—reaffirms a self long postponed. Often coupled with an outside job, the shift toward the independence of which Sandy spoke so powerfully can be a heady and disruptive experience as she struggles with the conflicting demands of work, study, and family. As Merriam and Clark (1991) richly illustrate, the three seldom mesh smoothly. One of the most important of all our interventions as teachers and advisers of adults is to acknowledge in our female students the poignancy of this struggle.

In our third vignette we meet Monique, a twenty-six-year-old secretary. She was one of my first students, and the conversation that follows occurred early in our career together. The central question for Monique has to do with how one distinguishes between good and bad, right and wrong. As you read, take note of how she views authority; consider how she construes the nature of knowledge; and notice how she views herself as a learner. What lies behind her misunderstanding of the assignment on sexuality? What makes for the breakthrough at the end?

Venturing Out

For a woman with little formal education, one of the few ways to edge out of the pervasive poverty of the Northeast Kingdom is to become a secretary. For a few years, money for job training was available to employers in these parts, and a number of women seized the opportunity to ground their meager high school secretarial skills in solid experience. As soon as she could, Monique began to take college courses, seeking to expand her knowledge and move into a more important administrative position. It irked her that people with less experience and whom she considered less competent than herself held authority simply because they had "that piece of paper" and she did not. As far as she could see, the sole difference lay in that college degree. It did not—indeed could not—occur to her that perhaps another difference might lie with the very way she thought, interpreted her experience, and made sense of the world.

After being in the program for a couple of terms, taking courses in office management, business communication, and the like, she decided, quite on her own, to take a weekend course entitled "The Challenge of Sexuality." I was a bit surprised but encouraged the choice, feeling it was important for her to move outside her narrow vocationalism. The instructor, Bill, had designed the course in a loosely structured discussion format, providing some basic information but restricting his part chiefly to guiding the class in its own discovery of the values that society places on sexuality and gender. This might be a good chance, I thought, for Monique to view with some distance a topic I knew she had strong opinions about.

She could not have been back home more than a few moments after that first weekend when she called.

"I'm not going back! That Bill must be sick. He must get his thrills by making people tell all about their private sex lives. It was nothing but a sex counseling session. I learned nothing. Nothing!"

I listened for some time. Knowing Bill, I was quite certain that he had more conventional means of excitement at his disposal. Apparently Monique had run squarely into a deep prohibition. To discover an authority, it seemed, who ought to know better than use such obscene words as *penis* and *vagina* in public was profoundly disturbing.

She was required, she went on, to write a fifteen-page paper about her private sex life. "There's no way I'm going to do that for him. No way. That's for sure."

When I asked her for the specific wording of the assignment, it turned out that it was "to discuss your own life in terms of what you have been taught about sexuality." Assuring her that I too would be reluctant to discuss my own sex life with a stranger, I explained that the assignment was simply to examine her own beliefs about sexuality, not to tell about her sex life. She cooled down at this, and we talked of how she might go about writing the paper.

Although she put it off until the last moment, she did eventually complete the assignment and was delighted several weeks later to receive very good comments on her work. "For days after she got that paper back," said a friend, "she was a new woman—Monique at her best."

Curious about the impact of the experience on her way of thinking, I arranged a meeting in a nearby restaurant for an afternoon snack.

"So how are things going with your courses?"

"Well, the photography with Armand is going pretty good, I guess," she replies, speaking softly with a slight French-Canadian lilt beneath the Muzak. "You sure were right about him. He's a really sweet guy."

She giggles a lot when she is uncomfortable. Giggles now.

"What have you learned?" I ask, overanxious to move from him to her.

"Oh, a little bit about how to make a picture pleasing, I guess. A little bit about photography, the different styles, you know." But when I ask her what particular styles, she is stumped; she has forgotten the names of the photographers. She does recall several particular shots but seems to have no way of talking about more than one photograph at a time. Everything is isolated. She likes this, doesn't like that; remembers the content of a picture, but nothing of the form. *How does she make sense of this? I* wonder, and ask her if the course was worth taking.

"Armand did a pretty good job, I'd say," she begins, and I signal the waitress for more coffee while Monique describes Armand and what he did. Again I try to move from him to her, less gently this time.

"OK, Monique, that's a description of what *he* did, but what do you think made it a good course?"

"Well, let's see now." She scans the ceiling, looking for the answer. "Well, I liked his individualized style of teaching. I liked the content. I liked learning that a photograph should be a piece of art. I liked learning the history. I liked learning how to run a camera."

After another ten minutes of this, Monique is on her second piece of pie and I decide it's safe to broach discussion of the beast with two backs.

"How would you compare your two courses this term?"

"Well, I guess they were both interesting," she says slowly, then giggles uncomfortably. "But I liked Armand's better than Bill's." She giggles again and flicks a cautiously knowing glance in my direction. Armand's course, she explains, had a lot more facts in it. He lectured more and gave her the feeling that he would take care of her. He seemed to care for her personally, though her one criticism is that "he was too much of a mother hen."

"Bill's course didn't have enough facts," she says, avoiding my eyes. "Still, I guess he did the best he could. There's no way he could have done much differently than he did, either."

Looking for her sense of how she has changed, I ask her to recall how she felt about the course at the beginning. Does she feel differently now?

"I didn't like his whole approach," she replies, turning dark. "Some of the language in the class was too much for me. I didn't like the talk. I didn't like the discussion of sexuality; it made me feel as if I didn't even want to be in the room." Indeed, she contracted a cough that first weekend and found herself leaving the room frequently. I express my sympathy, acknowledging how difficult it can be when people say or do things we feel are wrong.

"I wish he'd given us more facts or maybe even some opinions from other experts so I could make up my own mind. Well, he did have some facts but not really enough." Without saying a word about herself, she is saying volumes about how she thinks. The word *experts* catches my ear.

"Were there any ideas from experts in your reading?" I ask, looking for a vein. "People you disagreed with or who disagreed with Bill?" This time we hit pay dirt.

She pauses and looks down, thinking hard, then looks up with a frown. "Well, one psychologist thought that children should be given a special room in the house where they can experiment with, you know...." Looking away, she giggles incongruously. Is it embarrassment or anger? "I'm gonna let my children do that?" Her voice rises and she holds the appalled expression an instant too long, to make sure I get the point.

"Do you have any idea why an expert would have suggested such a thing?" I ask, wondering how clearly she can see into that darkness. In reply she sinks back deflated against the padded Naugahyde of the booth. What was the matter with me? Couldn't I see how ridiculous that was? After a long silence she looks up from the empty pie plate, glances past my face, and fixes her gaze toward the plastic flowers on the jukebox against the wall.

"I suppose it might be a way of letting them get out their frustrations. Maybe he thinks it might be good for them?" She looks over, checking. I agree and then go on to restate what I imagine to be a more complete rationale. Then I add, "Now, this man's an *expert*. How can you possibly disagree with him?"

"Well, he's just too idealistic. Those ideas are all very well in theory, but he doesn't understand the way things really are—the practical aspects." She goes on to explain that experts sometimes do disagree with one another and that there's really no right or wrong anyway.

"Do you really believe that, Monique?"

"Well, there's no *one* answer. You have to look at all the facts and then make up your mind."

"Did you use to believe there was a right and a wrong?"

"I don't know. I think there might have been. I'm afraid I still have some old principles there that go down pretty deep." The boil has burst. She speaks softly now, concentrating on the space between our plates. Pensive.

"You're 'afraid'? What's wrong with the old principles?"

"Nothing. It's just that they're conservative."

"Is there something wrong with being conservative?"

"Not really. It's just that I'm trying to see things in a broader sense rather than in a narrow-minded way. I'm gettin' there, but some things still go down quite deep." I'm with her now. Gentle.

"What are those things—that go quite deep?"

"Well, thoughts about sexuality, I guess."

"Can you remember some of those things that you feel quite deeply about?"

"Well," she pauses, takes a deep breath, and plunges on. "There's one that I might be more liberal on now: no sex before marriage and no outside activities. I used to feel that there should be no sex before marriage and that if you live with a guy before marriage, that's terrible. Now I can recognize—at least see—their point of view and not even bat an eye about it like I used to. So I guess I'm relaxing a bit about that, and I'm not judging, which I would have judged before. I think I'm... relaxed more, more tolerant of other people's ways of doing things."

We talk for a while longer, and I focus on the word *tolerant,* a key word for Monique now. It's her word, and I underline it for her. I tell her I want her to use that word and to think about things in that way as often as she can so that when she finds things that bother her, she makes an effort to see things through others' eyes, to try to imagine how they might explain what they did. Perhaps that will help her continue to grow more tolerant.

We walk silently together back to her office. At the door, she flashes a quick smile and goes inside.

The Perry Scheme

Conversations like this are not everyday occurrences, but they do happen often enough to keep me alive; they're the stuff of my work, and for the insight the credit goes to William Perry, who has done more to illuminate important dimensions of the intellectual growth of college students than anyone else I know. Disarmingly simple, Perry's scheme offers a powerful way of understanding the struggle that Monique and students like her go through as they attempt to make better sense of what they think is right and wrong, and under what circumstances.

Much of the appeal of the theory is that it lends itself so readily to the metaphor of a journey. Indeed, in Perry's book *Forms of Intellectual and Ethical Development in the College Years* (1968), it is described as a "pilgrim's progress." Although the framework first grew from the stories of a highly select group of traditional undergraduates as their ways of understanding evolved during four years at Harvard, the model is now widely applied among students of all ages and backgrounds. The initial formulation has generally held up well, and a "Perry network" developed over the years to expand on his work.[3]

Briefly, the tale begins in an Eden-like garden where good and evil are clear and where Authority unequivocally divides right from wrong. Knowledge is concrete and readily available if Authority is properly courted. As students at this early point, we tend to see ourselves as passive vessels to be filled with Truth by authoritative teachers. We can become quite frustrated if teachers do not live up to this expectation.

But as we travel, clouds begin to roll in and obscure the light. Some things appear to be more readily provable and hence truer than others. In time, as authorities visibly clash before our eyes and as we lose the simple vision that once so clearly divided right from wrong, we find ourselves in a dark—and, for some, forbidding—Gethsemane, torn from the plain truths that once both blinded and preserved us. At one moment we are buoyed by a new kind of freedom; at another we are submerged beneath the weight of our own uncertainty. Some of us, unable to bear the dark, turn back to the safety of earlier truths; others, bemused and numbed by the swirl, temporize; still others, blessed perhaps with courage—or simply desperation—forge ahead through the forest of simple relativity toward new apprehension of truth. We discover that though there are many truths, not all are of equal validity, nor do they exist in isolation. Each has its own context, meaning, connections that rest on certain assumptions and contain their own inner logic. We too have a context from which we construct our own reality.

In fact, everyone does. With this realization, we negotiate the shift into contextual relativism and our view of the world is transformed. It remains now to acknowledge our place in this new world, to begin to make—and later unmake, and make yet again—commitments to values, work, and people, despite our bone-deep knowledge that the rock we once thought the world rested upon has been replaced by some sort of manufactured substance: attractive perhaps, maybe practical, but fabricated and surely not permanent. On it, nonetheless, we build our church.

With this in mind, the conversation with Monique, and perhaps the source of my frustration, grows clearer. I had known Monique for some time before and knew that she tended to color the world more black and white than gray. At the same time, she was a perfectly intelligent, capable person, and I knew that she felt driven to make sense of the new information she was picking up. Perry's model suggested that an exploration of Monique's notions about authority and about how one tells right from wrong would reveal how she was making sense of diverse and conflicting information and, more important, how her meaning making was changing in response to the new knowledge. That was what lay behind my questions.

It was clear that knowledge for Monique was fairly concrete and discrete. If the instructors in the two courses attempted to make connections for her, evidently she was unable to hear them. It is not surprising that things seemed so fragmented. She was still some distance from a position that would allow her to place such disturbing information in the context of a particular set of assumptions about human nature. She was simply incapable of making such abstract connections without help. Perhaps because of this and perhaps because of her consequent high need for external authority, Monique attempted to make sense of her confusion by discussing the instructors—comfortable territory—and the extent to which they provided meaning for her in the form of "facts."

Although I repeatedly asked her to discuss the course itself, she stuck like hot bubble gum to what she felt about her teachers. Far from a detached examination, evaluation at this position was a matter of personal feeling: one likes or dislikes the object in question. One cannot both dislike and consider something good at the same time. Given so personal an identification with the source of knowledge and a strongly traditional upbringing, it is no wonder that she found it difficult to handle the course on sexuality. She simply lacked the capacity to decenter herself from the ideas, to *have* her own ideas rather than *be* someone else's. She thus found it easy to feel attacked when her ideas came under question. This is why she was so quick to assume that Bill wanted her to describe her sex life rather than to discuss and evaluate *her ideas about sexuality.*

Perry's formulation all began, he tells us, when as a literature teacher he asked his students what they believed he wanted from them. Upon receiving the responses, he discovered each student to have quite a different teacher. To some, he was a pleasant fellow who wanted them to think for themselves; to others, he was an imposing authority whose job it was first to inject and later to extract from them the right answers; and to still others, he was an exponent of a particular point of view arguing for a coherent set of interpretations of literature. How to make sense of all this?

Like several others who later turned developmentalist, Perry was influenced by the massive study of authoritarianism carried out in the postwar years by Nevitt Sanford and his associates. It was clear to Perry that some of his students showed distinct authoritarian patterns. Yet over time, they seemed to change. Because he interviewed his students every spring, his experience of students was more akin to a motion picture than isolated snapshots—there was movement here. In most cases, the authoritarian students *changed.*

With his colleagues, Perry began to listen to students' answers to the least-loaded question they could devise, one borrowed from Robert Merton: "Why don't you start out with whatever stands out for you about the year?" Interviews typically lasted about an hour and commonly centered around how students made sense of the diversity of new information and experiences that college brought them. It took some fourteen years in all before Perry published the group's findings. The basic map of the journey, a nine-position continuum, appears in Figure 3.3, with a description of the itinerary.

Perry is fond of pointing out that "the first characteristic of any theory is that it is wrong in any particular case." He does not exempt his own scheme from this and advises that it be viewed with caution. On at least one occasion, having taken his audience

Figure 3.3. Perry's Map.

Perry's Main Line of Development

Position 1: The student sees the world in polar terms of we-right-good vs. other-wrong-bad. Right Answers for everything exist in the Absolute, known to Authority whose role is to mediate (teach) them. Knowledge and goodness are perceived as quantitative accretions of discrete right-nesses to be collected by hard work and obedience (paradigm: a spelling test).

Position 2: The student perceives diversity of opinion, and uncertainty and accounts for them as unwarranted confusion in poorly qualified Authorities or as mere exercises set by Authority "so we can learn to find The Answer for ourselves."

Position 3: The student accepts diversity and uncertainty as legitimate but still *temporary* in areas where Authority "hasn't found The Answer yet." He supposes Authority grades him in these areas on "good expression" but remains puzzled as to standards.

Position 4: (a) The student perceives legitimate uncertainty (and there-fore diversity of opinion) to be extensive and raises it to the status of an unstructured epistemological realm of its own in which "anyone has a right to his own opinion," a realm which he sets over against Authority's realm where right-wrong still prevails, or (b) the student discovers qual-itative contextual relativistic reasoning as a special case of "what They want" within Authority's realm.

Position 5: The student perceives all knowledge and values (including Authority's) as contextual and relativistic and subordinates dualistic right-wrong functions to the status of a special case, in context.

Figure 3.3. (*Continued*)

Position 6: The student apprehends the necessity of orienting himself in a relativistic world through some form of personal Commitment (as distinct from unquestioned or unconsidered commitment to simple belief in certainty).

Position 7: The student makes an initial Commitment in some area.

Position 8: The student experiences the implications of Commitment and explores the subjective and stylistic issues of responsibility.

Position 9: The student experiences the affirmation of identity among multiple responsibilities and realizes Commitment as an ongoing, unfolding activity through which he expresses his lifestyle.

Conditions of Delay, Deflection, and Regression

Temporizing: The student delays in some Position for a year, exploring its implications or explicitly hesitating to take the next step.

Escape: The student exploits the opportunity for detachment offered by the structures of Positions 4 and 5 to deny responsibility through passive or opportunistic alienation.

Retreat: The student entrenches in the dualistic, absolutistic structures of Positions 2 or 3.

Source: Figure from William G. Perry, *Intellectual and Ethical Development in the College Years: A Scheme,* 1970. Used by permission of Jossey-Bass Inc., Publishers. This book was originally published by Holt, Rinehart and Winston, Inc.

of several hundred earnest academics and administrators through his marvelous description of the scheme, he announced impishly, "Now, of course, you realize that this is all nonsense." People do not live, he emphasizes, inside little boxes marked with his position numbers, and development does not occur in a straight line; rather, those who have made the journey may think dualistically in some areas under some circumstances, multiplistically in others, contextually in still others. Nevertheless, we function predominantly in one range or another, and although a contextual thinker may on occasion operate dualistically, a dualistic thinker does not think contextually.

In accord with other stage theories, Perry's positions are hierarchical and essentially invariant: each rests on the one before it, and there are no shortcuts. At the same time, however, people may move through two positions in a brief burst, or remain for long periods at a single position. Occasionally they even retreat to an earlier stance.

Position 1, basic dualism, is essentially a construct necessary to anchor the scheme. It is at position 2 that movement begins. Things start to fall apart, first as the student discovers that there is more than one answer for most important questions, and then as she discovers that authorities differ in what those answers are. But the process may be a slow one. For many, it takes years. No one begins at the absolute beginning; almost all of us have discovered at least some moral ambiguity in our lives, even though some find it harder to accept than others. This is especially true of adult learners, some of whom have spent sixty or seventy years feeling its cold touch.

My own research (Daloz, 1981) suggests that most adults returning to college arrive carrying some degree of dualism and a good deal of multiplicity. That is, they are moving away from exclusive reliance on external authority as the source of "truth," toward skepticism of such authority (albeit sometimes rather dualistic skepticism) and the belief that any opinion is as good as any other. This is when the journey gets exciting, for it is during this time, as the old foundations begin to crumble, that the footings are laid for the transformation that Perry describes as the position four-to-five transition, the central transformation of his scheme and very probably of a good college education. Let's look more closely.

In the midst of multiplicity (that yellow wood this side of contextual relativism), two paths diverge. One route (position 4a in the description accompanying the map of Figure 3.3) is characterized by the belief that in the absence of authority any opinion is as good as any other. Since nothing can be known for sure, one's own experience is the most reliable guide.

Asked how he tells right from wrong, a person in this position is likely to respond as this student did: "Just my own intuitive experience, I guess. No one's gonna be able to tell you, and you just have to rely on your feelings." Hard work, which often served as a criterion of value before, seems pointless now. Said the same student a moment later, describing a literature course: "There's no end to how much I study, you know. I can work thirty hours and pass or two hours and pass." The classic stance of the 1960s hippy, which in many ways typifies this position, is as much a developmental statement as a sociological one. If there are no ultimate values, why work anyway? This is often disparaged as "mere moral relativism," unattractive to observers on either side. To those who have yet to venture, it looks anarchistic, sacrilegious, unkempt, and terrifying. To those who have moved through, it can appear spineless, destructive, cynical, and self-indulgent. One of the values of a developmental perspective is that it allows us to acknowledge all of the above and then go about the business of helping people move along, for there is no better place to begin rebuilding meaning than where all previous structures are in shambles.

The other route (position 4b), somewhat more worn, is also more tranquil. Here the paradigmatic student is one who begins to realize that "they (the authorities) want us to think for ourselves" and who proceeds to do what "they" want. Procedures such as use of evidence, weighing both sides, and testing hypotheses are seen initially as the right way to do things; later they are relativized and become a "better" way. Perry sometimes refers to this as the Trojan Horse effect: we take into our midst a foreign way of thinking that ultimately brings about the transformation. Less a giant to be slain than a benevolent voice urging its own demise, Authority paradoxically becomes the bridge to its own overthrow, a bridge as delicate as a spider's web: "It seems to be some loyalty to truth, a feeling that if the truth is really dubious, it is better to have a dubious truth than a false certainty" (Perry, 1968, p. 108).

Understood as a transitional stance, intellectual diffidence is important, confusion benign. If we help our students accept the uncertainty and feel safe with it, if we encourage them to enter the darkness and explore those terrifying opposites fully enough, there is a good chance they will move through them on their own and begin to discern a meaning in "the starless air." As they find it safe to let go of their self-evident ways of making meaning, discover the considerable limitations of common sense, and begin to risk seeing through the eyes of other people, other cultures, other times, they begin to construct a world first of multiple opinions but eventually—and more importantly—of multiple ways of arriving at those opinions. The discovery that things can be related—that connections can be made rather than truths found—begins to dawn, and the world is reborn on a whole new level. In short, our students begin to think about thought itself. It is this recognition that lays the groundwork for the critical shift from multiplicity to contextualism—that is, for the essential difference between the way Monique thinks and the way her teachers think.

But she is not there yet. Indeed, her thinking seems most like that found in late dualism and early multiplicity. Consider her approach to authority. Perry found it fruitful to ask how students dealt with conflicting authorities. Monique recognized that experts might legitimately differ, but she stopped short of standing up to them herself. (Full-blown multiplicity allows us to do this by denying that *anyone*, expert or not, "really" knows anything.) Instead, she resorted to the old that's-all-very-well-in-theory ploy, asserting her own expertise to reside in her direct, practical experience. Because she was unable to imagine how an opposing point of view to her own might be constructed, she was powerless to argue against it except in the ad hominem way she chose. This is one reason why it is so important to encourage students to articulate positions different from their own. Until they can do that, they have no way of constructing an argument on the basis of reason rather than their gut.

Nonetheless, at this point in the conversation we began to move. Her assertion that "there's no such thing as right and wrong" struck me as a bit facile, knowing her as I did, and I questioned it. From there, she was able to recognize important elements in her own growth and see that although she did indeed continue to hold some strong "principles," she was becoming better at see- ing some parts of the world through others' eyes. By continuing to practice suspending judgment, by holding that word *tolerant,* she would continue the direction of her growth toward greater understanding.

This episode drove home to me the meaning of Perry's wry ob- servation that "too early a moral judgment is precisely what stands between many able students and a liberal education" (Perry, 1969, p. 105). To remain ignorant, judge everything. By sealing great chunks of the world into boxes marked good and bad, right and wrong, we effectively choose to remain ignorant about large areas of our experience, saying, "I will learn from this but not from that."

In this way, the kind of "entrenched dualism," as a colleague calls it, from which Monique is emerging has a self-fulfilling quality; by defining in advance the lessons we learn, we safely protect ourselves from both nasty surprises and useful lessons. This is not to say, however, that the obvious course for enthusiastic mentors is to lay about them, shattering dualism wherever it occurs. Monique's stance, like all of ours, represents a delicate truce with the truths of her life. We all presort what we let into our lives. The task is not to stop sorting; rather, it is to seek ever finer and more fitting instruments. For Monique, the time has come to retire a tool that is no longer up to the task and to forge something better.

"I'm getting there," she says and quite by herself comes up with exactly what she needs: tolerance. Clearly, she has a sense of her own direction despite what she herself acknowledges is fierce resistance. She knows her question is about tolerance. Our job in cases like this is least of all to push. Rather, what we can offer is simply a little light in the right places and lots of support. Monique can take it from there.

In concluding this chapter, let us return to Eric, whom we met earlier, and consider his story in light of the three maps we have just reviewed. We begin with Levinson's perspective.

In the adult development seminar that I set up for several of my students, selecting particular theorists for particular students,

I chose the Levinson study for Eric. Several years before, he had begun to realize that his present career path was taking him as far as he could go. He had prepared himself in his teens for an engineering career that took him through his twenties. But by the thirties transition, he came to see that if he wanted to continue to move ahead, he would have to make a leap into management, a field in which a degree would be a virtual necessity. Right on schedule, he returned to school in search of the ticket.

But as Levinson says, transitions are times of the breakup of old structures. If Eric were to rebuild a new structure adequate to his thirties, one that would allow him to secure a satisfactory place in the adult world and become his own man, he would need to make some qualitative changes, letting go of some of the assumptions that got him through the earlier decade. *More* education wouldn't do. He needed a *richer* education, one that would provide the breadth of understanding necessary for leadership.

It took a while for him to realize this fully. Surely it was not clear when he first came into the program, at the first meeting. But over time, especially through his association with Dave and Milt and to some extent myself, he began to see not only that he would need to change but that he could, and that it would be all right to do so. A good deal of that change had to do with Eric's willingness to let go of the tough facade with which he first greeted me and that he always used for protection and advancement in his career.

Human development is rich with ironies, and it is no accident that Eric was most able to start moving ahead in his career at precisely the moment when he could let go of the single-mindedness that had brought him to where he was. It is a lot easier to let go of one thing if we are holding onto something else, and for Eric the something else was the positive quality of his other and more reflective self—the Eric who drew his strength from being alone in the woods. This is the extraordinary impact of his experience with the deer, his readiness to respect another life in a way he had not done before. What he did not want to stop, it seems to me, is the delicate emergence of a new, more vulnerable Eric.

In Kegan's terms, this looks like the leading edge of the institutional self, the fresh determination to define ourselves in our own terms rather than as we would have others see us. To be ten feet from a deer and not shoot *is* crazy in the eyes of the prevailing and conventional ethic of hunting. "You just don't throw fish back in when they're big enough to keep," says the voice of the culture. "Well, *I* do!" retorts Eric. He is listening more and more to a new voice, one that was inside him for years but only recently able to find ears. It's still tender and needs plenty of privacy, but in the right setting, where it is safe, the voice yearns to be heard.

For his final paper, I encouraged him to write a personal application of the various theories he was studying. He was reluctant at first and asked if he could submit it in longhand since he did not type and wanted no one else to see the work. I agreed, and he later told me that he had spent hour after hour of intense concentration writing pages and pages, many of which he was unwilling to show anyone, including me. He discovered the journal—at last he had a friend in himself who would listen. For people like Eric, at the delicate transition from conventionality to a new independence (a point that Jane Loevinger insightfully terms the self-aware stage), self-disclosure can be both extremely threatening and extraordinarily powerful. The journal, with various safeguards for confidentiality, is an effective device for helping people find their voice at this period.

Eric's course in organizational behavior was important in giving him a new perspective on his workplace and a language with which to describe the pecking order of his bosses. But the emotional force underlying his description, the relish with which he declared their simian proclivities, comes, it seems to me, from the new voice. Because he was strengthening his roots in soil other than the work world—finding new nourishment in an inner self, acknowledging openly the love he bore for the silence of the outdoors—he was able to view his job with more detachment and was consequently able to make his decisions in greater freedom. "I'm just not as attached to that place anymore," he told me later. "I know there's so much more to me than that now."

For Perry, an important dimension of development is a movement from reliance on externally validated truth to internally coherent explanations. Such momentum is clear in Eric's story, and an important roadmark is his willingness to see varied and competing approaches to the same problem. Working with Milt, coming to trust him—largely thanks to the older man's willingness to be open about his own humanity—Eric was able to let go of his need for a single right way of doing things. He grew increasingly able to acknowledge that other points of view may also be valid, have their own inner logic.

His current way of addressing a diversity of solutions is "to try to put them together and come up with the best approach." This has about it the ring of intellectual compromise and lacks full recognition that "the best approach" might be more than simply an amalgam, but Eric has come a long way from the simple expectations of his earlier days. His current stance still maintains that absolutes always exist in some fields—engineering, for instance— but he is quick to affirm that "there's no simple right or wrong answer when it comes to dealing with people."

Given reasonable faith in the maps, the journey ahead is clear. In his work life, Eric needs to consolidate his new position of leadership. Assuming that the administrative climate surrounding his job is sufficiently flexible to acknowledge his broader perspective, Eric should be able to flourish and move ahead as the cultural script dictates. If he can continue to care for his new self as he moves up the corporate ladder, and if that self maintains its respect for the legitimacy of his working world, his path ought to be fairly smooth.

As he grows more familiar with his new, inner self and becomes more willing to share it openly with others, he may find new capacity for intimacy. His family and close friends may take on a new meaning for him. Increasingly able to listen as well as talk, he gains a deepening appreciation for the complexity with which others live their lives. In time, if he can remain open to the continuing challenge of the new diversity that his growing openness reveals, he will grow more adept at building bridges, making connections among people, ideas, differing values. If his teachers can reveal to him their own fears and uncertainties, their own humanity, he will come to see that they too—even mentors—are creatures of their contexts.

All this, of course, is laced with ifs, as any prognosis must be. Maps can never substitute for the journey itself, nor can they ever be more than representations of the territory. People, Perry reminds us, are always bigger than our ideas about them. Those deep trenches of Eric's do not lie on anyone else's charts. They are his own, and the choice to enter them is his.

Learning as a Transformative Journey

Chapter Four

The Deep and Savage Way
The Unsettling First Steps
of an Educational Journey

> *"Thou hast so disposed my heart with desire for*
> *the journey by thy words that I have returned to my*
> *first intent. Now go, for but one will is in us both,*
> *thou leader, thou lord and master."*
> *Thus I spoke to him, and when he set out I entered*
> *on the deep and savage way.*
> —DANTE, THE DIVINE COMEDY

As they head off on the first leg of their journey, students often sense that their educational travels will require them to let go of old ways of seeing. They react in a variety of ways to this discovery. For some, ready to make changes in their lives, the new demands bring a welcome freshness. For others, the journey can be a stiff challenge, one they complete only after considerable turmoil. And for still others, the pressures prove too great and they turn back to the simple haven of a home too safe to leave. But for those who stay on the downward path, the rewards can be unimaginable—quite literally, for it is the nature of transformation that we are changed in ways we do not foresee. If we are not surprised by where we come out, as one student commented wryly, we may not have been there at all.

As mentors, it is important that we understand something of the nature of the changes we are asking our students to undergo so that we can adjust our expectations to their particular strengths and weaknesses; what is a snap for one may prove a challenge to another and overwhelming to yet a third. In this chapter, we listen to the voices of students as they head down "the deep and savage way," on the first leg of their transformational journey.

Opening with a discussion of the emotional tenor and intellectual stance of the first part of the journey, we meet three students as they and their mentors attempt to sustain a fruitful balance among the challenges and supports of their educational work. We meet Betty, who despite her teacher's best efforts chooses to retreat to the shadow of her former worldview; Jean, who struggles with mixed success to free herself of the tangle of family relationships; and Richard, who almost reluctantly manages to break through his own dogmatism.

Like all of the examples in this book, these cases have emerged from my interviews and personal experience over the course of several years. They describe real people who did not always deem to follow the scripts written by theory. The reader is advised first not to see these as polished illustrations but rather as the kind of coarse approximations that reflect most of life's refusal to behave itself; and second, in searching for lessons, to look not simply at what went right or wrong but rather at what happened. What these vignettes have most to offer is not a set of neat generalizations but a model of a certain kind of passionate relationship, a relationship in which mentors care deeply about their students' welfare, win or lose. The greatest practical value of this book is that it offers some new ways of asking questions—of students and about them. This chapter concludes with a set of concrete suggestions for how to do this.

Let's begin then by asking what motivates adults to return to higher education. Why do they begin the journey? There are, of course, as many reasons as students, and as Merriam and Caffarella (1991) remind us, the research on motivation is thick. But most do so because of some transition in their lives (Aslanian and Brickell, 1980; Schlossberg, Lynch, and Chickering, 1989; Galbraith, 1998). For women, one of the most common precipitating events is the children leaving the house, either for school or for good. Said one mother, as she began to build a new career:

> I had been very busy raising my kids, and I loved it. My youngest
> son was going to kindergarten, and I think it occurred to me that
> I wasn't doing a darned thing. Somehow I wasn't satisfied with that;
> it was depressing me; I didn't like it. It wasn't the way I wanted to
> spend my days, and I thought, "Another ten years of this?"
> Something had to give.

For men, the event more frequently revolves around work. "I work for the state," said one man who, like Eric, had reached the limit in his job, such that to advance further he needed a college degree: "And in order to advance it is always beneficial to have a degree. I have gone quite far without one, but to go further I need to go back to school and get that piece of paper. One day I saw an ad in the paper about how it's never too late to go to college, and so I called them."

People working with adults in transition have heard variations of these stories many times over. The tales extend far beyond the classroom, because when tales of transformation are told they often begin with a glimpse of a simple, happy scene just before the descent. King Arthur was a wise and successful ruler; Cinderella was of unparalleled goodness and sweetness of temper; Adam and Eve were naked and not ashamed. Yet usually there is a cloud on the horizon; the serenity is flecked with portent. Something doesn't quite fit, and so they move toward the threshold, impelled outward.

As anyone who has ever stood on such a threshold knows, however, the excitement we feel is usually mixed with a good dose of fear. A glance at departure points in many great tales reveals travelers almost paralyzed as they face the unknown terrors ahead: Dante on entering Inferno, Christian before his pilgrim's progress, or Gilgamesh and Enkidu before the events that were to make of their lives an epic.

So it should not be a surprise that the most common emotion experienced by adults as they return to the classroom is fear. I once asked a group of students to write about their educational experiences using the metaphor of a journey. What were they feeling as they set out? More than four out of five described fear in one form or another. At one level, the fear is born of simple anxiety about an unknown future. For many of these students, school is a reminder of former failure and thus understandably carries grim memories. But there is more to it than that. Whether in terms of Levinson's life structures or Kegan's balances, transformation involves both breaking down and rebuilding. Since we can rarely see far ahead, we are much more aware of what we are about to lose than what we might gain. Fear of the unknown may be irrational, but it is not unreasonable. Here Martin talks with Joanna, his mentor, about it. She has asked him whether he learned anything new in his psychology class:

Martin: I think the biggest thing that comes to mind was that before the class I had an idea that psychology was similar to a technical field where a molding machine in Denver was the same as a molding machine in Boston, and by that sense a psychologist in Orange County Mental Health would believe the same as someone who had the same training any place else in the country.

Joanna: And the training would be the same?

Martin: That's right. And where now I see it as—there really isn't anything that's black and white that you can cut a piece out of. And as you go through, two people might seemingly have the same ideas and agree on the same things, but if they were to write it down, it would be different. I guess that's probably the biggest thing I learned: that nobody really knows what's right or wrong, best or worst, good or bad.

Joanna: Do you have as clear a sense of what's right or wrong as you did before?

Martin: No. When I talk, when I say no, I'm talking about right here, sitting here today. Last week or even last month might have been completely different. I can't even remember. But I know that right now, no, I don't.

Joanna: That must be unsettling.

Martin: Very much, to me right now. Yeah. It's hard for me even to admit to myself because I've always had at least one foot firmly planted somewhere, and I always knew where it was. And, gee, it's sort of like jumping from one iceberg

to another. You don't really know how solid the next one's
going to be when you jump.

Joanna: Does that feel exciting, or is it all negative?

Martin: I can't... I can't put it together. It's [long pause] I just
can't get my hands on it.

Joanna: You feel as though you're in the middle of quicksand right
now?

Martin: Yeah. And it's... kind of frightening, really.

No nineteen-year-old sophomore, Martin was until recently
a prominent official in the Presbyterian church. At thirty-seven,
he is the father of nine children, holds an important industrial
management position, and is well respected in his community. But
along with many of his fellow students, he feels an old, dualistic
world breaking up under him. He has left home, and he's scared.

Being human, when we are afraid most of us turn to other
people for help. It is fitting that we seek Mentor just as we need
him. Dante found his Virgil, Martin his Joanna. Joanna was of
immense importance to Martin as he proceeded to negotiate those
ice floes in the following year. He told her he could not imagine
undertaking the passage without her; he was extravagant in his
praise. Had he been the only student to speak so glowingly of his
mentor, this book would never have been written. But we heard
such expressions again and again.

The early phases of the relationship are frequently characterized by adulation, though occasionally by terror or a paradoxical
failure to recognize the mentor at all. To understand this, it is important to recall that fear both blinds and paralyzes. When we are
frightened, we don't *want* to see too much. At such times, mentors can appear, lantern in hand, helping us to see the way ahead,
perhaps strengthening us in our downward journey, promising in
some way to help us fill the void left by the loss of our former
certainty. At such times, we need to think of them as part divine,
and it comforts us to believe that they have been here before, that
they can see the way through. Most of us are in no hurry to learn
that our teacher is only human. That can wait.

The speed and quality with which the mentorship grows more
equal seems to depend to a great extent on the student's ability to

grow a conscious inner self that can mediate conflicting information effectively. Students at early positions seem to need to invest
the mentor with power as a defense against the fear of rampant uncertainty. Until they can develop their own inner voice to sort right
from wrong, they understandably rely on external authority. This
correlation between Perry's dualism and a high need for authority has been well documented (Adorno and others, 1950; Perry,
1968; Belenky, Clinchy, Goldberger, and Tarule, 1986). Teachers,
advisers, and mentors are all important authority figures during
this period, and it is a safe bet that regardless of how we name
ourselves, we are called on to fulfill this need for some students.
Consider for a moment what Perry observed about how students
in early positions view authority:

> From this position, a person construes all issues of truth and
> morality in the terms of a sweeping and unconsidered
> differentiation between the in-group vs. out-group. This division is
> between the familiar world of Authority-right-we, as against the
> alien world of illegitimate-wrong-others.... Morality and personal
> responsibility consist of simple obedience... of committing to
> memory, through hard work, an array of discrete items... as
> assigned by Authority. In this structure's most primitive form,
> Authority's omniscience is so taken-for-granted that no distinction
> is made between Authority and the Absolute. "Truth" and "what
> They say" function as tautological alternatives of expression, as do
> "right" and "what They want" [1968, p. 59].

Few adult students are so naïve as to believe that only one
source of authority holds all truth (though for some the Bible
comes close). Most acknowledge at least several authorities. These
students know their teachers to disagree with one another and
tend to side with their favorites. They may further attempt to
resolve conflict among authorities by dividing them into good
authorities and bad ones—thus maintaining the essential dualistic structure. This tendency to consider some teachers good and
others bad, of course, persists for all of us. But the reasons differ
tellingly. In early developmental stages, good teachers are those
who really know the subject and tell us what is right and wrong.
The others either do not know what they are talking about or

refuse, for their own arcane reasons, to come clean. And because knowledge is concrete, good teachers provide lots of facts.

But teachers are not the only authorities in a classroom. A classic conflict arises if a teacher and a textbook differ. The dialectical movement begins to heat up as the student shuttles back and forth between—and later among—authorities, trying to find out which one is right. The breakthrough comes if she is able to realize that perhaps there's something amiss in her basic formula, in the assumption that there must be a right and a wrong in the first place. At this point, something—usually a very small something—shifts, and she finds herself allowing that perhaps in some areas (such as literature or art) there are no absolute answers, at least not yet. This shift is described as central to "transformative learning," as the concept has been developed by Mezirow (1978, 1991), Brookfield (1987, 1995), Clark (1993), Cranton (1994); and Kremer (1997), among others. We see how this works in more detail in the next chapter.

With this realization, the student is forced to reevaluate her view of authority as well, for how can one authority be better than another if there is no single truth to know? Seeking some basis for judgment, she turns elsewhere. Good teachers are the ones who want you to figure it out for yourself ("Ah, so that's why Dr. Scruggs never gave us the answers."). They may or may not have a lot of facts, but good teachers *care* about you; they try to get you to learn. Sometimes, as one student had it, "[they] let you do things your own way. Maybe if you're writing, they let you break a rule or something in English to make your point. They let you do your own thing. They don't make you adhere strictly to the rules."

Note that in the eyes of this student there are still rules. But as the old structure thaws, "good" teachers seem to become more permissive. They too seem to be searching for their own truth, no more dependent on authority than we. Accordingly, good teachers are less concerned now with grading. After all, if there is no right or wrong and if what really matters is our own personal experience, how can we be graded on that? Good teachers are supportive and nonjudgmental. Among psychology students, Carl Rogers (through no fault of his own, we might add) attains new heights of popularity. He becomes truly a teacher's teacher because he *seems* to say that all you have to do is let people do their own thing and they will learn. Wow.

Perry notes that as the former structures break down and as authority loses its hold, some students turn to cynicism and bitterness. Teachers who once were seen as paragons of knowledge now appear pompous and empty. For adults like Martin entering this intellectual sophomore slump, it can be a time of considerable trial, demanding patience and care from the teacher. A good deal of anger may well up to fill the void left by authority. It is a hard time for families; given the welter of stress on adult students, the loss of such fundamental security can be a backbreaking straw.

The bridging away from authority that goes on at this time is probably paralleled by a tentative shift away from the assumptions about proper behavior and conventionality that have sustained people up to this point. It may gain early impetus in a countercultural thrust, a "pushing away from the dock," as Parks (1986) puts it in her important and engaging study of this shift among young adults in college. But for years older students have been a part of that conventional culture. It may take a profound jolt to help them see for the first time that others may not only differ from them but may do so *legitimately*. As long as we have to be right or wrong, it is difficult to question our culture's givens and to form our own *considered* value position.

It is characteristic of the journey metaphor that mentors may be seen as gatekeepers as well as guides. They stand at the boundary of the old and the new worlds, and as such they hold the keys for successful passage. They understand the cryptic passwords and, like Virgil in Hell, seem to be able to move undaunted among the inhabitants of a frightening world. That they are in a position to make judgments and to select or reject us gives them considerable power. Their refusal can be a terrible blow; their acceptance of us, a tonic of magical force. Though some take to it more readily than others, such power makes most mentors uneasy. Handling it is delicate work, since to dissemble too soon can lead to confusion and even resentment from students. Yet to accept it too easily or hold it too long denies the student his or her own power.

Indeed, managing power over the life of the relationship is a central problem for both partners. Almost always, the relationship begins in a "complementary" mode in which the mentor is clearly

dominant (Bateson, 1972; Huang and Lynch, 1995; Mullen, 1997).
As the partners come to know each other more intimately, there
is pressure for the relationship to become more symmetrical and
interdependent. But the movement is seldom smooth; sometimes
one, sometimes the other partner resists. In many cases, the strain
is too much. One partner moves too fast, the other is unwilling
to change, or the changes are inappropriate, and the relationship
collapses. Betty and Ken are a case in point.

Searching for the Rock

Student and teacher in a special-access program for adults who
have been away from education for a number of years, Betty and
Ken first met when she enrolled to take "Dimensions of Learning," the centerpiece of the program, a course explicitly designed
to provide a review of basic learning skills as well as to promote
student development. In it, students practice solving problems,
taking tests, reading analytically, and writing. The book list includes Plato's allegory of the cave from *The Republic; Revelations:
The Diaries of Women;* and *1984*—all readings intended to promote
the ability to carry on thoughtful discussion of matters existential
and epistemological. This is a skill considered by Roger Cranse
(1982), the program's designer, to be "more basic than basic."
Classes are kept small, the atmosphere personal and supportive.
The teacher's role includes acting as formal program adviser to
students in each class, so the teaching load is relatively light.

Betty's ruddy appearance belies the strain of her forty-three
years. The central fact of her life is that two years ago she "threw
away [her] life to Jesus" and was born again. Her faith has been the
galvanizing force for a life gone tragically awry with her husband's
conviction for incest, consequent destruction of her twenty-year
marriage, and her forced departure from the family home where
she had spent most of her life. A Christian fundamentalist group
took her in, and she felt cared for in a way she had not experienced
since childhood. Through them, she obtained work in a nursing
home and returned to college to learn the skills she felt she would
need to hold her job.

In our first interview, she explained that her former life was
"communistic," a term she used to mean "evil" rather than to

describe a social system. Now that she had "come to Christ," she knew that certain things were right and others wrong; the Bible was an absolute authority in these matters. At the same time, she was fully aware that not everyone agreed with her and they had a right to their opinion (even if it was wrong). Furthermore, she did not believe "we're stuck with saying everything is bad or everything is good." Some things were gray, and good things could come from bad. Her own life taught her that.

Her job as a student was to listen carefully to what she was told by her teachers, respect their authority, and do the assignments faithfully. Yet she did not always expect her teachers to tell her what to do; sometimes they would want her to learn for herself from her own mistakes. She held Ken in high esteem as her mentor. He was "very knowledgeable" and spoke distinctly. His chief responsibility to her was to "lead me into clear understandings," and she joked about being in love with him "in a girlish way." Asked to describe an ideal mentor, she said it would have to be someone who was "so perfect I wouldn't have to find flaws in his life." Although Ken was not that perfect, it was extremely difficult for her to be critical of him.

As an anthropologist, Ken prided himself on his blend of scientific rigor and deep caring for people. Developmental theory held a special fascination for him, and he enjoyed the "magic moment" when a student would move from belief that her own point of view, her "campfire," was the only one, to a recognition of "multiple campfires."

His role as teacher was to help students see a complex world more intricately by exposing them to "a world bigger than they know... in a gentle, supportive way." Although emotional engagement with his students was essential because significant learning required trust, it was important for just that reason that a certain separateness be maintained: "There are boundaries that we all have to accept."

Ken's greatest satisfaction as a mentor would come when a student became aware of herself and "took off," by which he meant "grow philosophically, begin to explore bigger, more complex, and less self-centered questions." His job was to be a catalyst, helping students develop a "multiple campfire perspective." The student's part was chiefly to be "receptive" and "want to fly." An ideal relationship would be one in which the student and the adviser grow progressively closer and in which the student's respect for the teacher changes from blind to earned.

He held a high regard for the power in his position and was cautious about "intervening with people who are reasonably content with their lives." He did not wish to risk hurting people by forcing change upon them. On the other hand, helping those ready to fly was what teaching was all about. "For us to grow, we have to help other people grow. You have to give it away to get it."

When Ken first met Betty, he was impressed by her openness, that New England charm, the intelligent wit. He was aware of her Christian fundamentalism but felt confident that she had sufficiently sophisticated reasoning at her disposal to reconstrue her religious experience in less narrow and dogmatic patterns without losing her faith. She was, he believed, ready to fly.

But this was not to be.

Now, a year later, disillusioned with Ken and discouraged with her work, Betty talks to me of dropping out. "I guess when you come right down to it, what I want to be is more mother and things like that than a working woman." Work with the elderly no longer holds a reward for her, and thus much of her reason for study is gone. In addition, she failed a psychology course, an event that was, she acknowledges, "more important than you want to admit."

The lecture format of the class moved too fast, she said, and the instructor and the text did not always agree.

> He spewed out all his knowledge, and I was writing it down, and what he told us and what the book had sometimes was different stuff, so you had to study all your notes from him. So I knew I wasn't going to do that great.... It was like "How can I do anything but flunk this class?"

Moreover, much of what she was hearing conflicted with her faith, and she resented "being put in a block" and "having to fit their pattern."

During the previous semester she had not taken a class from Ken, but she did see him occasionally and recently had a long talk with him. She felt she was talking to her father. Asked what that felt like, she replied it was having somebody who knows things she does not, someone who could guide her, give advice. "My father usually saw things that I didn't necessarily see," she said, and broke into tears. She later explained that she was feeling "homesick for parents I don't have."

Betty strongly feels she needs a guide now, and even though Ken has "been there all right," their relationship is not what she has been hoping for. She knows he feels that "probably religion got in the way." But she cannot separate her faith from other aspects of her life as he would have her do, and she feels that to do so would be "like building a house on sand that's going to sink and fall in; it's there but it has no foundation."

If anything, her religious faith has strengthened during the past year. When she "came to know Christ," she became a new person:

> By doing that, I feel free to be myself, and I wouldn't want to give up being free to be myself anymore because I'm no longer my own. I was bought by a price and I think Christ paid a dear price on the Cross to die for me, and now I'm on that road of seeing that, I would never want to change it.... There's something that's going to make this life worthwhile regardless if it's a hard life all the way through. So I'll never turn back and I'll never look at anything probably the same as I did before ... such as evolution.

She feels her conversion has protected her against the danger of future error; her faith gives her a kind of sterile environment guarding her against intellectual infection.

Yet she does not feel that religion is a barrier to her relationship with Ken. On the contrary, it frees her to be more herself, more objective about what she reads and thinks. Although she finds it difficult to believe that "baboons turn into people," Betty goes on to say that "it is possible there is something to evolution.... There could be reasons that God allowed some evolution.... I often feel like God has not revealed any answers to some things, specifically for us just to trust."

By the end of our final interview, Betty makes it clear that although she is discouraged, she will not stop learning. What has changed is her certainty about future training; it is beginning to look as though her education might take a lifetime.

Riding on the surf of his own midlife transition, Ken describes the past year as having brought tumultuous growth: "I've been living more for the present... gaining some modicum of humility... becoming less self-absorbed... a better listener." All of this narrows the gap between vocation and avocation—a positive development, he says.

His views about teaching and learning have not changed significantly, though he acknowledges that his humility may have some relationship to the experience with Betty. He shares her disappointment, describing the association as "difficult, challenging, and fairly unproductive."

"She's a very bright woman, very observant, has a good sense of humor, a great deal of charm and potential." But he finds it difficult to deal with her fundamentalist religion. What he sees as her "reluctance to move away from a kind of safe haven in her religion" runs against his own belief in the value of multiple perspectives.

Whenever he attempted to discuss ideas that were at variance with her interpretation of the Bible, "switches began to shut down." That might have been all right except that she would turn to Scripture for support rather than her own powers of reason whenever a tough question arose.

He suggested that she try reading materials from other religious traditions to strengthen her Christianity, but she "saw this as a very dangerous area." At one point Ken tried confronting it directly:

> Betty, we've got two tanks in our head. One is our *faith* system...
> our *belief* system that can't really be tested empirically. We all have
> that. Whether we're communists or capitalists or Christians or
> Buddhists, we have that. We believe in *something*, even if it's only
> ourselves. We've got a faith system. And the other is the *logical*
> system, the observable world, the observable, knowable universe
> of cause-and-effect relationships. We're not talking about
> theological stuff.

Betty listened politely and then replied: "You can't separate the two. It's either God's way or it's not God's way. It's either right and just in God's way or it's not. And frankly, there are things in this class that are not God's way."

At about this time, Ken realized that he had run into "a blank wall." Although he felt considerable frustration, he was reluctant to "get out the pry bar" and increase the pressure. He saw Betty's belief system as an important "stability factor" in her life and felt it would be wrong to "mess around" with it:

> I'm not a faith buster. I'm not a reprogrammer. I don't deprogram and reprogram people.... I see nothing sinister or unacceptable in a firm Christian belief. I find my own spirituality is quite well developed, and I respect the spiritual development of others, but there's so much in the way of knee-jerk response ... unthought-out response among fundamentalists.... [They] think in terms of black and white extremes.

So he chose to "pull away from it," hoping that over time some of what he said or she read would settle in and she would feel more willing to extend her reason into presently unquestioned areas.

But there was another reason things fell apart. Partway through the first semester, Ken came to believe that Betty was infatuated with him. It was a painful situation, for not only was it one-sided but he felt that in any event it would be ethically inappropriate for him to reciprocate. She was very vulnerable at the time, and he did not want to hurt her feelings.

> I tried to let her know in every way that I could, in every civilized, gentle way, that I was unavailable. I kept her at arm's length. And this led to a downturn, too, because I couldn't see her in the same light as a protégée after she started declaring this romantic interest in me. So that further flawed the relationship.

By the time of the final interview, the relationship has tapered to the point where it is "not quite as warm or respectful as it was." Ken is saddened by this, but resigned. Betty's case, he feels, is an exception.

What happened? Clearly Betty's traumatic experience of betrayal contributed to her subsequent immersion in religious fervor. It might well be argued that we are treading here on the borders of psychotherapy, theology, or both—territory conventionally off-limits to educators. Ken felt that way, and his intuitions and respect for Betty's delicate balance led him to back away from a situation he feared was beyond him. At the same time, it is apparent that Betty's capacity as a student and her potential for intellectual growth—both being concerns properly within educational bounds—were linked to the event and her way of dealing with it. The spurious separation of intellect and affect is too often a convenient excuse to avoid asking hard but important educational questions. It takes but the slightest deepening of focus to see that both education and religion are centrally about growth of the spirit, and it is no accident that in less specialized societies healers, teachers, and priests are often the same person.

In any case, Ken felt that Betty was using her religion as a protective device—however necessary—to keep from asking herself the sorts of questions that would lead to greater intellectual flexibility and complexity. When he sensed her precariousness, he backed away. At the same time, he has noted that someone with Betty's own religious sensibilities and somewhat less dogmatism might be able to help her "loosen up." His use of that phrase is interesting, for like someone wounded by a flying object, Betty is suffering from spiritual injury. As with a laceration in which the area around the wound stiffens to protect it from further harm, so has she stiffened her epistemology against further insults. Recovery would seem to involve gradual loosening of the area as the traumatized region shrinks.

In certain ways, the healing metaphor is appropriate here.[1] Betty found herself in a spiritual intensive care unit, a caring community that gave her the support she desperately needed when she needed it. The question, of course, is whether she wants to recover the flexibility. Can she do so without either rejecting her community or losing her faith? Ken hoped she could and would. It was apparent to him that her dualistic bifurcation of the world was limited to certain particularly sensitive areas. She was willing enough to acknowledge that some things were intrinsically gray, and on the whole she was probably more multiplistic than dualistic. Perhaps he could help her recognize those areas and then, bit by bit, transfer horizontally her gray areas toward the injured zone.

But she found it difficult to handle a class in which there appeared to be two differing authorities; she felt helpless. Her tendency to see the instructor as a fount of knowledge rather than herself as a source of learning meant that it was hard to organize the material in ways that made sense to her. After all, what good would that do? Her task was not to make sense of disparate information; it was to learn the truth. Given that, she was right; how could she but flunk? It wasn't that she *did* something wrong; it was that she understood the situation inappropriately.

And then she got sweet on him. Transference, as the psychoanalysts call it, is what gives the mentor-protégé relationship its fire. Commonly understood as the process by which patients project their fears and aspirations onto the therapist, it occurs in modified form in virtually all mentorships. Therapists are taught to use it to help patients move through their particular problems. Ken had no such training, and for him it was simply an inappropriate infatuation. He did not wish to use it for anything; he just felt uncomfortable and wanted out. One can hardly blame him, since it appears from Betty's association of him with her father that her expectations were substantial. Ken's reluctance to play that part may contribute to her own discovery that she can care for herself, that she doesn't need a perfect mentor to protect her. If she can accept that and learn from it, she will continue to heal.

As every teacher knows, love in its many forms is central to the whole enterprise. It only becomes a problem when it moves in some way out of the bounds that we consider legitimate. This seems to happen rather frequently in close situations of this sort. Occasionally it works, and things go smoothly, but far more often one or the other partner—usually the student—ends up hurt. Some (though by no means all) of the growing number of sexual harassment cases now emerging on campuses may chronicle such relationships gone bad. Though it may sadden us, we ought not be surprised that sexuality so frequently becomes an issue; mentorships have a special intimacy, and the bounds are not always clear. Because the teacher holds the power in the situation, the primary responsibility for drawing the line falls in his or her hands. The decision can be painful; we know that in the intensity of the connection lies the power of the teaching.

Still, neither Ken nor Betty has entirely shut off the relationship, even though it seems to have gone into temporary storage. It would be a mistake to assume that nothing happened. Indeed, Betty could use much of what occurred for her own healing. Whether she will or not remains to be seen; for now she is very much in the wilderness, wandering (as she acknowledges) on sand, unsure of her footing, still believing that somewhere there must be solid rock.

For his part, Ken wound up feeling frustrated. He chose not to challenge Betty beyond a certain point for fear of hurting her delicate balance, but he found his efforts at support misinterpreted. The result was a stalemate. The transformation went unrealized.

But sometimes a student's difficulties lie outside the bounds of the relationship. Sometimes the only thing a teacher can do is be present when she is needed. It can be helpful at such moments to be able to step back and know that the best intervention is simply to be there. This seems to be what happened with Jean and Dolores.

Family Ties

Three years before our first interview, Jean's husband was disabled. To support the family, she was forced to leave the home where she had raised four children into their teens. She took work as a chambermaid in a nearby resort but soon dissatisfied with menial labor, she began secretarial studies at the local community college. Though the decision was hardly a free one, she says, "it was something I always wanted to do," expressing a deep desire to better herself. Jean is now thirty-five, and her children are well along in school. "I feel it's time—it's now or never."

Most of her courses were job-related: typing, office procedures, shorthand. But she also enrolled in "Dimensions of Learning," a course she entered with great fear, feeling "very, very lost." Here she met Dolores, her teacher, who turned out to be "super easy to talk to." Dolores's job, as Jean saw it, was "to get everyone through," and she was "fantastic" at it. Dolores seemed to know everything, was very patient, was committed to her work, and loved reading. "She's got it all together, and I definitely haven't." Yet this did not mean Dolores was perfect; Jean might disagree with her teacher on occasion.

Math class was fairly comfortable because it was "pretty black-and-white; there's a set way to do it and that's it." The Dimensions course, on the other hand, "has a lot of levels of doing it right." Anyone's opinion there could be as good as anyone else's, though some opinions didn't make as much sense as others because they lacked the facts "to back them up."

Jean felt a good deal of frustration with herself for "always doing the things [she was] supposed to do" rather than what she wanted for herself. She admired her teacher's independence and looked to Dolores to help her set goals and to keep her "on the track." As long as she remained attentive and honest, she felt confident that Dolores would be there.

For her part, Dolores loves her work and talks with matter-of-fact amazement about her first class. When she first asked if anyone knew who Plato was, a hand shot enthusiastically into the air: "He's a dog, ain't he?" *and nobody laughed.* They all agreed.

Dolores didn't laugh either. Her job was to provide a climate where students could talk freely without embarrassment, think aloud without being put down, and experiment with sometimes frightening ideas. Education ought to help students to see themselves in a new way. It should move them from "narrow rights and wrongs" to where they could "work with ideas and not have to see the world as black-and-white." To do that, they had to feel safe from scorn. Her part in that was to act as a "sounding board for ideas, one that encourages rather than ridicules."

The term *mentor* only recently came into her vocabulary, but she liked it. It had a reciprocal, two-way quality that appealed to her. Far from placing her on a pedestal, she felt the term allowed her to reveal her clay feet. This was important, because she was put off by students idolizing her. They needed to see her survive errors so they could learn to do the same. As long as they were hooked on their failures, they would have difficulty seeing their successes.

Dolores had a special fondness for Jean. Like herself, Jean seemed to be honoring an inner voice that said it was time to care for herself. Jean's curiosity, eagerness, enthusiasm, "inner sparkle" appealed to her. Dolores was aware of her student's insecurity, her fear of the journey she was undertaking, so it was Jean's courage that Dolores admired most of all—her "determination to get on with her life plan despite horrendous family problems." She held great hopes for Jean:

> She's so ready to push ahead with some new ideas.... She's going to move into doing a lot of independent thinking; she's going to be doing a lot of challenging because you can see it now, just those little sparks. I think she'll be able to move tremendously.... She's just standing at the threshold.

A year later, after mixed success in her secretarial science courses, Jean is confused, discouraged, and frustrated. She is still "hanging in there, still battling," but more than once she has almost quit. The reason, she insists, is not so much her schoolwork as her homework. Her husband has not made the progress she hoped he would in recovering from his disabling accident, her nineteen-year-old daughter has moved into the house with a baby, and Jean feels almost completely without support:

> Last semester I tried getting out of the house to do my homework, but that didn't work because my husband was upset because I was gone so much. And I'm trying to do my homework around the telephone ringing and the TV going and the radio going, not having any room to go into by myself; or even if I go in and close myself in the bedroom I find that they're coming in and interrupting me even when I'm in there and even after I've asked them not to.... They don't feel how important it is for me. You know, they haven't even begun to grasp that yet, how important it is for me to do this.

Her frustration is all the greater as she feels the impact of her education, both *what* she is studying and *that* she is studying. She enjoys being with other students, feels as though she is "into the world" and "participating in something." And although she is not sure she is "on the track I was when I started," this does not worry her. There seems to be something more to it now than just learning how to be a secretary and more to her life than being only a mother.

Knowing she is heard has allowed Jean a greater sense of her voice during the past year. She is no longer as afraid as before to speak up in class; she feels freer to ask questions. If someone calls her on the phone, she feels more authoritative, more self-confident than she used to. Though she is ambivalent about it, she sees her goal as somewhat closer now, feeling that even though her family may not know (or care), "inside myself, I'm growing."

Asked how she would resolve a situation where two experts offered conflicting opinions, Jean says:

> I would probably go with the one that was closest to my own opinion, if I had an opinion on it. If not, I would just weigh the evidence and then state who I feel was right.... We act on the

evidence we have right in front of us. We take a step in that direction. If everything comes out all right, we feel it's right. If it doesn't, we feel that it was the wrong choice and just learn from it and try again.

Faced with a difficult real-life moral choice, she may not have an answer. Pressed, she would turn to the religious principles she was brought up with. She believes in God but is not "overreligious." "I guess I basically live by the rules," she says. "That's been set for us from generation to generation, and it was there for me."

Jean has not seen her mentor much since the Dimensions class ended, even though Dolores has invited her to drop by numerous times. When they do talk, however, it is refreshing. Jean never fails to feel Dolores's interest, concern, and warmth, knowing she can talk to Dolores about anything, "not just the school." At the same time, Jean senses that her teacher will not tell her what she has to do but rather will let her make her own mistakes. She values that.

Despite their relatively minimal contact in the six months preceding the second interview, Jean feels that Dolores is not far away, that the choice is hers to make if she wants to talk. Even in absentia, she says, "I see her supporting my goal, and I see her challenging, because she's where I want to be some day—not, say, this given job but her emotional attitudes toward her job and everything. I see her being where someday I want to be."

Dolores represents for Jean someone who has been where she wants to go. Her mentor incarnates her dreams and gives her encouragement to see beyond her immediate surroundings. She has begun to wonder whether the track she set out upon is the best one for her and has begun to dare to imagine something more:

> I'd like to be able to carry on a conversation with somebody and know what I'm talking about, have opinions—not like it's a math problem, right or wrong period—but just being able to give an opinion and know that it's really my opinion because I know what I'm talking about.
>
> In the back of my head I've always wanted to go back to school just to learn and to be more qualifying, to be more worldly about what's going on in the world. Not just the history of the world and how are math problems done, but just to be more learned about what's going on in general—everything.

I was beginning to feel like I was just a mother, and I felt important to my kids and to my husband, but outside of that house I felt like a stranger. And I don't have that feeling so much anymore.

Yet the questions raised by her family remain: not only whether to study secretarial science or literature but whether to continue studying at all.

Dolores shares Jean's sense of frustration. She wishes they could have more time together and fears that "things have fallen apart" between them. Yet to an astonishing degree, she is aware of Jean's difficulties despite what she feels is inadequate contact.

Limited finances, family problems causing severe barriers to her own education . . . resistance from a spouse who feels threatened not only by her intellectual growth and curiosity but by her being away from where he can see her and exercise that sort of control he feels he needs to assure himself that she'll stay with him. . . . And there's an alcohol problem.

In addition to occasional phone calls and passing conversations, a current work-study student and friend of Jean's has been acting as an intermediary between Dolores and Jean: "A lot of messages from Jean come to me through Anne. . . . We send messages back and forth through her."

Describing her student's past year as a journey, Dolores has this to say:

It's a journey with a lot of potholes and trees across the road, and thunderstorms, and needing to take detours. Last term she really had to take a detour, and maybe she's had to fill in a couple of potholes this year, but she's underway again, still moving ahead.

What is her responsibility as a guide to Jean?

Maybe just trying to be there with the flashlight and keeping the door at various places of the journey open when she wants or feels that she is able to make it in . . . helping her find balance, looking at the different piles of stuff in her life with the old flashlight and saying, "Where are you going to add this chunk called school? How is it going to balance you?"

It is particularly important as she works with Jean, as with all her students, Dolores says, to keep in mind the whole of Jean's life, not just her academic curriculum. There is a temptation "to steer students into courses you know would be good for them," without regard for their capacity to handle the work, given the rest of the forces in their lives.

> I need to understand Jean's whole life; I need to be able to see all the pressures on her. . . . We can't assure everybody success, but I think we can work with the whole framework, the holistic approach, so that the chances of success are going to be much greater than if we don't focus on the whole picture of the adult.

Dolores has heard her student's growing concern with larger questions, and it frustrates her to think that Jean may be unready to nurture this movement in herself. Yet she recognizes that her student needs practical training right now, and she respects the need. She sees the distance Jean has already traveled, but she also senses the threads that hold her student, and from this perspective comes the wisdom to decide when to support and when to challenge her student.

Jean's story is all too common. Her tale of trying to read in the midst of whirling family life—often at the kitchen table—brings a grimace of recognition to her sisters everywhere. For most adult learners, the return to study, however exhilarating at moments, entails long hours of sheer drudgery, often at a cost to family life. Dolores's recognition of the importance of seeing the *whole* student cannot be overemphasized. This is particularly true for female students, who tend to be more concerned than men about the effect that their study may have on other people in their lives for whom they accept responsibility. Recent research on gender differences suggests that if study is seen as demanding a choice between cost to others and benefit to oneself, women are likely to sacrifice their studies more often than men are (Evans, 1985; Josselson, 1987; Taylor and Marienau, 1995).

Frequently, campus-based teachers fail to recognize that their commuting students live very different lives from residential undergraduates. And although no one (least of all the students themselves!) seriously argues that we should relax standards for these students, it is imperative that the boundaries that make sense for eighteen-year-old full-time students be reexamined for their usefulness to the growing number of working students of all ages. Class hours can be changed, completion deadlines made more flexible, study methods made more appropriate, and a range of more dramatic and imaginative reforms introduced to provide the kind of supports and challenges appropriate to students whose lives are demonstrably different from those for whom colleges were designed in earlier times.

But there is more than institutional rationale for attending to the whole lives of students. Knowing what is important to our students as individuals, we can more readily help them find connections between the lives they live and the subjects we teach. Effective advising is more than simply spewing out distribution requirements and interpreting regulations. A colleague describes his job as "accountant, lawyer, and philosopher king." Thus, we may shuffle credits and distribute requirements, but more important is our support and advocacy for the student, and more important still is our loyalty to a tradition of learning and intellectual accomplishment. If the first is allowed to eclipse the other two, we compromise our students and betray our commitment.

In the end, it is simply *better* to see human beings as wholes rather than isolated minds, bodies, or souls. It is phenomenologically better because it recognizes that the world is intrinsically connected and respects those connections *before* sundering them for purposes of analysis, not after. It is intellectually better because it allows more complex and dynamic understanding of living phenomena in flux, a grounded and contextual grasp rather than the abstract and conveniently frozen vision of a cadaver on a table. And it is ethically better because it represents a stance at least approaching a loving, caring respect for the inherent worth of the other person.

Having said all that, let's return to Jean's words. She says she has grown even though others in her family may not recognize it (and, she implies, may not want to). But has she? Few people, if asked, will deny that they have grown in some way; our culture smiles on the word. Indeed, Jean's way of thinking about knowledge seems essentially as it was a year earlier. She said then that some things like math were black-and-white, others gray; and she seemed to have no particularly sharp tools for deciding whether something was right or wrong. After a year, she acknowledges that she would "weigh the evidence" but is still some distance from the kind of ease with the tool that characterizes contextual thinking; pressed to make an ethical decision, she would finally turn back to her upbringing rather than forward to her own developing principles. They seem still to lie ahead for her.

Yet, speaking of her "voice," she is unmixed in her assertion that she has become stronger in important ways. She speaks up in class, she disagrees where she would earlier have buckled, and she can talk with others now about things she would have bottled up before. Especially among women, voice has been shown to be a particularly clear metaphor for growth (Gilligan, 1982; Belenky, Clinchy, Goldberger, and Tarule, 1986; Marienau, 1995). Jean confirms this resoundingly. Her movement is echoed as she describes her new sense of self on getting out of the house and into the world. As she moves out, her angle of vision expands, and secretarial study no longer seems the only choice before her. Although her voice has yet to find the strength of Sandy's "I want to be a legitimate member of the world," it is the same song, no doubt about that.

What has to happen is for the *figure* of the outside world to become *ground*. That is, moving out of the house is still an aberrant act for Jean. The house is where her home is, and under stress she retreats there rather than stay in the world where her supports are still so tentative. In time, perhaps this will reverse so that the world becomes the background, her house a special case. That day is some time off, of course, and may never arrive. That is what lies over the horizon toward which Jean is trekking. As she continues to move, the choice becomes increasingly real.

As I reflect back on their partnership, Dolores's part is difficult to see at first. Like many mentors, she feels she could do more. But it seems clear that Jean didn't ask for more. She had ample opportunity to see Dolores and decided not to. As near as I can tell, this has nothing to do with negative feelings between the two. On the contrary, each speaks warmly of the other. Rather, it seems to be a mixture of Jean's own guilt about her family struggles and her strong inner sense that she can handle things by herself. Given that, Dolores offers perhaps the best gift she can: her caring presence.

By remaining receptive and available to Jean when she is needed, Dolores lets her student know that she matters enough to be cared about by someone important in the world. That's potent tonic, even on the shelf. Dolores's mere presence seems to be a powerful support for Jean, for she knows that she cannot drop out with Dolores around, she knows that someone who cares is watching her, and she knows that Dolores will be there if she really needs help. Mentors sometimes seem to function this way, as guardian angels, invisible but present and guiding. Just in case she needs to check to see if the angel is still there, Jean can send her friend Anne, the intermediary, to make sure.

But if Ken thought it unwise to challenge Betty's beliefs and Dolores found her steady presence to be her best choice for Jean, the next case illustrates what can happen if the situation is ripe for a happy blending of challenge and support. Notice how Hank supports his student, Richard, by encouraging him to speak in his own voice, yet challenges him to hear other voices as well.

Growing Doubt

Richard had dropped out of college his freshman year. Ten years older now, something about him still appeared younger than his age. It was not his long hair and earring that set him off so much as a certain forced, carefree quality. Many of his fellow adult students were well ensconced and even advanced in their careers. Richard was still undecided. Commitment, he maintained, was OK for some people, but he believed in freedom.

During his years at large, he lived in several communal situations. None worked out very well for him, yet he would spend hours in conversation with fellow students arguing the superiority of such collectives over private living arrangements, which he labeled selfish and archaic. Other students soon tired of the game, however, and complained that he rarely had anything fresh to say; whenever someone questioned him, he would revert to his party line. This was particularly true when he spoke about education. "Schools should be abolished," he would say. "If we just let kids alone, they'd grow up much more healthy; people should be free."

He rejected the idea of authority, saying that it was responsible for all the wars of history. If people would just be free, there would be no war. Asked what it meant to be free, he replied, "Well, you have to reject authority." For him, Summerhill, the progressive English school, represented the only legitimate form of education. He counted A. S. Neill, Baba Ram Dass, and Marshall Parks (an obscure anarchist) among the few thinkers he respected. "It's not because of their authority," he explained; "it's because they know the truth." He looked forward to his independent study on educational philosophies with Hank; Hank would understand.

"It's almost as though he sees me as a potential convert," was Hank's opening description of Richard. "He seems to need confirmation of his beliefs so badly."

Hank made these remarks on the basis of a brief conversation with Richard and twenty years as a teacher of adults. His early training was in English, and like many of his colleagues who were fascinated by underlying thought structure, in recent years he was drawn toward adult development theory.

"One of the intriguing things about all this stuff," he said wryly of the growing body of developmental research, "is that knowing about it doesn't keep it from happening." He was emerging from "a tumultuous midlife crisis" that saw the end of his fifteen-year marriage and "an astonishing new freedom." Yet Hank's idea of freedom differed sharply from Richard's. "Freedom is like breathing," Hank said. "You have to keep doing it all the time ... and there are times when you wonder if it's worth it." For him, the end of education is the enhancement of freedom. A good education should free people from their past and from their own cultures, without depriving them of either.

The most important thing he learned over the years about his work was how to listen. For him, listening well meant "actually trying to enter the world of the other person, see through his or her eyes as clearly as possible, without making assumptions or judgments—just plain 'get' their world as they see it." In this act of listening, one could not only understand better how to work but "listening like that is teaching in the profoundest sense."

Hank described mixed feelings about his first contact with Richard. He was at once attracted to the young man's sincerity and passion; he liked and agreed with Richard's views, yet found them remarkably rigid, and was disturbed that an idea as important to him as freedom could be so casually made into what he called "a canned religion."

Six months later, at the conclusion of the study, Richard is noticeably subdued. Asked about this, he replies, "I guess the biggest thing that stands out for me is that I'm not so sure of things anymore." This is not bad, he goes on, "only that I'm not so confident now as I was, you know? There are so many sides to things. It kind of makes you think."

The study went "really well" at first. He decided, with Hank, to look at a variety of ideas about freedom and education through history and in different cultures. The idea appealed to him because he saw it as an opportunity to confirm his views about society's destructive effects on the young through educational institutions. What happened?

> It turned out a whole lot more complicated than I had expected.
> I mean you look at a guy like Plato and it's pretty obvious . . . that he
> put society ahead of the individual, you know? But then you start
> looking at why you have to do that sometimes, like in Tanzania, for
> instance, or what happens if you have too much freedom.

Pressed for conclusions, he replies that "there just isn't any way to know for sure." He guesses that it "might depend on the situation" as to what would be the best approach. Perhaps surprisingly, he is not particularly uncomfortable about this. He seems to take a kind of new refuge in his tentative intellectual diffidence and denies that it is a major change for him.

> I don't think I've changed my opinion all that much; it's just that
> I have to think more about whether my opinions are, you know, any
> good. [What is a good opinion?] Well, I guess one that has some
> facts behind it, maybe some research to back it up. That's what
> I mean by "think"—you have to consider something from all its
> aspects before you make up your mind. And I kind of like that, you
> know? I mean it almost feels better to not know about something
> than to know it. Does that make any sense?

At one point, about midway through the study, Richard felt "pretty discouraged." He began his work with considerable momentum, but as his reading progressed, he came to see there were more sides to the problem than he realized. He found it extremely difficult to write his second paper, a description of Plato's view of the role of education. In part this was because the language was difficult, but more because he found it almost impossible to describe a position different from his own, as Hank specified, without injecting his own opinion. In the end, he wrote a largely subjective reaction and did not receive a favorable response from his mentor.

He was angry at first, but Hank's critique was not wholly negative. "He said that what I had written was OK; it just wasn't the assignment, and he pointed out particular passages in the reading that I should go over again for the meaning." The second time Richard tried, he said, "I got much better comments." He was beginning to get the idea of distilling someone else's ideas, though he wasn't sure he saw the point. "I remember thinking, 'Why should I use these guys' ideas instead of my own?' and it sort of got me." As the term's work progressed, however, he found it easier to understand the readings, and by the end he was able to produce a final paper that combined the ideas in his reading with some of his own. Did he reach any conclusions? No, he explains, but "I think I learned a lot—about how much there is to know."

Hank was pleased with the study. "Richard came a long way," he says. "I think what he learned most maybe was some humility." The first assignment was simply a paper about Richard's own ideas—"a strictly personal statement" to let him feel that what he had to say was important, but also to give both Hank and himself a starting point from which to see what difference it would make, as Hank wryly notes, "if he learned anything."

Like Richard, Hank considers rewriting the second paper to be a critical incident. "I think that's when he began to get it that his own subjective impressions—which were really not his own but were cloned from his countercultural heroes—were not going to be adequate." But Hank emphasizes the importance of his having provided positive support along with his criticism of the effort: "I tried to tell him that it wasn't *what* he was saying that was the problem, but *how* he was thinking about the question. He was still looking for answers from authorities, even though he outwardly rejected the idea."

The support was particularly important, Hank says, because he was really asking the student to let go of "some pretty important external supports" in his preexisting doctrines, and he had to be willing to be leaned on for a while during Richard's transition to "self-propulsion."

Hank is less sure that any substantial changes occurred in Richard's view of freedom, a goal that he held at the outset of the study. The final paper did not deal very thoroughly with the topic, and Hank's feelings about this departure are mixed:

> I guess you can only expect so much. He did loosen up a whole lot, and the final paper was a classic case of sophomoric multiplicity, where you have gotten the idea that there are a million ways of seeing but haven't yet figured out how to make them cohere. . . .
> I think he still believes freedom is some sort of Nirvana, and Baba Ram Dass is still on his throne, I think, but the world has gotten more complicated for him, that's for sure. And—isn't it interesting—he's a whole lot quieter.

Richard's movement was clear and fairly direct, if undramatic. As he acknowledges, he loosened up from his doctrinaire stance, allowing himself, with Hank's help, to move around and look at the phenomenon of education from several vantage points. In doing so, he discovered that the floor did not fall away when he took a step out; he could immerse himself in a different way of seeing and still return if he needed to. His world, initially cast as an island of freedom surrounded by hostile authority, began to lose its harsh edges as the study developed. The movement stopped short of a complete transformation of his idea of freedom, but it is apparent that as Richard's thinking becomes more complex, this idea too will grow richer.

When their collaboration began, Richard viewed Hank as the only teacher who would be sympathetic to views that he considered too radical for most faculty. This was not because he knew what Hank actually believed but rather that he saw Hank to be more open, less judgmental—and consequently less threatening—than the others. In this sense, Richard never actually saw Hank at all in the beginning. It was only as the study got under way that the young man realized that he was under some sort of pressure. Initially encouraged to express his own views, Richard could then invest himself in the work in a way he almost certainly would not have under more conventional circumstances. Hank was wary of his student's tendency toward counterdependence, a stance that Parks (1986) describes as still a part of reliance on authority. He did not want to get thrust aside with all the other jetsam in Richard's wake.

Richard is not clear about his feelings during the difficult middle of the study. Off the record, Hank acknowledges a certain sadistic twinge as he sent Richard's paper back. He knew it would be difficult for the student. Yet Richard simply describes himself as "quite upset." He seems unwilling to acknowledge anger toward his mentor. Later, as he began to "get it," and as the praise became more abundant, his esteem for Hank grew. By the end of the study, he sees Hank as "incredibly supportive, I mean just incredibly. He seemed to know just what I needed, and when I needed it. I couldn't have made it through without him." It's almost as if he has forgotten who threw him in there in the first place!

Richard seems to have made the kinds of change we tend to call progress. He moved undeniably toward greater multiplicity, his thought grew more complex, and—considering where he was coming from—the decrease in self-confidence is healthy for him. This part of the journey often witnesses such change, as uncertainty becomes more prevalent and legitimate. He was fortunate in having a teacher who was both skilled and sensitive enough to make the right moves at the right time. The change in their relationship is not dramatic, but the two men certainly moved closer together in the course of the study, coming to know each other better even if there is no indication that they will continue the friendship after the formalities are over.

Looking Ahead

Yet as we have observed, it would be a mistake to consider the other two relationships presented in this chapter to be less successful in any profound sense.[2] If a collaboration between mentor and student is fruitful, its primary task is to enable the student to work with the business she has before her. What is important in Betty's case is that she learn to be more comfortable in the uncertainty that surrounds her. If it means that she must wander for a while and do so alone, then perhaps that is what she needs. As long as she can know that someone is there when she is ready to move on, it need not be Ken. There may be another, or perhaps she will find she can travel by herself.

Jean's movement is fragmented, not at all uniform, but she has spoken strongly in her new voice, and while the way ahead is dark, it is clear that she knows Dolores is there for her when she needs her. In Perry's language, she is temporizing. Some part of her knows it is not yet time to move on. Yet the foundations of her former world are shifting. As of this writing, although she is still a stop-out it is significant that she has retained contact with Dolores and with college. It is almost as though she is just waiting until the ties that still hold her to her family slip a bit more, until she can move into a new family and new self without forsaking the old.

Richard's next step is to continue working with his new insights about the complexity and multiplicity of truth. As he does so, he may well begin to ask, perhaps with some anger, what right the institution has to make any judgments at all about him or his work. Like Emerald, the accountant we met in the first chapter, he is at a vulnerable if occasionally exuberant position, and it may be a while before he is able to move ahead and make the sorts of clear commitment that some of his fellow students have made. But he has finally broken free of the stuck place of his earlier fundamentalism, and with care and support he will be able to move ahead without retreating to the safer but less adequate world he has left behind.

It is important to note that all three students are moving. With the help of their teachers, they have lost their balance, and each is struggling to regain it. With the possible exception of Betty, when they do, they are virtually certain to find that they are no longer standing in the same place.

But these cases are all situations where teacher and student worked closely together. Are there lessons here for those in the more traditional classroom? Clearly the answer is yes, but I want to emphasize that the lessons do not require individualizing instruction. Rather, they involve enriching our teaching so that each student can take from it what she or he needs. Here are some thoughts.

First, there are few college-level subjects in which there is no legitimate controversy. It may indeed be wise to emphasize a preferred approach, but teachers should attempt to *present a range of perspectives* on their subjects and on the topics within the subjects. What are the great controversies in the field? How do the antagonists support their positions? What are the differences in methodology? Practitioners in the field can be invited as guest speakers to present controversial positions. This is not simply so that each student can seize on a preferred approach. It is so that all students can recognize that there may be many paths up the mountain. This is where the developmental press occurs (Knefelkamp, Widick, and Parker, 1978; Merriam, 1993; Cranton, 1994; Tennant and Pogson, 1995; Courtenay, Merriam, and Reeves, 1998).

Second, teachers can strive to provide a broad overview of their subject. What are the assumptions underlying the field? Is it possible to imagine other assumptions? Are the given truths universally accepted, or do other cultures handle matters differently? How did the subject evolve through history? How was knowledge accumulated in the field? How is it related to other subjects? What impact has technology had on the evolution of methodology? Who are the putative experts, and how did they get where they are? In short, we can *provide a context for our subjects*, a map of the field to remind students that all knowledge rests on a web of assertions, not some absolute, immutable Truth. Regardless of how practical or applied the field may be, graduates who see the big picture and can think independently on their feet are far more valuable than those who can only do things the "correct" way. This point is driven home for subjects as diverse as engineering, business administration, and education in *The Modern American College* by Arthur Chickering and his colleagues (1981).

Third, ample *opportunity to discuss and debate* the material is important. One of the greatest values of class discussion is the chance that it offers for students to role-play positions with which they may overtly disagree. An avowed liberal might be asked to present impartially the conservative position on an issue, for instance, or members of different ethnic groups might reverse roles. This need not be done formally or artificially. Rather, the instructor can periodically ask one or another student to assume a fresh stance in addressing a question. "I know you are a feminist, Alice, but how would a supporter of Jesse Helms respond to this issue?" "How do you suppose an inner-city black might react to what you just said, Nathaniel?" Development is closely related to enrichment of inner dialogue, and class discussion helps students process material, hear different accents, and try speaking in new voices.

Finally, a quick survey of age, sex, and interests of a class, informed by knowledge of developmental patterns, can help us to make some reasonable guesses about *the tasks confronted by our students*. Readings and written assignments can emphasize issues of concern to each group. In particular, appropriate selections from great literature help surface developmental challenges. Maxine Greene (1990) brilliantly summarizes the "emancipatory potential" of this approach.

It is a given that what distinguishes Betty, Jean, and Richard from their teachers is not the size of their brains. Nor is it their age. The students simply think in ways that fail to match the complexity and intellectual dexterity expected of a college graduate or demanded by their expanding worlds (Kegan, 1994).

It is a given, too, that these folks *can* change (though their teachers may well despair) and it might take more drastic alterations in their lives than simply attending courses to bring change about. In many ways, the traditional ages of college attendance are ideal for the sorts of change we value in liberal education: greater independence from authority, a new perspective on one's culture, the capacity to think hypothetically and contextually, and the ability to see the connections among things. This is the time for reassessing family and upbringing, enhancing formal operations (Inhelder and Piaget, 1958), and making new commitments in a new environment. As Chickering (1969) richly illustrated, campus life is ideal for developing autonomous identity. But for adults, few of whom live on campus and all of whom are deeply embedded in real-life relationships, such change comes with a good many strings attached. In a case like Betty's or perhaps Jean's, the strings may just prove too constraining.

Therefore, as teachers and advisers there is much we can do to help our students decide how far, in what ways, and even whether they continue the journey. We can seek to understand the ties that hold our students in their present lives so that, like Ken, we can better judge how much challenge is enough. We can work to extend our respect for their struggle and communicate our support regardless of whether we happen to approve of how they are conducting it. We can encourage our students to look clearly at their own motivations for returning to college, ask themselves the hard questions, and respond as honestly as possible to those questions. We can do this individually in conversations after class or in comments on written work; or we can take time to encourage classroom discussion of the impact of class content on the outside lives of our students. Whichever way our students finally decide to go, we owe it to them to help their decision be a conscious one, chosen in the fullest light we can cast between us.

Guiding Principles

Before we move next into the heart of the journey, here are some guiding principles that have emerged thus far.

The primary task is to *engender trust*. One of the best ways to do this is to listen well. This means suspending our own agenda for the moment and attempting to enter the student's world. It also means asking questions that move the student's reflections onto a level where the meanings are made. "Why have you come back to school?" is often a good starter, allowing both teacher and student to understand the place that education occupies in a student's life. "What are you learning?" can open the discussion more fully, followed by questions ("Why is that important?" or "How does that relate to what you said earlier?") that move beneath the content answers that frequently come first. "Can you tell me about a good teacher you have had?" is another question that moves to issues of authority and what is worth learning. Needless to say, the task at this early stage requires that we simply acknowledge the legitimacy of the answers, not that we judge them.

It is important in the early phases to *see the student's movement*. During an opening conversation, we can make a rough assessment. How is she moving: away from simple blacks and whites toward gray? Away from tribal anonymity toward a more visible self? Or is she rebuilding a frame of meanings in a more contextual and interrelated way? And how does the return to education fit with life, family, work? This is a time for an initial diagnosis in which we look not so much for strong or weak points as for growing and withering edges, as new perspectives succeed old, like cells on a growing organism. It can be helpful to remember that narrow thinking is less an affront to us than a limitation of the relationship. It is a place to begin.

Throughout, we need to *give the student a voice*. As in any dialogue, it is important to grant space to the student's own views at first. This can be done individually or with classes. One accounting teacher tells of an early assignment in which he asked students to write a brief paper on what most people don't know about accounting. This yielded material with which he laced subsequent lessons and allowed him to connect the subject freshly with the lives of his students. Not only does this allow the teacher to learn more about the student but students then have a clear record of their own opening position in the dialogue, and they know they have been heard. In courses or studies where there is reasonable latitude for individual exploration, such questions as "What would you like to learn about if you really had your choice?" or "What burning question would you like to pursue in this subject?" can often help students find an emotional core with which to fuel their investigation.

As trust is established and a way charted, it may be time to *introduce conflict*. An appropriate dose of conflicting or counterintuitive information can raise questions about the student's givens. This might be done by calling attention to the major disputes in the field or introducing data that do not fit the prevailing paradigm. Or one might ask the student to take an unfamiliar perspective or to explain in a sympathetic manner a position with which she disagrees. A subject such as history (which places our absolutes in the context of time) or anthropology (which does the same across space) has special power because it can relativize our cultural givens and force us to construct new ways to hold the conflicting facts. A historical or cross-cultural perspective, introduced to any subject from engineering to business administration, can have this effect and help students learn that before they agree or disagree with a position, they must first *understand* each side fully.

As students respond to the questions, in conversation or writing, it is important to watch for the growing edge, like a coach photographing their forward movement and replaying it for them. This may mean being very explicit about what students have done well. It is generally more effective to show people when they are on track than to tell them where they should go or to criticize when they have strayed. *Emphasize positive movement,* underline it, restate it, praise it. By spending undue time on the negative, we run the risk of simply helping our students construct a vision of the impossible, whereas our job is to help them imagine the possible and then move toward it. Always we are guides, encouraging movement.

Throughout this part of the journey, it is valuable to keep *one eye on the relationship* itself. Most often, as student and teacher come to know each other better, the distance between the two that characterized the early days narrows. As greater intimacy develops, some of the student's unreflecting deference to authority may diminish. No longer based on superficial trappings, the relationship has the potential to be transformed into something more profound and powerful. This has major implications for the growth of both partners, as we shall see in the next two chapters.

Chapter Five

The Dynamic of Transformation

How Learning Changes the Learner

*The person is most of all a motion, a motion that neither
we nor she can deny without cost, and a motion which
includes experience of balance and imbalance, each as
intrinsic to life, each a part of our integrity, each
deserving of dignity and self-respect.*
—ROBERT KEGAN, *THE EVOLVING SELF*

It's time now to take a closer look at the meaning of the word *growth*
and to suggest some useful ways to understand it. We consider two
questions about growth: What is its direction and how does it work?
We look first at how the word has been used normatively by stage
theorists. Then we cast more broadly, turning to a discussion of the
idea of dialectic, emphasizing the importance of understanding
underlying structure. We conclude with a conversation with Irma,
who chose to move through her fear and land upright on the
other side.

Transformation: The Meaning of Growth

The problem with the term *growth*, as commonly construed, is
that it implies a continuous, rather unbroken process of "more-
ness." For the first eighteen years or so of our lives, as Topsy had

125

it, we "just growed," getting bigger. The word seems to offer few intellectual crevices. It has a seamless and rather magical quality about it. Yet clearly growth is not simply a matter of quantitative increase; there is a qualitative kind of change as well, a shift not simply in meaning but in the very ways we make meaning.

Since the term is so closely identified with living creatures, it is not surprising that biologists have led the way to closer understanding of it. It is clear, after all, that living things pass through a number of quite radically different forms as they grow. A dandelion is at one point a seed, at another a rooted cluster of new growth, then a golden flower, then a balding headful of gray seed, and again a cluster of leaves. Likewise, an *egg* and a sperm become androgynous embryo that then differentiates to a male or female fetus, later emerges as an androgynous child, again transforms to a young man or woman, and finally matures to a new androgyny. In fact, we change structure dramatically as we grow. The notion applies equally to our mental and spiritual growth as to our physical maturation.

Drawing on his early training as a biologist, Jean Piaget laid the groundwork for much of the extraordinarily fruitful marriage of organic metaphors and epistemological speculation that has since spawned developmental psychology. He understood growth to emerge not from the individual in isolation, nor simply in response to the environment, but from interaction between the two. Organisms function in equilibrium with their environment. To maintain equilibrium, they must *adapt,* they must change in some way as the environment changes. They can do this in two ways: either they modify the environment (by eating part of it, for instance) so that it *assimilates* to their structure, or they modify themselves (for example, by extending leaves to photosynthesize sunlight), thus *accommodating* their structure to that of their environment. Growth involves the simultaneous interplay of both assimilation and accommodation as the organism adapts to its shifting environment.

Intellectual growth, says Piaget, proceeds similarly. As a child develops, she moves through a series of accommodations, transforming the way she organizes information in a regular and predictable sequence from relatively simple, global, and self-centered ways of making meaning to increasingly complex and differentiated forms as the world she encounters grows more diverse and complicated. This doesn't happen, however, simply in a series of forward froglike leaps. Rather, the child makes a new conceptual breakthrough in one area at a time (say, in counting objects), remaining at an earlier stage in other areas. By a kind of sideways movement that Piaget calls *horizontal décalage,* the child gradually extends the power of the new insight to other parts of his or her experience. The term literally means a shift sideways, a kind of intellectual waltz step to the side as we move ahead. This concept is particularly helpful in explaining why some adults seem to be so aware in some realms but so "behind" in others. As we shall see later, it explains why the quality of the environment is so crucial to how we develop. Under stress and threat, we tend to hold to those earlier parts of ourselves with which we feel safest; conversely, when we feel safe, we can trust our growing edge more fully.

The irony is that we often react with primitive behavior to environmental changes that demand all the adaptive capacity of our better selves. This seems to be as true in dealing with an intransigent neighbor as with Saddam Hussein. Those who have developed the capacity to feel relatively comfortable with change seem to cope most productively with its demands.

Piaget's model deals primarily with intellectual growth and culminates with what he calls formal, abstract thinking somewhere in the teen years. Some researchers building on his work have suggested that many adults never attain that level, whereas others continue to develop beyond it. The stage theorists mentioned earlier are among them. Although I have chosen to discuss only Kegan's and Perry's work in any detail, there are others whose research is of special value in helping us understand what growth looks like.

Probably most familiar is the work of Erik Erikson, whose eight stages of man constituted the first major effort by a psychologist to work out a systematic scheme of stages throughout the life span. Erikson seems to be neither stage nor phase theorist, falling somewhere in between. But I have found his work of great power, especially his emphasis on basic trust, identity, intimacy, and generativity. Erikson describes a sequence of "crises" that each of us must resolve as we progressively engage with the tensions of our lives. Though they are age-linked, we cycle through them again and again as we mature (Erikson, 1950). Thinking back on Eric from Chapter Two, recall how his growing ease with his own deep trenches emerged in concert with his more intimate relationship with Milt. Perhaps one thing that prevented him from killing the deer was a dawning sense of his own participation in the growth of others, of his generativity ("I don't want to stop something").

Erikson reminds us that growth is fundamentally seated in a sense of basic trust, a capacity learned in the parent's arms but arching through a lifetime of progressive reaching out to others. To the degree that we can find this sense of basic trust in ourselves (a touchstone to which we must return again and again), we are enabled to take the growing risks of defining ourselves, sharing ourselves, giving ourselves to our children, and finally affirming meaning where there is only uncertainty.

In the late 1950s, Lawrence Kohlberg, then a doctoral candidate at the University of Chicago, began asking schoolchildren to tell him what they thought was right and wrong. To do this, he told them several little stories without endings and asked the children to talk about them. One of these hypothetical dilemmas has attained a certain limited notoriety since then. Known as the Heinz Dilemma, it tells of a man (named Heinz) whose wife is dying of cancer. He cannot afford the only available medicine and is unable to borrow money. What should he do? The case is designed to force a choice between stealing the drug (thus breaking the law) or obeying the law and allowing the woman to die. The actual answers the children gave were less important to Kohlberg than the *reasons* they offered for their choice. On the basis of the forms of reasoning that they used to reach their judgments, Kohlberg (1969) was able to construct a series of levels, a hierarchy that he later argued was in fact a sequence of moral development. Thus, "It's wrong to steal because he might get caught" is a less sophisticated answer than "It's wrong to steal because it's breaking a law and society needs laws."

Kohlberg's stages move from early self-protective and manipulative levels (an act is wrong because you might be punished) through those dealing with maintenance of the social order (an act is wrong if it is against the law, and we must obey the law) to those based on loyalty to overarching and, he argues, universal principles (an act is wrong if it violates the principle of justice). Needless to say, the scheme is highly controversial (Gibbs and

Schnell, 1985). Yet it has been employed in various forms in schools, prisons, and youth programs around the country for some years with considerable success. Although it is now buried under layers of criticism, one suspects that history will regard Kohlberg's contribution as foundational to our understanding of human development.

Influenced by Kohlberg, Jane Loevinger, a psychometrician, worked out a sequence of six broad stages and several sublevels based on lengthy analysis of a sentence-completion test (1980). Like Kohlberg's, her scheme runs from early stages characterized by impulsive and self-protective orientations, through middle positions typified by conventional morality, to higher and more autonomous stages. Her work has proven of particular applicability to understanding the movement of adult learners as they return to higher education. Rita Weathersby, for instance, found that people in early positions tend to seek education as a means of making up a deficit; education is a *thing* to *get*. People in middle stages see education as a way to *be* someone; it helps them get a better job and improve their status. With further development, however, people come increasingly to see education as a way to enhance first their sense of competence and ability to achieve, then their own inner growth. Education becomes intrinsically valuable rather than practically useful (Weathersby, 1981). Monique, whom we met in Chapter Three, seems to be moving from the first to the second of these orientations, and clearly Sandy is moving to the third as she leans on her education to help her become "a legitimate member of the world." For Loevinger, the general movement of development is from early impulsivity through conventionality and toward autonomy and integration. It is interesting that although Loevinger's methods differed from those of her colleagues, her stages closely parallel theirs.

An early protégé of Erikson and Kohlberg, James Fowler has constructed a particularly intriguing sequence of faith stages— "transformations along the journey of faith"—moving from essentially childlike mythic and literal interpretations of our place in the universe toward more conventional understandings and on through universal and self-transcendent expressions of our relationship with "the ultimate environment." Fowler has done more than any other stage theorist to acknowledge and explicate his indebtedness to other developmentalists. His major work, *Stages of Faith* (1981), contains a delightful set of imaginary conversations about human development among Erikson, Kohlberg, and Piaget.

For increasing numbers of adult students like Emerald, whose story began this book, questions of deep meaning that can only be called spiritual lie at the heart of the journey. As academics and educators, particularly those of us in public institutions, we would often prefer to skirt this particular briar patch. Yet if we are to address the developmental needs of our students as whole people, it is important for us to find ways to honor the longings of the spirit as fully as those of the intellect.[1] In one of the most useful books in this regard, *Teaching and Learning in Communities of Faith*, Linda Vogel (1991) details how "the teacher as guide and companion" leads adult learners along their various spiritual pathways.

But always we need to remember that what we hear from our students depends on what we have asked. These developmental shifts happen in various ways, along a range of fault lines in the same person. The shift Perry describes is different from the one Kegan or Piaget might discern. And yet they are connected too, for contextualism would be impossible without formal operations, Kegan's interindividual balance unthinkable without contextualism. The important point is that growth in our species is an enormously complex matter, best observed through many lenses.

Regardless of the differences among these theorists, most assumed that the broad direction of growth pointed toward greater autonomy and ability to act separately from the demands of one's environment. In 1977, however, an article in the *Harvard Educational Review* rang a resounding challenge to that idea. The author, Carol Gilligan, had worked for years with Kohlberg and knew his work intimately. Over time, she grew uneasy with the fact that disproportionate numbers of women seemed to fall into his third stage, a position in which "the good" is conditioned by the actor's intentions (rather than an abstract principle) and by the expectations of others (rather than by one's own inner ethic). Unwilling to accept the implied slur, she questioned the theory itself. The emphasis on autonomy and separateness as the "logical" end point of development, she maintained, betrayed a fundamentally male bias. She went on to develop this notion in her groundbreaking book, *In a Different Voice* (1982), in which she drew on an impressive array of evidence from interviews, mythology, literature, and psychology, arguing that in contrast to the male vision of a "hierarchy of power," women view the world as "a web of relationships." Thus, to be on top and separate is less important to women than to be part of a fabric of interconnected associations. And though the greatest failing for a man is to violate his personal integrity, to a woman the greatest wrong is willfully to hurt another person.

Gilligan then proposed a sequence of "perspectives" that she argued more adequately describe developmental movement for women. Adhering essentially to the notion that we move into, through, and then beyond our cultural conditioning, she rejects Kohlberg's implicit ladder metaphor, suggesting instead an involuted, organic form. As women develop, they spiral through a three-level evolution of responsibility to themselves and others. The early orientation is characterized by primary concern for one's own survival in the face of powerlessness. This gradually gives way to a stance in which one equates the good with caring for others, and self-sacrifice is considered the highest virtue—the antithesis of the earlier perspective. The synthesis is attained with the recognition that "It is OK to care for myself as well." The self, as she puts it, becomes "a legitimate object of care." Out of this insight emerges a "morality of nonviolence" grounded in the ethic of care.

Gilligan's work has had a profound influence, for she has righted a critical imbalance in how we have thought about human development. By demonstrating so powerfully the deep importance of a sense of connectedness with and responsibility for others as well as oneself, she has affirmed for women the centrality of a way of being that has traditionally been undervalued, and she has reminded men that growth toward full humanity includes recognition of their own need to affirm their connectedness with others. Justice, men are prompted, must be tempered with mercy—a willingness to loosen their sole reliance on rules and welcome *compassion,* a "feeling with" the other in the service of a larger understanding of responsibility. This insight generated a decade of popular and academic works about gender difference. The most far-reaching of these in the field of higher education was the award-winning *Women's Ways of Knowing* (Belenky, Clinchy, Goldberger, and Tarule, 1986), which subsequently led to an edited volume

(Goldberger, Tarule, Clinchy, and Belenky, 1996) of implications and applications, surely containing the richest lode of references ever compiled in the field.

Throughout all these approaches to development, including Gilligan's, was the idea that growth proceeds from an early preconventional way of seeing in which our primary concern is with self-preservation in a narrow sense, through a conventional stance where we are moved as much by how others see us as by our own needs, to a postconventional position in which we work to resolve the tension between our own needs and those of others. For the most part, this final level entails a certain willingness to flout both authority and convention in the service of some transcendent value or principle. All of these researchers maintain that growth is more than simply adjustment to the norms of our own particular culture; consequently, most would argue for some sort of universalistic notion of what it means to mature. They trace their lineage, after all, through French structuralism to Kant and in a sense back to Plato. They are not mere relativists. There is more to the universe than what we alone make of it.

The objection is almost always raised in this regard that these are dangerous ideas, ethnocentric and elitist. I have no desire to put that debate to rest,[2] but perhaps it helps to associate movement through stages with climbing a ridge having a number of ascending peaks. Virtually everyone ascends the first few, but as the climb continues, more and more people pause along the way, choosing their own favored peak for its unique view, saying it may be true that later peaks are higher and one can see more broadly from them, but it is unwise to presume that the view from one is more pleasing or in any absolute sense better than another. I have climbed in the hills of Vermont and the Himals of Nepal; it would be plain silly to proclaim one superior. It depends, after all, on what you want to see. Yet this is not to say that climbing is unimportant. There is something within us that must grow, and there are those among us who will ascend. We must honor that—in others and in ourselves.

A more prosaic way of putting it is simply to note that the value of a particular level of development depends on its context. Some environments and some people fit each other better than others; they are more appropriate to certain ways of seeing than others.

Whether a given environment is good in an ethical sense is more a philosophical than a psychological matter. Few would maintain a value-neutral stance about Auschwitz, but out of that hell Viktor Frankl, the psychoanalyst author of *Man's Search for Meaning* (1959), emerged whole to write an inspiring testament to the value of his journey through despair. What enabled him to survive—and to help others survive—was his recognition that despite apparent hopelessness and radical threat to meaning, it was possible to emerge whole if one were willing to take responsibility for one's own sufferings, to weave of them a fabric of meaning. Frankl was not born with that capacity. At the very least, one might argue that richer development increases our ability to make sense where none appears. In a world of growing violence and impending environmental collapse, this ability may be all we have between ourselves and despair.

Taken together, these ideas suggest that growth can be understood as a series of transformations in how we make meaning. As infants, we are embedded in an environment that demands relatively little of us. Virtually our every need is cared for (if it is not, we let our environment know in no uncertain terms), and what we learn if our world is trustworthy is to trust. But as we grow, we place increasingly greater demands on our world, and it on us. In time, we find that we can no longer get what we want from our parents in the old ways; we can no longer continue to assimilate without doing some changing ourselves.

So we begin to accommodate our structures of thought to the shifting environment. Over several years, as Piaget has demonstrated, we form new, more adequate ways of organizing the world, of making sense out of it. And looking back, we wonder how we could ever have been so simpleminded. Thus we move through progressive transformations as our world grows more complex and as we see more from each standpoint: first our home, then neighborhood, institutions, humankind, and all Creation. Each new horizon demands that we form new, overarching ways to make sense of the diversity and conflict we see with increasing clarity around us. For each, we need to learn to think in whole new ways.

In the late 1970s, investigating the effects of women's consciousness-raising groups, Jack Mezirow (1978) coined the term *perspective transformation* for this kind of shift. Over the years, his work has become the benchmark and primary catalyst for transformative learning theory in adult education (Cranton, 1994; Taylor, 1998). For Mezirow, "the central process of adult development" entails the shift toward "a more inclusive, differentiated, permeable, and integrated perspective" (1991, p. 155). Thus, as we grow, we develop ways of knowing that can include more information and experience but make still finer distinctions; ways that are ever more open to new learning but integrate and pull these learnings together in more comprehensive patterns. I know of no more terse description of developmental direction than this.

Meanwhile, Mezirow's colleague at Columbia, Stephen Brookfield (1987), richly described and illustrated how the transformation happens through discerning, exploring, and challenging one's own underlying assumptions about the self, society, and reality. More recently (1990, 1995), he has offered detailed and practical guidelines on how mentors and teachers of adults can become more "critically reflective" themselves in their practice. He is generally recognized as one of the leading voices of critical pedagogy in adult education.

Learning to Swim

What, then, does this experience actually *feel* like? Here's how a friend, who learned later than usual, once described learning to swim. He was out wading on the lakeshore when all of a sudden he stepped off an underwater cliff; the bottom fell away. He panicked and started kicking with his feet and pushing with his hands. Somehow that allowed him to keep his head above water and get turned around until he got his feet under him again and made it to shore. "I guess I didn't exactly learn to swim at that moment," he said, "but I got the idea. You can't move the same way when the water is over your head as you do when it isn't."

Indeed. In a certain sense, my friend accomplished a transformation, however brief, in the way he moved in the water. His environment suddenly changed drastically, and he accommodated; that is, he changed how he moved to fit his new environment. The cost of failing to do so in this case was rather more drastic than the cost of passing up a developmental transformation, but the idea is the same. The feeling, at least for a flash, is fear. My friend didn't actually change once and for all at that moment, but he "got the idea." So it is, I think, with transformations. Some change in our world suddenly forces us to relate to it in a sharply different way, and though we may revert once we are back in safer waters, we have learned something enduring. The next time it happens, we will swim.

Recall how Sandy, who longed to be "a legitimate member of the world," described her transformation from a conventional and dependent self largely defined by her family toward greater "inner-dependence" (Parks, 1986) and a mind of her own as she moved into deeper waters:

> I feel like that the way I guided myself through life was to go back to my family and say, "Tell me what to do. Am I OK?" . . . rather than seeing, looking, understanding how *I* operate and finding out how *I want* to think and how *I want* to deal with myself and how *I want* to treat other people from my own perspective and my own point of view.

Notice here the deep transformation, not in what she thinks about but in the very structure of how she sees what she thinks about. It is a shift of *perspective* from viewing herself through the eyes of others toward increasingly seeing through her own eyes ("from my own perspective and my own point of view"). It's this fundamental shift of *stance* that we are looking for. In the next chapter, we hear her again as she quite literally likens the feeling to being underwater.

Similarly, Perry gives us the words of a student who is just in the process of discovering that the bottom of his lake has dropped away—a transformation from multiplistic to contextual thinking:

> I know that, ah, there is more to me, and more to the things about me than I knew before. I won't say I understand them; I just know they're there and that I may never fully understand or appreciate them. Before, I had ideas about where I was going and what I was going to do. I had a plan. I had a certain program about what I was going to fulfill. . . .
> Well, what I've appreciated is this: that I may get something I wasn't planning on, and that some of the things I'm planning on I may never get. . . . What I'm saying is that I don't think I'm in

perfect control of myself and the world anymore. And I think I'm probably the better off for it, because if something should come up, if the bottom should be pulled out, I wouldn't have been aware of the fact that this could happen [1968, pp. 118–119].

This sense of the "bottom pulled out" is common to descriptions of transformation. Buddhists refer to the sensation of enlightenment as being akin to what happens when the bottom falls out of a bucket of water. For some time it seems that more has been lost than gained, yet beneath that lies knowledge that the exchange was immeasurably for the better. "At least," the student says later, "I've started to think now." As Perry describes it, one begins thinking when one stops believing. The shift into contextual relativism is "the point of critical division between 'belief' and the possibility of faith. Belief requires no investment by the person. To become faith, it must first be doubted" (1968, p. 131). It is at this point that choice becomes real and responsibility takes on new meaning. The ground of our being must shake and be sundered before we can take the radical leap of faith that may carry us across the chasm.

This loss of meaning lies at the heart of the mythic quest; when Dante confronts Satan, the world literally turns upside down. In Zen's famous series of ox paintings depicting the journey toward enlightenment, there comes a point where both ox and self disappear; the frame is empty. We have so fully entered our opposite that the system self-destructs and the screen goes blank. An old self dies so a new one can be born. That's what goes on down there in the dark.

Carol Christ suggests the need for an "experience of nothingness" to mediate woman's spiritual quest for a "new awakening" and a fresh naming of her self (1980). In his work on personal transitions, William Bridges (1980, 1991) points out that major changes require "the transformative experience of the neutral zone," a time in which we welcome emptiness and surrender to chaos. "Chaos," he reminds us, "is not a mess, but rather it is the primal state of pure energy to which the person returns for every true new beginning" (1980, p. 119). In popular songs, in mythology, in religious canons, in literature, the three-part syntax of transformation seems everywhere.

Dialectic: The Dynamic of Transformation

If growth means transformation and transformation means the yielding of old structures of meaning making to new, then how does it take place? What actually goes on during the process of transformation?

Let us look again at the journey Perry describes. The pilgrim moves from dualism (in which one construes the choice to be a simple matter of *this* or *that)*, to multiplicity (when the simple two-part frame turns multiple), to contextualism (in which we realize that right and wrong are more useful labels under some circumstances than others). The choice is no longer external, no longer about absolute good or evil; choice has moved dramatically inward and is now understood to be about choice itself. Perry describes this journey in exquisite detail, giving us student-eye views of the lunging struggle to accept, then reject, then reconstrue the meaning of knowledge, authority, and truth in our lives.

Some years after Perry's work was published, one of his former students, Michael Basseches (1985), suggested that dialectical thinking actually represents a developmental advance beyond formal operations and offered a detailed description of the many forms that this may take. More recently, Rybach, Hoyer, and Roodin (1986) and Commons, Sinnott, Richards, and Armon (1989) have pressed postformal thought further.

In any event, the three-part movement from former, simple meanings to loss of meaning and on to new meaning is hardly new; it bears a keen resemblance to the "romantic descent" of nineteenth-century Romantic literature as well as to the mythic quest so powerfully captured by Campbell. At the nadir of his journey, the hero enters most deeply into the source of his fear as he confronts the formerly irreconcilable opposites of being and nonbeing, male and female, time and eternity, good and evil, light and darkness, hope and despair. At this point, transformation demands not that he choose one or the other but that he move *through* those contradictions and become whole—not again, but anew. It is what Campbell (1949), deliberately punning "atonement," calls "at-one-ment." Not for nothing is it called the moment of truth, for it is a new form of the self in which the old truths are radically revised and the old schisms not simply healed but obliterated. It's a whole new ball game.

Consider the idea of *dialectic*. The term shares with the word *dialogue* its roots in the Greek *dialektos*, to "speak across." As Plato used it, the term referred to a discussion aimed at discerning the truth about some philosophical matter or other, and Socrates stands as the acknowledged master of the art. Without entering into a discussion of Socrates' sometimes questionable rhetorical tactics, it is safe to say that the ostensible intent of a dialogue was that each party would put forth an observation for examination by the other. Out of the give-and-take of their discussion would emerge common agreement on truth. *Dialectical thinking* thus refers to a process of thought that relies instrumentally on formal logic but, more importantly, on the relationship of one idea to another. It presumes change rather than a static notion of reality. As each assertion is derived from the one before, truth is always emergent, never fixed; relative, not absolute.

Most simply, it can be diagramed thus:

To begin, a "thesis" is stated or an assertion made (A). This is countered by a contradictory statement or "antithesis" (B). Out of the two positions emerges a "synthesis," which, in turn, becomes the thesis (C) for a further dialogue, countered by a new antithesis (D), and so on. In theory, the process goes on forever; there is no resting point. Truth is where the disputants choose to take a break.

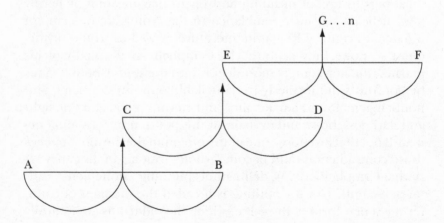

But a synthesis is not formed simply by merging thesis with antithesis in a kind of intellectual détente. *Synthesis is not compromise.* If I suggest that an object is black and you counter by calling it white, our synthesis is not that it is gray. Rather, to reach agreement, we must come up with a formulation that accounts for both positions, doing damage to neither. We do this by leaping to a higher abstraction, by distancing ourselves from it sufficiently that we can *see the whole process,* not just our own side of it. The object, we might agree, is both black and white, *depending on where one is standing.* We thus avoid the either-or trap, not by backing down but by moving through and above the problem to see it afresh. We come to recognize that our own version of the truth is conditioned by where we happen to be standing at the time. The only route out is through an understanding of the opposing positions. This is why listening to positions different from our own is so important. To reach deeper similarities, we must acknowledge existing differences as fully as possible.

The current struggle to define more humane gender roles for our rapidly changing culture is a case in point. As long as we fail to distinguish between equality and sameness, we remain trapped in a gray androgyny as unappealing as a universally tan human race. The way out is to recognize the enduring differences between men and women, yet hold them in the broader context of our common humanity and the imperative of mutual compassion and equality. But encounters across gender are only one of many kinds of differences that can lead to transformation if we engage them fully. In *Common Fire* (Daloz, Keen, Keen, and Parks, 1996), our study of how people come to care about the *common* good rather than their own well-being alone, we found that just such a "constructive engagement with otherness" was fundamental to formation of enduring commitment to the common good. Often those differences were across race or class, but sometimes also across age, physical attributes, sexual preference, culture, or even species.

The paradox seems to be that we best see ourselves in the mirror of the other; we move forward by going sideways. Robert Frost (a notably contrary man) put it this way in his poem "West-Running Brook":

> Speaking of contraries, see how the brook
> In that white wave runs counter to itself.
> . . . . It has this throwing backward on itself,
> So that the fall of most of it is always
> Raising up a little, sending up a little.
> Our life runs down in sending up the clock.
> The brook runs down in sending up our life.
> The sun runs down in sending up the brook.
> And there is something sending up the sun.
> It is this backward motion toward the source,
> Against the stream, that most we see ourselves in
> [1949, pp. 328–329].

Speed skaters and sailors know this. In unsure waters or on slippery ice, the best offense often looks like a good defense as the skater thrusts her blade from side to side or the sailor tacks first one way, then the other to move into the teeth of the gale. We move by contraries. This is useful to remember, for when we seem to be swept away from all sense of purpose, when we fear we are heading in precisely the wrong direction, our movement may have purpose in a larger frame. Much of the fear we experience at such times is a consequence of our inability to see the larger frame, is rooted in our unwillingness to let go, to risk a transformation that at the moment may feel more like disintegration. At such times, we need experienced travelers to tell us that it is safe to go that way, to trust in our own contrary movement toward the source.

To understand transformation, then, it helps to see it as containing a tension between, and subsequent resolution of, contraries. Gregory Bateson, an anthropologist who saw the interconnectedness of all things to an extraordinary extent, notes that an English schoolboy trained to defer to authority may become an ideal model of what is expected of him or he may reject it all and become a pariah, but the boy "cannot conceivably acquire irrelevant patterns." Bateson goes on: "If we know that an individual is trained in overt expression of one half of one of these patterns, e.g., in dominance behavior, we can predict with certainty . . . that the seeds of the other half—submission—are simultaneously sown in his personality. We have to think of an

individual, in fact, as trained in dominance-submission, not in either dominance *or* submission" (1972, p. 92).

Only when he recognizes this intrinsic ambivalence can the
boy himself transcend his "training." History is marbled with tales
of oppressed people who overcome their masters, only to become
oppressors themselves. It's what anthropologists sometimes refer
to as "tacit enculturation" and educators as "incidental learning."
Marshall McLuhan knew it when he coined the phrase "the medium
is the message." We learn as much or more from *the way* we are taught
as from the content itself. Put more succinctly, *forms instruct.*

Paulo Freire, the Brazilian educator who saw so clearly the
innate relationship between education and transformation, points
out that real freedom can never emerge out of the unexamined
struggle of the oppressed against the oppressor, for in that struggle
are only the seeds of a new oppression. Rather, we must recognize
that the problem lies with the nature of the struggle itself. In doing
this, we circumscribe both combatants and name the problem
from a perspective that includes the legitimate aspirations of both.
Oppressed and oppressor must each come to see the trap they are
in; they must see the whole wheel, not just their own spoke, and
rename it. Says Freire, "To exist, humanly, is to *name* the world,
to change it. Once named, the world in its turn reappears to the
namers as a problem and requires of them a new *naming*. Men are
not built in silence, but in a word, in work, in action/reflection"
(1970, p. 76).

The act of new naming reifies the unseen and draws us upward;
at once it adds a new rung to the ladder and calls us to climb. From
"I am right" to "you are right" to "we both have rights," the idea of
justice allows us to break out of the trap.

Note that when a synthesis is struck, when the two ends of
the tension are resolved, they are not resolved in the same terms
that led to the tension in the first place. Always something quite
new and unexpected emerges. Notice how this happens in the
exchange between Morrie Schwartz, the dying professor in Mitch
Albom's (1997) *Tuesdays with Morrie,* and his protégé. Morrie explains that life is

> "A tension of opposites, like a pull on a rubber band. And most of
> us live somewhere in the middle."

Sounds like a wrestling match, I say.

"A wrestling match." He laughs. "Yes, you could describe life that way."

So which side wins, I ask?

"Which side wins?"

He smiles at me, the crinkled eyes, the crooked teeth.

"Love wins. Love always wins" [p. 40].

So, how does all of this relate to the idea of development? Recall the lifelong dialogue within ourselves, between self and other, that Kegan considers the central developmental tension of our lives. On his map, we move from early inclusion in the family to increased separation during our school years, to a new kind of fusion with others in our teen conformity, to formation of new boundaries around the self during our early adult years, and then back to higher integration at the interindividual stage. Throughout, we move back and forth in saccadic fashion between self and other in ever-widening ripples as the boundaries of each "evolutionary truce" form and yield and form again.

Moreover, Kegan emphasizes that transformation requires resolution of old dichotomies within a frame that accepts both old and new. "It is important to bear in mind," he says, "the distinction between *abandoning* the old longing on behalf of the new, and *integrating* the new with the old, a distinction essentially between the dichotomous and the dialectical" (1982, p. 154).

The most intriguing aspect of Levinson's work as well lies in his recognition of the importance of dialectic. Here he has this to say: "Every developmental transition presents the opportunity and the necessity of moving toward a new integration of each polarity. To the extent that a man does this, he creates a firmer basis for his life in the ensuing phase. To the extent that he fails, he forms inner contradictions that will be reflected in the flaws of our next life structure" (Levinson and others, 1978, p. 198).

Thus, to move ahead into the next phase we need to attend to the tensions we have created by moving into this one. Those tensions are located along the four polarities he has described. Their resolution is accomplished as we are able to name ourselves anew, manifesting fresh mixes of youth with age, femaleness with maleness, creativity with destructiveness, and attachment with separation.

Although in a somewhat less dramatic and mythic fashion, Irma, a mother of four, underwent a similar transformation. At the age of forty-five, her last daughter safely graduated, she decided to return to school. I became her mentor.

She was having difficulty around the topic of evolution as taught in an anthropology class. This led to a series of conversations about the role of religious teachings in her life, about how they were conflicting with what she was now learning in college. In an attempt to resolve the tension between secular and sacred teachings, she took a class in ethics. One late fall afternoon, we met in her home to talk about it.

Beyond the Other Side

My God, even the spices are in alphabetical order! I think, as Irma speaks carefully across the immaculate kitchen table about the abortion debate in her ethics class. Through the window, I see the wind picking up, the predicted storm slapping wet flakes against the pane. Inside not a thing stirs.

"... maybe the more you think about it, the less you're certain what your response in the situation would be because every situation would give you a different outcome."

A woman of strong, conventional religious belief, Irma has found the class's open attitude toward sexuality, and particularly abortion, to be both disturbing and fascinating. At the moment she is struggling with a paper on the topic. I ask her how she plans to deal with all this gray matter.

"I have what seem to be just disconnected thoughts that when I put them down don't jell," she replies. "I can see both sides, and I'm not sure which side has the better claim; I'm not sure which way I want to go. I've picked up so much material, and it's so hard to settle on a point of view."

This is clearly painful for her; she winces as she speaks, squints toward the spice shelf as if looking for help from all that order. Yet I have a clear sense that she is staying with it. It's almost as if her keen mind demands the challenge, leans into the struggle to make sense of the onslaught of new material, sorting, sifting, carding through her notes. She could, after all, simply close her eyes when the flashes grow too bright. That's a chief function of fundamentalistic thinking—to keep information manageable and reduce painful ambiguity. But Irma has clearly not done that; she has instead risked learning more than is good for her.

"There were two conflicting points of view, and I could identify with both sides. But you can't take a position if you feel both sides strongly because again you're caught between the two. And I suppose that's been the story of my life these last couple of months: being caught between the pro and con of the subject matter of a paper, or between duties at home and family relationships versus the responsibilities of school and life."

"Is it worth getting educated?" I ask, curious about how she pulls it all together.

"Well," she replies, shaking her head back and forth, almost as if to settle something out. "I don't know whether I'd call it getting educated or not, but certainly I've taken in a tremendous amount of new material!"

"What's it done to your head?" I wonder aloud. She laughs a bit grimly.

"Sometimes it just rattles around in there and just bangs against everything else." Her laughter again masks the pain trapped in the metaphor. I ask her what it feels like, and she talks at length about the frustration of sorting so much diverse information. Somehow it used to be easier, though she says she can't imagine how that could have been. But now it is important to her to align her ethical views with her political position, her religious beliefs with everyday commitments. The boundaries of her world have exploded outward, she has seen the form of her own thought, and the effort to locate herself, to heal the frayed ends is exhausting. As we part, I find myself torn between a desire to help her pull those ends together and a sense that it is a task she can best do for herself. She seems to know that too, and though she appears to welcome my concrete suggestions, in the end she takes her own course.

Months later I talk with her again and learn that she has begun to sort all of those pieces and feel an intensified need for commitment to something, to test the new fabric she has begun to weave. "I can't live with all these loose ends forever," she says with a laugh as we chat during her graduation reception.

Still later, we meet at her new place of employment: a volunteer agency providing alternatives to young women considering abortion. "I don't suppose I'm any more sure than I ever was," she says. "Probably less. But this seems important work. And I need to do something I believe in."

Irma chose not to turn back. Somewhere in the darkness of that ethics classroom she summoned the courage to look the hard questions in the eye, slide down their haunches, and slip beneath their feet to the other side. She did not so much *answer* them as acknowledge their legitimacy. By truly hearing the other side, by confronting her polarity, she was able to build firmer answers of her own—answers that she knows are not absolute but that she has woven strongly enough to hold her weight as she makes her way home. Her choice of work is thus a marvelous synthesis, allowing her to hold both positions without being paralyzed—a genuine transformation.

I attempt in this chapter to show that significant learning and growth involve qualitative, developmental change in the way the world is viewed. We grow through a progression of transformations in our meaning-making framework, from relatively narrow and self-centered filters through increasingly inclusive, differentiated, and compassionate perspectives. I also argue that dialectical movement is central to such qualitative change. What are the implications of these assertions for our teaching?

As teachers and counselors, it is valuable for us to be aware of the overall directions of growth, to consider our work in a larger frame. The idea of resolution of opposites, central to the dialectic, is a powerful one. It allows us to see that our students may be moving ahead even when they appear to be retreating or going hopelessly astray. Knowing that forward movement may occur paradoxically by going backward or from side to side, we can take a step back and watch our students more carefully than we might if we feared they were merely backsliding or wandering.

In addition, more subtle understanding of the dynamics of their development allows us more effectively to help our students move. For they will make meaning of whatever we do; knowing this, we can understand better why it may be of value to play devil's advocate, to ask them to argue conflicting sides of an issue, to explain a particular position through another's eyes. By offering opposed and juxtaposed frames of reference, we can help them make meanings that are correspondingly broadly based, that rest on a felt sense of the legitimacy of the other.

This is why it is so important for teachers to encourage students to immerse themselves in differing perspectives. It is why the traditional liberal studies, well taught, can be such powerful transformative experiences. History calls us to see the world as the medieval church did; literature offers a Raskolnikov; mathematics raises fundamental questions about how we symbolize reality; art shows us human torment through the eyes of a Picasso; philosophy asks us to leap from Hobbes to Berkeley; and anthropology argues the internal logic of cannibalism.

Yet as we offer our challenge, it is important that we also support our students in their dismantling of old structures and construction of new ones. As they begin to reassemble their worlds, we can offer them the tools of our methodology; we can model for them new ways of making meaning. At the same time, we should recognize that things have changed, and we may need to step back a bit. This is a time when students often begin to move out on their own as they make their own connections among ideas, see relatives and old friends in a fresh light, and reach out for new friends. We are still needed, but in a different way.

Chapter Six

Returning Home
Helping Adults Integrate New Insights

> *The final belief is to believe in a fiction, which you know*
> *to be a fiction, there being nothing else. The exquisite*
> *truth is to know that it is a fiction and that you believe*
> *in it willingly.*
> —WALLACE STEVENS, *OPUS POSTHUMOUS*

With the darkness met, it remains for the hero to return home bearing the prize. Enlightenment is not all there is. One must reconnect with the world, or the journey is not complete. Growth requires separation, reconnection, and new understanding of the journey itself. For Odysseus, returning those ten long years from his great victory over Troy, the overriding image is the vision of his wife, Penelope, at the hearth. For her part, she is fending off the usurpers of her husband's estate by weaving a shroud by day and unraveling it by night. He is drawn homeward by a call to heal, weave again a fabric, regain a sense of the wholeness of his life. For the return home is a completion of what Joseph Campbell (1949) calls the "cosmogonic cycle," the universal round, the great helix on which we are all drawn in the upward coil of evolution.

In this chapter, we consider how students heal, reconstruct their vision of truth, name themselves anew. Several homeward-bound students carry us along, describing in their own words how they managed to piece their worlds together again. We see also how their teachers helped—or managed not to hinder them—as they traveled.

In our work with the developing student, it is important to know when to move in and when to step back, when to support and when to challenge. This is a time for building, and it is often valuable at this point for us to grant students more initiative than we might have at an earlier point in the journey. It is, after all, their own world under construction. Close understanding of what the process entails helps us know better when the project is furthered by hard questions, when by enthusiastic encouragement, and even when by our absence. It also helps us better sense when our words will be heard and when ignored. Our work is about timing, and timing is about sensing what is going on inside our students.

Because it is building time, students must attend to the how of things. This is the time that we can help students gain sharper awareness of the *process* of their own development, to construct a platform from which they can see their own thought as they could not before. On an intellectual level, this means helping them recognize how the form of their writing and the logic of their answers provide a new kind of rightness so they come to recognize that the *method* may be as important as the result. We can also help them to this realization by being more explicit now about our own assumptions and methodology, so they come to see that even *our* truth is relative to its context. More broadly, it means helping them develop a new vision of themselves based on their own experience rather than images they have absorbed from others. We do not simply hone minds; we help people name their wholeness. The words *heal* and *whole* share a common root. This is a time for healing (Adelizzi and Goss, 1995).

But it may not be as easy as it seems. There are obstacles. One might, for instance, refuse to return, wallowing like Odysseus with Calypso in the easy irresponsibility of one's new intellectual indulgence. Perry noted this attitude among some students, calling it "temporizing." It may simply be recognition that "I'm not ready yet," or it may be a prelude to a more entrenched form of inertia: "escape" into alienation. Said one student: "I just don't see any need to draw any conclusions towards it at the moment. I'm perfectly satisfied with all of it in ways. Not to say that I don't get depressed, but I'm sort of satisfied with that too; it's very nice to be able to sit and think and smoke and play pool" (Perry, 1968, pp. 195–196).

Or we may simply find it more comfortable where we are. Our lives may call us to rest here, or simply fail to provide reason to move on. Developmentalist Loevinger places the "modal position in adult life" somewhere between conformity and individuality, stages analogous to Kegan's interpersonal and institutional balances. Many people, Loevinger says, seem to have found a comfortable place to rest midway in their voyages away from the tribe toward broader, internal sources of identity. There is awareness of an inner self, separate from the expectations of society. Yet ideas about what is right or proper are still quite stereotypical, and the secret self is not yet free to go public; the distinction between public and private selves is rather sharp, and the two need not have a great deal to do with each other.

Consequently, although the right to exercise one's individuality is granted, it remains an aberration, a departure from the way one "should" act. The journey into one's own shadow side has been considered but not yet taken (Zweig and Abrams, 1990). We still seek to eliminate rather than acknowledge the negative parts of ourselves, believing the purpose of the journey to be attainment of perfection. We have yet to learn what we can only know from the other side of the gulf: that wholeness is a far more precious gift than perfection.

The memory of lost innocence still pursues us, threatening to draw us back into the warmth and security of the unquestioned beliefs of our childhood. *Wouldn't it be nice,* we think, *to believe in something solid again just once?* This was much of the feeling behind Ellen's tale of crossing the river, the loss:

> You know, when you get over here, you leave something—you have to—and sometimes I wish I was that person back there. But I can't be, and I don't want to be.... I mean I can't ever be that person again. Once you cross the river the innocence is gone.

Don't look back! is the imperative of this point in the journey out of the underworld. Until we know in our bones that truth is relative to its context, commitment seems forever. To turn around is to risk turning to stone. Is it possible, we ask, to make a commitment to something without calcifying? What was that difference again between faith and belief?

So there are no guarantees. There can't be. This lesson, after all, is what the transformation is all about. If it were a sure thing, it wouldn't get you there.

Yet at the end of the journey lies a new identity. Traveled with integrity, the way home leads to a fuller and clearer sense of who we are, a new and broader boundary between oneself and the world. The struggle to be something more than the person others have made, to construct and then live up to a set of *our own* expectations, is one of the most compelling struggles of our adult lives. When we left Sandy back in Chapter Three, she saw the struggle coming. Describing herself as "pulled by a current" toward greater independence, she longed to become "a legitimate member of the world." What has happened since then?

Somersaulting Backwards

The contrast with my last visit to see Sandy could scarcely have been greater. In place of the brittle crust of the snowbank grew a swath of tousled grass; tiny clumps of chamomile made their incongruous place between cracks in the sidewalk where earlier the salt had failed in the bitter cold to thaw the ice. A soft breeze drifted up the hillside from Lake Champlain, and overhead the maple leaves rustled. Whereas before Sandy had opened the door not a moment too soon, now I found myself almost wishing she had forgotten our appointment so I could disappear in search of a soft patch of sunlight by the lake. The old saw about Vermont's two seasons (winter and the Fourth of July) makes days like this collectors' items.

Alas, the door was open when I arrived, and Sandy, looking like the day, ushered me into the living room, where we sat and got caught up, the tape recorder nestling between us under a potted philodendron. As she spoke, I realized with a growing sense of awe that a good deal more than the weather had changed since last December.

Recall that Sandy followed an intensely personal study of "family systems theory" with an effort to carry out a more "academic" study of psychology, for she had come to fear that she lacked the kind of detached, academic thinking that she believed necessary for success in graduate school should she go on and become a trained therapist. She also began to feel, like many students in programs of this sort, that she needed a general overview of the subject matter—the sort of survey conventionally fed to freshmen. She was beginning to feel a need to "enter the world" and make it on her own. A sense of independence was very important to her, and the language of movement in her speech was striking.

But back in December, the future was still uncertain; she felt less than confident of her ability to keep moving through the darkness ahead and looked to her adviser with considerable reliance and not a little awe. "She's an extraordinarily rich person," she said of Grace, who seemed able to maintain her balance amidst conflict in a way Sandy admired, who possessed an alluring sense of independence, who could listen so well, who appeared to be very clearly on a journey of her own, and—above all—who had been there before. "There's something, there's a feeling that she's been through something, and it's been rocky," Sandy said, "but there's something about her that seems accepting. Whatever her situation is, she seems accepting of it." These were, of course, the very characteristics Sandy sought for herself; what she chose to see as Grace's strengths were those that she projected at the end of her own journey—the ones without which, paradoxically, she would be unable to complete the journey itself.

With all of this in mind now, six months later, I turned on the tape recorder, anticipating a headline story of mentor and student moving bravely together into the murk of ignorance and uncertainty.

But the study had not gone well at all. Grace was the wrong person for what she needed at the time, Sandy said. She needed someone who knew a lot about the general field of psychology, someone who could give her the support and structure she needed. As an educator, Grace had insufficient depth in psychology and furthermore was overwhelmed with outside work and thus unable to be there for Sandy when she needed her.

My stomach sank. I began to wonder what would happen if all my subjects turned out to have disastrous relationships. Research can only stand so much of this stuff. How do I write my book? Then, somewhat petulantly reminding myself that just because the drama didn't go according to my script didn't mean it had none, I moved ahead with the interview.

Although Sandy took pains to separate Grace the person from Grace the teacher, the study had been frustrating. Most of the time Sandy felt adrift in a "huge ocean of psychology" with no one to give her the bearings she needed. Only toward the end did she begin to pull her ideas together, but by then it was too late. Her final paper left her vaguely dissatisfied, and the oral presentation to her fellow students was confused, scattered, and "very, very upsetting."

One time during the study, reading the work of a particularly difficult theorist, she felt "just devastated" to think that she might be unable to find the right psychologist for her, the one she could identify with and whose work would guide her in her subsequent practice. The more she read, the more she saw that "different ones would pull me in for different reasons, and they'd all have their point of view and they would all be significant. And so it was more me realizing that I've got to have my own point of view and take from whomever."

She laughs nervously as she says this, and I ask her if she can recall any moments when she knew "what had to happen."

"Let's see," she says, and leans back on the sofa, resting one arm along the back, gazing at the ceiling, tapping her lips pensively with the index finger of the other hand. Slowly she begins to reconstruct the previous term's work. The first part of the study went relatively well, but it soon became apparent that she was not satisfied with simply drifting where the currents led. That might have worked earlier, but not this time.

> I needed to define more what I was doing, and it was hard being so general and I wasn't sure where I wanted to go next. And I realized too that some of my own issues in the study weren't being met. I think that was the big thing. And so that's when I decided that I had to find my own narrowed goal to finish the study; and there was a time in there where I was trying not to but feeling I needed to, and that was the most difficult time. And I wasn't hearing from Grace at that point either, so I was tearing my hair for a while.

She laughs without a whole lot of conviction, and I ask her what that moment felt like.

I felt like I was under the ocean, you know, just sort of
somersaulting backwards [that laugh again], knowing that I would
eventually come up but not knowing where or quite how to do it at
that point, and still excited about where I had gone and just about
the study. I was excited about the study even though it was very
frustrating at times.

"What happened to get you through that?" I ask, hoping for
some sign of Grace.

"Well, I had to come up very quickly," she replies, laughing
uneasily again, "because I was getting to the end of the study, and
that's when I realized that I wasn't going to get it from Grace, that
I had to figure it out for myself."

She goes on to explain her fear that the study wasn't "legitimate"; somehow it wasn't all right for her to be studying psychology. So, she says,

I wanted to see [whether,] if I wasn't legitimate, why were other
people legitimate? Why was it legitimate for Maslow to study
psychology? . . . So I started reading their personal lives and that's
what straightened it out for me. . . . I saw how much people's
beginnings, their personal beginnings and their emotional lives, led
them right into the psychology they developed, and I was then able
to see how my personal life tied into what I was trying to do.

Despite her misgivings about the study itself, in discussing it
later with another faculty adviser who helped her gain some distance on it she felt a "great relief" about the term's work: "I understood where my confusion was and why it wasn't only me that was
making me confused, but it was the situation, the way the study
was set up."

In effect, what seems to have happened is that the study worked
at the outset because she could simply follow a set of initially
prescribed readings. But when the time came to take more of
her own direction, she felt lost because she was unable to ground
the study in any kind of context that had meaning for her.[1] In her
more dualistic days, the authority of the instructor might have been
enough to give the study meaning, but Grace was not providing
that sort of authority; for Sandy's more multiplistic self, personal
exploration would have done, but this time she needed more than

that. This time, in order to make sense of what she was learning, she needed her ideas *to make connections*—with her own experience, with the outside world, and with other ideas. Something in her knew that and drew her to the thought of studying the lives of the idea makers themselves.

That was the breakthrough. It allowed her to see how ideas are formed in the context of real lives, something she could grasp with her intuition. It thus bridged that intellect-emotion gap that was plaguing her. The gap crossed, she was then able to see ideas from *both* inside and outside. As she says, she understood "that the world doesn't only revolve around me, [but] that everyone comes from their own circumstances, and they have their own makeup . . . people come from their own perspectives, that one is not necessarily more right. People arrive at where they are because they come from their own circumstances, have gone through their own processes, and have arrived at something that works for them but doesn't necessarily work for everybody." In short, she was finally able to give the study meaning by placing it in the context of human lives, not only coming to understand how ideas emerge but seeing in a brand new way how she, too, was a product of her own history.

So despite a study that left her with mixed feelings, she was very clear that the term had resulted in growth for her. Last winter she spoke with urgency and passion of her desire to be "a legitimate member of the world." But the goal seemed well off in the future then; the tenses were markedly changed now. "The world is a lot bigger," she says, nodding to no one in particular:

> I feel pretty confident about who I am, and especially about where I'm going. I'm not as afraid of the possible future as I was. I feel confident that I'm in a process and the process can only keep building; and earlier, when I last talked to you, I didn't have that confidence of knowing what was on the other side.

She seems to have crossed some sort of a barrier between herself and that elusive "other side." "I've never seen a way that I can fit into the world before," she says. "I've always felt like I'm on the outside and I don't fit in, that what I'm doing is a game; it's not legitimate. Someone else is supporting me."

Legitimacy is an important word for Sandy, a kind of gatekeeper between the two sides of home and world. It has about it a strong connotation of belonging. Yet it is not the kind of belonging to be had in her old family world, or as a possession of her husband. Rather, to be "legitimate" she needs to feel that it is OK to be who she is, on her own terms. When she can do that, she will earn her new membership in the world.

In Kegan's terms, she seems to be suspended between the interpersonal and institutional stages, moving fast to the latter. At the same time, Perry's lens lets us see that she took an enormous step toward legitimacy when she saw that the ideas of her psychologists emerged from the contexts of their lives. As she became able to place herself in context as well, she could accept as fresh and quite liberating her own legitimacy. By reducing her fears about legitimacy, the study has allowed her to imagine much more realistically that she might, indeed, make it and become a therapist. For her, this new skill is the ticket for her emergence into the world as a fully contributing adult.

But something else seems to have happened, some other barrier crossed besides this. She speaks several times of a new ability to trust both others and herself—this despite a term with an adviser on whom she felt unable to rely. Out of this trust, she describes a greater ability to teach herself. What's that about, I wonder?

She is speaking slowly, thoughtfully now, her voice almost a monotone but tinted with urgency. "I know I'm much more comfortable with my intellectual abilities, and before I had this big question about whether I had any, and I really relied on my emotions to learn things and travel forward. Now I feel more how to balance those two things so they can go together." The travel metaphor appears several times as she talks, her voice trailing fire, picking up momentum.

> I'm starting to feel really excited about knowing that no matter what dimension I travel that it's me and there's something to it and it's all right and there's something to learn that helps the whole picture of who I am. And that's really exciting. That came a lot from reading James Hillman, you know, traveling into the black and not closing it off and running away from it but realizing that it's part of who you are and it's legitimate and it's OK and it's important.

There it is again, I think, and check: "Traveling into the black?" She turns to me, instructing.

> Well, there's a negative side and a positive side, and you try to keep in the positive side so it keeps you from exploring the fears and the sorrows—instead of seeing that there's no such thing as negative and positive.... I have trouble with words like *wrong* and *truth;* for one thing, it ties in with what I was saying—that there's a positive experience in life and there's a negative. And what Hillman has encouraged me to think is that between the positive and the negative is one that goes straight down [that laugh again] and that includes positive *and* negative, and it dissolves truths and right and wrong; that it's more of an encompassing of all of who we are—and seeing that all of who we are contributes to how we live our life.

I have no idea what expression is on my face as she says all of this, but it feels like watching a child being born. She goes on.

> And there's no such thing as wrong. I really believe that. And there's no such thing as right; there's no such thing as truth. It's more that there's a dropping down into something and broadening what we are that is unique and also universal—and understanding how we're universal and how we're unique is what I'm most interested in right now.

Later, as we talk about her relationship with Grace, the dialectic comes up again. When the study began, Sandy was "in awe of Grace" and "treated her like a guru a little bit." But now, she continues, "it's more in balance.... I think what I want in the end is to be friends with her and to feel like a peer; and I think I have to some degree."

In an earlier study, she explains, she took all the blame on her own shoulders when replies came late. She started to do that again this time, but being more willing to accept her own negative emotions, she acknowledged that "I was starting to feel annoyed and angry with Grace, frustrated with her that she wasn't doing it right, or that we both weren't, but it wasn't just her and it wasn't just me; and so that's when I started taking over more and just, you know, realizing *this is my study.* I wanted it to work for myself and began to feel just less that Grace was greater than me in all ways. And so I felt it started coming into balance because of that."

"What do you mean by 'balance'?"

"That we're out of the context of being student-teacher, that we're both human beings."

In this sentence, in one of the thousands of small ways that transformations happen, Sandy renames her journey. In place of an authoritarian teacher-student imagination in which Grace is flawless and she is by implication incomplete, Sandy has re-framed the relationship as one in which the primary element is their shared humanity rather than their differentiated power. This transformation has profound implications for how she goes on to understand herself as a learner, the education system, and the nature of knowledge itself (Goldberger, Tarule, Clinchy, and Belenky, 1996).

What was Grace's part in helping this come about? According to Sandy, rather little. Grace helped her clarify her initial goals and got her started with her reading, but as far as the content of the study went that was about it. From there on, Grace simply (!) served as a reader for what Sandy was writing, encouraging her and providing superficial proofreading. The result of this benign neglect was that "it made me realize that *I* was making the study work. I was putting all that in and . . . that she wasn't going to teach me. It was more that I was reflecting off of her."

Sandy sees advisers as guides now rather than teachers, adding that "I think there's more of an exchange than I'd realized before. I think *they're also* on a journey, and in a sense I'm a guide for them. I think I see it more that way now. It can't be completely onesided." Later, when I ask her what she feels is the most important thing she learned from her relationship with Grace, she pauses a moment, brushes aside the content, and replies, "that I have to— in a way I have to guide myself first before I get guidance from someone else."

As I leave the house a short time afterward, I have completely forgotten the weather. My mind is spinning. Here I am writing a book about teaching, yet Sandy's enormous learning emerges from what seems almost no intervention on Grace's part at all. *How will Grace see it?* I wonder, and head for an appointment with her in the state department of education office.

As it turns out, Grace is in remarkable accord with Sandy's account. She shared Sandy's dismay over the material outcome of the study and seemed relieved to learn that Sandy looked upon the study in such a positive light. Did she deliberately refrain from providing more structure?

"It was somewhat deliberate," Grace says. She prefers to work in a style that encourages students to take the initiative for themselves, adding that she felt strongly that even if she had provided more direction, Sandy would have resisted it. "There was always some resistance when I suggested she could do such and such; she was never very happy with it."

It would be easy to conclude from this particular case that Sandy made her way in spite of Grace, and there is certainly some truth to this notion. But I think it is important not to confuse invisibility with absence; Grace's profile, however low, hovered significantly in the background of the study. Sandy saw her as an independent person and knew that her own movement toward such a stance would be compromised if she allowed Grace too much space in her life. She seems to have held Grace as a transparent image rather than a concrete presence, shaping herself in response to Grace's outlines rather than in conformity to her wishes. Grace had the wisdom to see this and respect Sandy's need for autonomy, while acknowledging her concurrent wish for support. How did Grace do this? How did she respond to Sandy's appeals for structure?

"Well, we talked about what structure would mean, and we talked about what she was looking for in the class that she took and then dropped at the university—about why that hadn't been successful. Most of what we discussed was why it was that she wanted the structure."

Thus, rather than focusing directly on what might have been Sandy's "failure" and trying to fix it, Grace raised the discussion to analysis of the broader context—to Sandy's need for structure. This enabled Sandy to stay out of the old dialectical trap about whether she was "legitimate" or not and brought Sandy's attention directly onto the developmental issue facing her: her own growing strength, her increased willingness to care for herself and stand on her own. This is the evolution that Gilligan considers the hallmark of maturity, a step that "dissipates the tension between selfishness and responsibility through a new understanding of the interconnection between self and other" (1982, p. 74). In effect, Sandy came to rename her work not as selfishness but as an act of care for herself. Seeing it thus, Sandy constructed a new perspective on herself, a platform between and above the horns of her former dilemma.

And when Sandy eventually came up with the breakthrough idea of studying the lives of the psychologists, Grace was quick to support her. She knew that what Sandy was finally looking for was permission, and she readily gave it, recognizing that here was an important opportunity for Sandy to break out of her rigid perception of what it meant to be academic and scholarly. Evidently, as things turned out, it was.

Toward the end of the interview, as I do with everyone, I read a short statement and asked Grace to comment on it. The statement went like this:

> In my search for truth, I kept looking for someone who had the answers. But now I realize that no one has the answers to the important questions of life. The best we can do is construct our own answers from the evidence we have and act on them even though we might be wrong. It seems that on the journey to truth, we can never come home to stay.

As usual, I asked what "home" meant to her. Here is Grace's reply:

> Well, it means the place I was when I was about thirteen and beginning to think about the issues and knew for certain what they were, what my opinions were, what the truth was . . . certainty.
> ["And you can't come home again now?" I asked.]
> No. I guess if home is comforting, it is the relativeness of everything. It's somewhat comforting to know that a lot depends on circumstance, the relationship of one thing to another, on some confluence that's as important as any absolute. There may be an absolute, but just as important are the ways in which certain forces or activities or circumstances or whatever sort of come together at any particular point—which doesn't mean that there isn't any good or bad. I think there are, I mean for me there are some things that are bad and some things that are good, so it is not totally amoral. It's like *you can be held as securely in a big net off the ground, if the connections are good, as you can on a solid rock* [italics added].

The question was designed to get at contextual relativism, and clearly it worked in this case. It is just this kind of epistemology that

Grace describes here that we value as an end product of a liberal education (Gamson, 1984). If the journey metaphor as we're using it has any usefulness for understanding intellectual development, then surely home of this sort must lie at the end of the journey— not the home from which we are all banned from the day of our departure, the home of which Thomas Wolfe's novel speaks so eloquently, but the new home that we forge for ourselves, the home we attain on the other side of the journey through the dark. If the first half of the journey is characterized by a downward slide into dissolution and disillusionment, the second is the story not of reillusionment (at least not in a conventional sense) but of acceptance. It is necessarily through acceptance of the darkness, not its obliteration, that we can transcend it. It is only from the gift of multiplicity and meaninglessness that we can construct a new meaning—that we can, in fact, come home.

Because the mythology and indeed a number of case histories seem to emphasize the Sturm und Drang of transformation, it is easy to imagine that the passage must necessarily be a painful one. But it need not be so. For some students, the release from all-encompassing authority brings a refreshing freedom. One student, relaxing into the interview, described her feeling of almost voluptuous delight in all that freedom to learn:

> I love to learn. I read voraciously. I'm always looking things up. They asked me what I wanted for a wedding present, and I got a set of *Encyclopaedia Britannica* because there's always things I want to know [but that] I can't get my hands on. Umm. Which I love. You know, it's my favorite. I take them to bed, you know, and just. . . .

It was with this sort of multiplistic worldview that Emily, protagonist of our next vignette, returned to school. Bob, her mentor, suggested she study some literature along with her practical education courses, and she did. Her shift to contextual thinking was relatively smooth, as she found her new voice and came to see herself as a product of her history rather than an imposed stereotype.

Thinking Something Makes It Real

While in teachers college during World War II, Emily met a wounded veteran, dropped out of school, and married him. Over the years that followed, she raised five children, one of whom was severely ill much of the time. It was not until they were out of the nest that she felt she could complete her formal education. "That's why I'm pushing sixty and still striving to become a teacher," she explained with a wry grin. Even though she acknowledged that it was mostly for her own self-satisfaction, she was taking education courses to augment her experience as a substitute teacher in the hope that it would lead eventually to certification.

Emily was enjoying her studies thus far, but if she read two books with different views on the same topic she found it hard because

> when I read one book I can kind of agree with their theory, and then when I read the next book I agree with that. So then I have to go back and see what basically I believe and then put my belief against those two books and then take what I really believe. I'm not going to take what somebody else believes and adapt it for my own. I'm willing to read it, but I'm going to put my own beliefs in practice in judging which I would prefer. Or maybe neither. Maybe my own.

A practicing Catholic, she prided herself on her tolerance of other faiths. "They say the Catholic church is the true religion, but what religion doesn't? As long as a person is sincere and loves their neighbor, I don't think God cares what religion you are."

As a student, Emily believed that it was imperative for her to respect and listen to her teachers, especially her mentor. Yet she felt free to disagree if need be, and even though she "was scared to death of him" when they first met, she had come to admire him for his ability to get along with people. She felt equal to him "as a person," and her opinions were equal to his. What separated them was his greater knowledge, and she looked to him to guide her toward gaining more knowledge for herself.

Bob, her mentor, a radical seminarian in the late 1950s, had moved north and worked in public education, eventually becoming an elementary school principal. Forty-five at the time of our interview, he was the father of two children just entering school.

His greatest pleasure came, he said, from watching students take off, especially those who had worked for years to care for others and who now were turning to education as a gift to themselves.

He loved to help people "see the possibilities in themselves and the world around them."

Emily, whom he had known as teacher, adviser, and employer, was such a person. He admired her for her candor, compassion, curiosity, and particularly for her openness to learning. He hoped he could be a "beacon" for her, letting her see that "there are other points on the compass" and other people from whom she could be learning, for he was somewhat uneasy about her tendency to put him on a pedestal; it was a role he resisted. She needed to take some of the confidence she placed in him for herself, he said.

Being cast as an authority made Bob uncomfortable. Helping people become more self-reliant was of central importance to him. "I don't think I've ever wanted to be God," he said. "I feel increasingly at ease with ignorance—my own as well as others'" he added with a wry grin. "I am very uneasy with individuals who have The Answer to the problems that have been asked through the ages." If he had a bête noire, it was narrow-mindedness and dogmatism. The ideal student was always finding new questions to ask, and he hoped "that Emily will be asking the questions eventually if she isn't asking them now. Maybe there will be two of us asking the same questions."

A year later, Emily is looking forward to graduation. It has been a good year, and she has grown "intellectually and spiritually." She feels she can converse more readily with people now, she feels "more adequate, better equipped," and she knows she has done it herself. "I'm making myself a bigger person," she declares.

"I have learned the power of words. Don't you find me talking more powerfully than I did last year?" she asks rhetorically and then goes on to explain that she is much more able now to express her feelings rather than "just *doing* and hoping people understood." It was hard for her at first to speak up in classes. She was afraid of being laughed at, but over time—and it helped that Bob was her teacher in several courses—she came to feel that "I'm enough of a person so I can state what I think and if they don't want to go along with that, they don't have to." Along with her greater loquacity, however, has come a decrease in her earlier tendency "just to blurt out" her opinions. "I think longer before I speak," she says. "Now I really sit and think things out."

She seems to have found a new distance from her work, an ability to distinguish between who she is and what she does that allows her to take criticism not only more graciously but perhaps more productively as well. At one point, a writing teacher criticized one of her poems rather bluntly. "A couple of years ago," she said, "that would have devastated me because I would feel I had done my best.... I might have thought, 'I'll go right back in and never show anybody my poem again. . . .' But really if you look at it, it's humorous. I wrote a poem and there's no substance to it, but it would look good in a Burpee's Seed catalog. On the other hand, that's *her* opinion. Maybe I like the poem."

A year earlier she described herself as others saw her: a "flexible, tough cookie." Now, asked the same question, she offers a detailed description in terms of her own history:

> I am what I am because of what has happened to me in my lifetime. I am a product of the depression, I'm a product of the Second World War, of the Korean War, the Vietnam War, and my viewpoint is going to be much different than those students [I teach] who are probably fifteen, sixteen, seventeen years old.... What I am is a combination of the things I learned from my parents, what I learned as an adult, as a single adult and as a married adult, and what I learned as a waitress for many years.

Commenting on an affair between two married neighbors, she notes that she would earlier have simply seen it as wrong; now she thinks it is not wrong so much as foolish, because the man, who is much older, is only going to be hurt in the long run, and "it seems such a foolish waste."

Does she feel that she has made any gain in the knowledge gap she described in her first interview? She still feels unequal to Bob in that regard, "but I'm catching up." Although she has added to her knowledge, she points out that she can now "put it to better use.... It's the use you put knowledge to that is beneficial. It's not keeping it in your head."

Of Bob, she has little to say aside from her affection for him. She saw relatively little of him after the "Bible as Literature" course she took with him a semester earlier and does not seem to need him for much any longer. But she remembers how he asked each student to bring a Bible along. She was surprised to discover that everyone brought one that was somewhat different. "I think the most important thing was learning how to cope with other people's beliefs that are different than yours. I think that's the most important thing I learned from Bob, ever." She goes on to explain that not only do others have a right to their opinions, but those opinions are real in an important sense. "Thinking something makes it real," she says, echoing Hamlet.

Bob tells with enthusiasm about how he encouraged Emily to undertake a local history study that allowed her to combine her knowledge of the area with her love of storytelling and her own inquisitiveness. The study taught her to ask good questions, he says, and to sift among many answers for the best (not the right) one, adding "if she could leave from my influence with a seeking mind, then I would have accomplished something. And in some ways I think that happened. I think that took place."

Although he is pleased with his influence, "in some way you don't want to question 'why' too much because there may not be any answers . . . to know there has been some influence, that's satisfying enough in itself." He is quick to point out that oftentimes students grow "in spite of you." Emily did it by herself in the end, he says, and that is as it should be.

The relationship, as he describes it, was not a particularly intense one, but it was characterized by warmth, trust, mutual concern, and "a growing friendship along the way." He knows the religion course had an important influence, as did his ongoing encouragement. But he feels that the local history study was a fitting culmination because it led Emily to examine disparate data and seek to make connections. Even though he stops short of saying that she is a full-grown intellectual, she has clearly begun the process of intellectual growth as he defines it:

> Intellectual growth . . . is to maintain that sense of inquisitiveness and the ability to be able to see connections; and in seeing those particular connections to be able to arrive at a synthesis of how things fit together, how things are integrated, how the world and the universe are a whole. But also to realize that you as a part of that whole don't necessarily understand it totally . . . there are exceptions, gaps in our understanding.

Bob is quick to agree that love plays an important part in his work. By this he means a sense of concern and caring that he feels matters if a mentor-student relationship is to work at its best. It is important, he says, because it allows him to see the student as a total human being rather than simply a mind to be trained. It lets the mentor acknowledge the reality of the student's "problems or concerns in that particular phase." "But," he adds, "you also have to be able to care enough to let them go." His relationship with Emily "will probably taper off" shortly after her graduation, and that's fine. He offers a kind of benediction:

> In some ways it's almost like the parent-child relationship, knowing that you have had an impact on some individual and gone beyond just setting up a program. But within that particular program and that particular relationship things have happened. [And when it is done you can say,] "Now you're on your own. There are other people that are going to come along in your life who are going to be helpful, who are going to grow with you, who are going to fall in love with you, who are going to be concerned about you. And I thank God that I've had the opportunity to be a part of that whole process with you."

Such benedictions, which mentors often provide, serve as little graduation ceremonies to mark the change in the terrain. They are especially important if the relationship is to continue on a new plane or terminate cleanly. Without some acknowledgment of the change, one or the other partner may feel cheated or hurt, a feeling that often turns to anger, a convenient if inappropriate way to end.

Although mentors often leave just as the traveler crosses the threshold back into the world of light, some stay on to aid in the transition, for the time of coming home can be one of considerable turmoil. After an experience of transformation, Campbell reminds us, "the first problem of the returning hero is to accept as real ... the passing joys and sorrows, banalities and noisy obscenities of life. Why reenter such a world?" (1949, p. 218) In its way it is analogous to the dilemma of the returning Peace Corps volunteer or Vietnam veteran—travelers reshaped by the demands of a distant world, no longer able or even willing to fit comfortably into the old slots. Said one returned Peace Corps volunteer,

"I tried and tried to readjust, but it didn't work. Finally I gave up and adjusted to being unadjusted." Here again, the transformation is accomplished not by coming down on one side of a dichotomy or the other but rather by standing back and renaming the whole operation. This is the synthesis of which we spoke in the last chapter.

The question is especially poignant as we teeter on the brink of commitment, the point where we decide to move ahead and begin walking on that "big net off the ground" that Grace was willing to call reality. It is easier if in the course of uprooting our notions of right and wrong, of teaching us that we construct our own realities, the transformation has also displaced our sense of what is normal. The returning traveler is always just a little crazy in the eyes of old acquaintances. Ella, whom we met back in Chapter Two, is one such traveler, crossing the border on her way home.

Living on the Border

It is May. Ella and I have driven off along the threads of dirt road that brush the border with Canada, to the edge of a small lake. We talk quietly, she standing randomly on the tiny beach looking across the flat water, I sitting on a half-submerged boulder. Warblers flit among the alders, listening and commenting erratically.

"Back when you first started all this," I ask her, "what did you think you'd be like when you finished?"

"I dunno. Maybe freer than I am. Solve more things maybe. Thought it would prove something." She talks in a low, almost sullen way. She's angry, I think.

"What was it going to prove?"

"I thought it would just shut up that stupid nagging that was always after me to do something. I thought it would be like, 'OK, you get your degree, it's over, and then you can get on with other things.' That's what I thought. But the only thing it proved was how far I've got to go. Opened up another whole can of worms." She looks back at me, hostile and pleading at once.

"So you're not what you thought you'd be?" I ask, smiling to glaze the obvious.

She snorts, enjoying the irony, then looks away, across the lake. "I'm a lot more than I had any idea I could be—as far as being a person goes." Then she turns back, releasing the sarcasm slowly, like her breath. "I always thought that with a little knowledge you could make the 'right' decisions. You could tell right from wrong and you could go around telling everybody that 'You're right, you're wrong; this is good, this is bad.'" And she shakes her head with a short laugh, almost as if she is trying to get something unstuck. "I sort of thought it was hooked with education somehow, and you learned *that* somehow through books." She is silent for a moment, eyes somewhere at the edge of the shore and water. Then she adds, mostly to herself, "You lose."

Grappling for balance between my delight at her struggle and compassion for her disillusionment, I try to help her come out.

"And it didn't turn out that way," I say, muting the question.

"Nope. Now the only thing you do is say, 'Well, you could be right and then again, you could be wrong, and it might be good for *you* but it certainly wouldn't be good for me.' It just colored the whole world gray."

"So, the world is different?"

"No," she replies, clear this time. "It's not the world. It's me."

The certainty in her tone provokes me to follow it. Who, I wonder, is this "me"? Commitment is the issue for her now; she needs to be thinking about this new person, a person who can come into being only as she begins to act in her new world. I ask her if she feels more certain or less so than she used to.

"I know for sure I'll take care of myself!" she replies with a broad grin. "I never knew that before. I never thought I could. But..." and her voice fades again; she looks down at the sand, "... it's the whole thing about endings and beginnings. I used to dread having anything end. Or begin. And instead of getting it cut off now, it just keeps going in circles. There aren't any beginnings; there aren't any endings." She looks back up. "But I don't fear either one anymore."

Recalling our conversation on the way here in the car, in which she talked about a recurrent dream of herself sitting by the water fearing to go in, I smile and say to the far shore, "Sounds like you better get into that water next time you have that dream."

"Why?" she asks with a laugh, knowing.

"It sounds like you're ready to swim," I reply. She tries a last maneuver.

"Maybe I'd choose not to."

"You don't have any choice until you get in," I respond, and she agrees. We both fall silent.

Later, heading back, I talk about my notion that for many people the degree is a kind of grail that—once attained, they believe—will transform them. What they don't realize, at least until later, is that it's not the degree, it's the education that transforms, not the goal but the journey.

"Yeah," she says. "I've been rereading a lot of the papers I did for different courses. I keep thinking, 'I wonder who did that?' There's, like, no connection with me. If I had them to do again, I could never do them like that. Same person couldn't do them." She pauses and gazes out the window at the manure pile trailing from the tip of a crippled conveyer belt as we bump past. "Same person doesn't exist anymore."

"What would the new person do now?"

"Probably be a whole bunch more wishy-washy about the whole thing. Everything is so damned definite in those papers."

"Is the new person definite about anything?" I ask, curious about her slipperiness.

"I dunno. Don't know. Hope not." The irony is back.

"But you said that you were surer that you could do things now. That there was a confidence there."

"Well, there's a confidence which is . . ." She searches a moment for the sense, ". . . which is like a core I never had."

"What's in that core?"

"I guess that's what I'm looking for," she replies and falls silent again. Then: "Maybe I don't want to know. Maybe it consists of nothing." She turns to me. I feel her eyes against my temple as I drive, boring in. "You create your own reality. I really believe that. You *do*. As long as I know that, I can take care of myself; let's leave it at that. Don't tear it apart [another pause] 'cause maybe it's not there."

Perhaps it had nothing to do with her return to education, but Ella's relationship with her husband went into severe fibrillation after that. She was already beginning to lose friends, a condition she wryly referred to as "leaving friends on the tracks." It was hard for her to tell whether the choice was hers or theirs. She would tell herself that she wasn't really any different, but she knew better. It was a good thing she was no longer as ready to define herself through their eyes as she used to be. They thought she was crazy.

At the same time, she became friends with a new range of people, "people so different from the ones I knew before. It's like having a whole lot of doors open." She found she valued her sons' dawning adolescence in a whole new way. She could welcome what lay ahead rather than regret the loss of their childhood. Swimming as she was—as we all are—through a sea of friendships, she was learning to let go of some in order to dive, but learning also that she could reach out in whole new ways to others as she became a more graceful swimmer.

I was an important part of Ella's new world, but our friendship grew slowly. Recalling her first impression of me, she said:

> You breezed into the room and were so casual and everything was fine. And I thought "Oh my God, no!" There was this air of confidence. "Everybody's gonna get through this and there's no doubt in my mind"—and I was thinking, "Ha, I'm not at all convinced." I was very, very much in awe of you for a long time.

For my part, quite simply I had never seen anyone with an intellect like hers. She put together a self-assessment portfolio for her community college degree entirely without help, and it was the best I'd seen. I was impressed. Needless to say, I encouraged her to continue her studies as my student.

Over time, we came to see each other increasingly as human beings, less as mentor and student. But for a long while Ella felt herself to be the more vulnerable of the two of us. She was the one, after all, putting her work out there for criticism; all I did was lean back and make comments. She wanted to know me as a human being more than I did her. Yet as the months passed, I was able to let her know that I didn't have all the answers, and she, for her part, grew less interested in getting them—from me at least.

I was able as well to talk more about my own feelings, about what was going on in the life I kept at home, away from work. This was hard for me, perhaps partly because of who I am but partly too because like most men I separate, more sharply than many women do, my home life from my work life. "What," I would find myself asking no one in particular, "do my children have to do with how I conduct my work?" But for Ella the answer seemed to be "A lot!"

"Where are you inside that shell?" she would ask in a hundred ways. "Who are you in there?" And as I struggled to answer, she was able to reach out to other people as well. I was, in a certain sense, someone safe with whom she could practice her own swimming lessons. For that matter, she wasn't such a bad teacher herself. More than any other student, Ella taught me that I could share more of myself too.

Self-disclosure from the mentor seems to play a crucial part in the full evolution of a mentorship from hierarchy toward symmetry. Often flayed and vulnerable, the student needs to know that he can trust his teacher. In the early stages of development, authority is enough, but as the student grows, his willingness to trust an authoritative mask without knowing what lies behind it dims. He comes increasingly to ask, "Who are you? What lies behind that façade? Can I really trust you?" If the reply is inappropriately muted, if the mentor is unable or unwilling to doff the mask and attempt to answer the question, things begin to die. The relationship grows hard and eventually cracks.

Listening to protégés talk about the early development of their relationships, the pressure from beneath erupts again and again: "I just wanted to know *who* she was. I wanted her to let me see her as a person!" Describing his own particularly powerful association with his business instructor/mentor, one student told me this:

After our initial contact, we would talk after class a lot and it was pretty clear that he liked me as a student, but nothing really changed a lot beyond that. I mean it was a warm relationship, but somehow it just wasn't special. But one afternoon I had a meeting scheduled with him and stuff at work had been going badly and my wife was getting on my case, and I just felt shitty. I hadn't done the assignment and called him to let him know I wanted to cancel. He said, "C'mon over anyway," and so I did. We got talking, and for some reason, I just decided to spill out how I was feeling. I mean, I never did that before with another man. But he was listening and really seemed to care what was going on with me. I really felt better after that, and the next time we met, he started talking about his own life a little. I mean not a whole lot, not like I spilled on him, but he told me some stuff about his own life, about troubles with his work and with his kids, that really made me say, *Hey, this guy is really a human being after all*, you know?

With only a little reflection, it is apparent why it has to be this way. Continued development for the student mandates a decrease in the power of authority; a greater need to see through appearances; a new sense of the value and importance of an inner, personal, emotional self. Clearly, the kind of relationships that both appeal to and sustain a person moving in these directions must be the ones that are capable of penetrating and discarding masks.

But it works the other way as well. To the extent that the mentor is able to become human, the student is empowered to see more deeply. Mentor becomes a practice ground for seeing all human beings with richer insight; she or he prepares a safe plot for intellectual and emotional growth. In the next vignette, we catch a glimpse of the power of intimacy to enrich learning. Although mentorships of such intensity are rare, they do suggest the remarkable connection that can occur between an open heart and an open mind.

A Tender Power

Robin and Alison worked together for six months largely by mail, in contact directly only at the beginning of the study for several days, and again at the end for the conclusion. Yet they developed a relationship of extraordinary intensity and power.

In her mid-twenties, it is obvious from the outset that Alison is a contextual thinker. She has not been drawn to the relationship out of any kind of awe for the authority of her mentor. Likewise, Robin's attraction to Alison is less that of an authority toward a willing pupil than of an older person who sees in a younger something very precious, something she values in herself as much as in Alison, twenty years her junior. Here, they talk about their study together.

When Robin first saw Alison, she thought, "Boy, this is a really sharp woman." But because Robin was a teacher of mathematics and Alison an artist, she didn't imagine that they would work together. As it turned out, however, Alison had studied math and was more than competent in the field. She attended one of Robin's classes and decided to study with her. She saw in Robin "a certain warmth, balanced by enthusiasm . . . a very direct person, a very sincere person, and sincerely interested in what she was doing."

At the same time, "she was still serious; she demanded a certain standard; she was knowledgeable about her material." For Alison, respect was important:

> I felt a respect for her. She was able to give me ideas about things I was unfamiliar with. She inspired in me a sense that she does know what she's talking about, and that was important to me. It seemed so natural at the time, but I think that if there hadn't been the respect, that I wouldn't have considered her for the study—if I hadn't just naturally respected her. I respect her ways of thinking, a certain sharpness of mind, a quick mind. I like someone who in a conversation can sit down and grasp your way of thinking and go along with the idea. It requires a certain balance so their mind is working and they can take in certain patterns of thought too.

Robin shared her student's respect. At first, she was uneasy with what she saw as Alison's "speed-thinking," a characteristic she viewed in herself with mixed feelings:

> But I felt very early on that she was very solid, that she really knew a great deal and had a real depth inside of her, and I could identify with that [quickness] because I'm a very speedy person too . . . we run a very similar kind of basic energy. . . . I have enormous respect for her mind and intelligence and integrity and ability to go to the sources and to find things for herself; and one of the things that impressed me right off is her intellectual honesty. . . . I just was so comfortable with that with Alison right from the start. She would always say what she didn't understand, and I found that so refreshing, so good to work with.

As the study progressed, Robin felt "really overwhelmed" by both the depth and breadth of Alison's work. It was graduate work, very abstract and of high quality. For her part, Alison reveled in the work, giving her curiosity free rein yet not hesitating to move deeply into problems she herself would often pose. She felt that Robin was helpful to her in just the right ways, assisting Alison to "pull out important questions," pointing out interesting new directions, encouraging reflection on "what it meant that the study was developing that way." Robin was accessible; she was encouraging. Yet if she disagreed or felt Alison was unclear, she would say so directly:

We would share on a very honest level. That kind of directness with
each other made the bond strong, and I never felt frightened to be
honest with her, to share with her the fact that I had forgotten all
my geometry or something very basic like that; and the humor in
our relationship was nice. She could kid me about something that
I didn't know, and I felt very good about that. At the same time,
I respect her in a way that I would not really kid her, but we could
share humorous things. I think respect is extremely important. She
respected me and could always criticize me, but it was always in a
very respectful way . . . a mutually respectful attitude.

Although their association began with a high degree of mutuality, as it grew it became richer on many different levels. Alison
felt it was particularly important that Robin was willing to share
her personal opinions and some aspects of her inner life during
their correspondence. Knowing that she was dealing with a whole
human being rather than a disembodied mind allowed her to understand *how*, not simply *what* Robin thought. Conversely, in the
personal sharing, Robin would come to understand *how* Alison put
together her ideas. For Alison, the context of ideas was essential,
and it could be experienced more richly in a personal relationship
than through a disembodied and abstract one:

Some very personal opinions came up because we both were
explaining ourselves to the other; we came to be able to hold [a
different] opinion and yet share it with the other; and I respect
somebody who can have an opinion but who's not arrogant in that
opinion and is willing to share it and explain it and defend it in light
of your opinion . . . you maintain respect by being there to share
what you have. If you always keep this incredible distance, I lose my
respect for someone because I feel they're hiding something.

The dialogue of learning is of special importance to Alison as
well, and she distinguishes between "a follower of someone" who
simply absorbs the ideas of an authority at face value and a true
"student-mentor relationship" in which there is an "exchange of
ideas *and feelings*." Clearly, a sense of mutuality and equality in the
relationship is important to her—not simply because it feels right,
but because it makes for better learning as well:

I felt very connected to Robin in a most positive way, as somebody I was growing with. Interesting, I say "growing with." I did feel we were growing together, but there's still a sense that we are both developing something together. Again, it's not the sense of "I'm way above you," but there's communal growth, and sometimes just a growth in our own dialogue . . . a sense that we were sharing and growing in our communication. Anything, no matter how deep your idea is, I think you gain in perspective when you share it. I think our relationship is stronger because of the constant dialogue.

As we talk about the study in her office, Robin describes a deep sadness as the tutorial comes to an end.

"What do you most want to give her?" I ask.

"Just self-confidence, you know, and just a good life—whatever that means. A good life." She laughs, a short, birdlike warble. "She's so worthwhile, and she's been through so much pain, like so many people have." She laughs again, but it seems more a release than an expression of delight. She is letting something go, I think. Robin goes on.

"She's just so . . . she has so much to give the world with herself, and she really doesn't—hasn't quite learned, I think. She's learning, but I mean how to fully nourish herself is what she hasn't quite mastered." Robin laughs again in that almost sobbing way. It is clear that Alison has touched something deep.

"Is part of her in yourself?"

She replies that in some ways they are very different. Then adds, "But there's a part of her that's very much me right now because she loves mathematics as I love mathematics, and she sees its wonderful connection with the world and with life in ways very few people see." Her eyes have grown red as she speaks, and the tears come. I wait, feeling awkward. I'm less comfortable with pain than many people, and less able than Robin to let it have its way.

"What's responding in you now?" I ask, as gently as I can. "What is that?" She laughs again. After a long pause, she replies, slowly, haltingly.

"It's so many things. It's hard to articulate or to try to get it into a linear thing. . . . It's not just mathematics, although a big part of it is. But I mean there's a kind of commitment. . . . It's kind of hard to talk about. It's embarrassing because, you know, to be in that position, to feel that you know someone else is kind of looking to you for something, and you feel inadequate and unable to give . . . and at the same time, not completely." She pauses a long while, then speaks again, more steadily this time. "There's just a lot of fullness connected to it, and a particular sadness too. Tremendous pleasure, tremendous joy that one could have shared so much in common with someone else and that one could be so privileged to think one is actually contributing to the real intellectual and full awakening of another human being . . . it's very moving."

At just that moment the phone rings. She dabs up the rest of her tears, answers it, and a few moments later it is time to leave. As I stand in the doorway, she says, "I just hate to call it love; love is so many things, and the word has lost its power. But I just care tremendously. We had such a powerful connection, such a really powerful connection."

Students like Alison are the ones we usually call bright and whom we delight in teaching. They are self-directed, ask excellent questions, grasp ideas and their implications quickly, and though unafraid to disagree with us are usually savvy enough to do so carefully. Indeed, there is a demonstrable correlation between high grades and contextual thinking. We like these students. They may not agree with us, but we think alike.

Looking back on my own shift into contextualism, it is sometimes difficult to see a single moment clearly. But as a student in American history and literature at the time, I do know that I was spurred on by a *range of diverse content*. My teachers demanded that I integrate it around central questions. I still have those papers today. "Lewis and Clark's Journals: A Study in the Making of an Empire." "A Theory of Art in *The Marble Faun*." "The Role of Women in Works of Henry Adams." Each of these and others forced me to integrate my reading with my historical knowledge, with art, with ideas from other material as well as in relation to the outside world.

Here, as I write, is a paper of mine comparing Plutarch's version of *Coriolanus* with Shakespeare's, and there a piece of "original research" on local dialect in New Hampshire. I was being asked to *consider original sources,* discovering in the process that what we view as historical truth is inevitably constructed through human observers conditioned by their own times and purposes.

On top of them all, yellowed and fading, rests a major paper I wrote for Fred Rudolph, a mentor to this day. "Humanity, Identity, and the American Negro," I called it, pulling together around the issue of identity such authors as Genet, Tocqueville, Douglass, Booker T. Washington, and W.E.B. DuBois to make what emerged as a personal statement of commitment to the emerging civil rights struggle in the South. How could Fred have known that as a senior in college I was reaching out for a new identity, that I sought a dream to capture my youthful idealism, that I needed to move toward making commitments as a basis for the future work now looming so close? How astonishing, I think, that Fred could have known me so well to have placed that needle in precisely the right place at just the right time![2]

Rudolph was, of course, working intuitively, as many great teachers have. But intuition and magic need not be entirely mysterious. To look more deeply at what helps students move into contextualism, let's return to the principles that surfaced at the end of Chapter Four and see how they might apply now that the student's job is no longer to dismantle old structures but rather to construct new ones.

To engender trust is central to any strong, nurturant relationship. But although the trust that characterizes an early relationship owes much of its strength to the ascribed authority of the teacher, more mature trust is sustained increasingly by the shared commitment of each partner. It must be constantly recreated. Like any living thing, trust wants tending. To keep it alive requires a small but steady stream of risk—the will to drop the screen that protects our eyes from the full glare of another's presence. This is especially true as a relationship matures and the growing student asks more of the teacher's humanity. In the strength of a maturing trust, the partners are freer to challenge each other's ideas, knowing they are held by mutual commitment. Conversely, with diminishing need to protect a mask, each can afford to hear the other more fully and can learn more deeply. Thus the relationship becomes the caring context for the dialectic, the culture out of which a transforming synthesis springs.

Watching now to *see the student's movement,* the mentor looks for signs of rebuilding. The student is now capable of removing herself from immediate identification with ideas; she can talk about them as existing in some measure apart from herself. She can attend to their form, ask about the logic and flow of an argument, check for use of evidence to support a position, consider how the historical setting and evolution of a phenomenon has conditioned it, and identify underlying assumptions (Brookfield, 1987; Mezirow, 1991). This is a time to note a growing sense of voice as the student increasingly clarifies the new boundary between herself and others, broadening it to include more, honing it to discriminate better.

Now is the time to *encourage the student's own voice* as he moves away from echoing outside authorities, and away also from simple self-absorption. The contextual learner can understand differing perspectives but is not overwhelmed by them; he has developed sufficient internal power to use the ideas of others but can do so in support of his own voice. The teacher's job at this point is to help the student complete the dialogue: from "They think," through "I think," to "Given that... it seems..." complete with evidence. This is what moves thinking out into the world, where it can stand or fall on its own.

Whereas the earlier purpose of *introducing conflict was* to aid in the breakup of calcified thought, now the value is that students can come to see that the power of one idea over another rests in how well it incorporates diverse information, how well it is constructed, how elegant its form is. Moreover, by giving several different interpretations of an event—whether the results of a physics experiment, the outcome of labor negotiations, or the meaning of Van Gogh's last painting—we encourage students to form their own theories, marshal their own evidence, and ultimately express their own emerging selves through their ideas.

As before, we encourage a sense of progress by *emphasizing positive movement.* Growth is seldom steady; it inevitably comes in fits, starts, and contraries. But by watching for and reinforcing those moments when the student performs at her best, by restating and underlining language that seems to construct an image of forward movement, we can help the student develop, even if the word's full meanings may yet lie ahead. By positioning herself just in front of her charge, the effective mentor thus acts as a magnet, drawing the student forward.

Finally, with *one eye on the relationship*, we can help it grow deeper and more balanced. We need not develop the intimacy of a Robin and Alison. Indeed, no one could sustain many mentorships of that intensity. But we can preserve an appropriate sense of balance as the time approaches to let go and watch our students fly on their own. At departure we are rarely equals in terms of the subject matter, but like Socrates we owe it to our students to remind them that ultimately it is only by recognizing our profound ignorance that we can grow toward something like wisdom.

Part Three

Fostering Adult Learning

The Ecology of Adult Learning

Barriers and Incentives to Learning and Growth

In the beginning is relation.
—MARTIN BUBER, *I AND THOU*

In the search for a more workable understanding of human growth, it seems only logical to focus on the part most obviously growing: the individual. For this reason, most of the research thus far has followed people's trails as they become older and sometimes wiser. But human beings clearly do not develop in isolation any more than tadpoles evolve without a pond. In recent years, developmentalists have paid increasing attention to the nature of the environment in which development occurs—or stalls (Merriam, 1993; Fogel, 1993; Kegan, 1994; Belenky, Bond, and Weinstock, 1997). Without a fuller vision of the ecology of development, we are sharply limited in our understanding of the role that other people, particularly teachers, mentors, or advisers, play in the growth of adult learners. To understand what mentors do, we must understand how they influence the environments that hold students as they grow, how they help to orchestrate the transformative dance between the self and its shimmering, changing world.

We begin with a brief introduction to three basic ideas from general systems theory, moving next to a more detailed discussion of how environments interact with evolving individuals, specifically in light of Kegan's thought. The principles that emerge from the discussion then light up a conversation with Anne, a thirty-five-year-old mother of three who is fighting for her balance amidst a whirlwind of family and cultural forces. A discussion of how these forces work for and against her development concludes the chapter.

General Systems Theory

General systems theory, an idea originally constructed by naturalists as a way of comprehending growth and change in nature, brings fruitful explanatory power to the study of human beings as well. Rather than resting simply on the most obviously changing objects in a field of possibilities, the eye of the general systems theorist looks at the *relationships* among those objects; it seeks the invisible threads of influence within which any action inevitably occurs. Systems theory thus allows us to see not only how individuals behave but how individuals and environments interact.[1] It reminds us that we must look to complex sets of contingencies that variously affect the developing person. In short, what are some of the barriers and incentives to learning and growth?

We teachers sometimes speak of pushing our students to higher stages of development. We want the best for them, after all, and we need to know that we have made a difference in their lives—an important difference. Yet this seems a risky way to think about helping people. Not only does *push* have an unsavory whiff of coercion about it, but it probably isn't the way things actually happen anyway. To push a person to change is about as effective in the long run as trying to push a chain uphill. People develop best under their own power. As teachers, we have a lot to say about the conditions under which our students may find the power, but we must remember that the power itself is theirs.

This realization may come as a disappointment at first, but it is in the end a gift, for if we believe we have such power and in fact do not, then we are caught in a foolish delusion; but on the other hand, if we really do have that power, pity the poor student. Better to recognize that we are only a part—however important—of a whole set of forces affecting the growth of our students. A systems perspective provides a valuable inoculation against the illusions of omnipotence endemic to our trade. In a fascinating series of case studies, Anthony Storr (1996) describes how such "gurus" as Jim Jones, Rajneesh, and Gurdjieff fell prey to these illusions and ultimately to paranoia. It is probably no accident that among the characteristics of these men was a marked hostility to worldviews other than their own and an equally strong need to be surrounded by those who agreed with them.

But there is more. Environments do not simply stay put; they too change—in response to external factors, their own inner dynamics, and changes in the behavior of the particular organism in question. Everything, as Bateson points out, is in motion: "The evolution of the horse from *Eohippus* was not a one-sided adjustment to life on the grassy plains. Surely the grassy plains were evolved *pari passu* with the evolution of the teeth and hooves of the horses and other ungulates. Turf was the evolving response of the vegetation to the evolution of the horse. It is the *context* which evolves" (1972, p. 155).

Environments respond to us just as surely as we to them. In the interplay of individual and environment, we can hear a kind of dialogue between the two, each responding to the response of the other. Movement—evolution—proceeds from the silences, from the gaps in the conversation. This is an essential point, as we shall see in a moment, for in a perfect fit between self and world there is no movement, any more than there is learning in a conversation where neither partner hears the other.

A third insight from systems theory is the idea of subsystems. Any system can be seen as being part of a larger system and having smaller systems within it. The analogy is similar to that of focus in vision. We see different realities depending on whether we focus our eyes on a cluster of grapes, a vine, or a vineyard. What we see depends on where we look. This seems obvious enough. What is often forgotten, however, is that where we look generally depends on where we are standing. It is much easier to insist that what we see is what any reasonable person would see; we *want* our truths to be universal. But universality is more a matter of vision than of determination. If Walt Whitman could see something universal in a leaf of grass, and Martin Buber the same in a human relationship, it is because of the depth of their insight, not the force of their will.

In any case, it seems apparent that the transformations we are concerned with can be understood as having something to do with a radical change in vision, with perception shifts from smaller to larger systems, a metaphor echoed in Novak's notion of growth from "horizon to horizon" as we ascend (1971). Thus, when we speak of the environment in which mentors and students work, we are speaking of a *perceived environment,* one that includes the student's view of parents, spouse, children, significant others, and the mentor—as well as ideas, memories, dreams, values, external events, old patterns, and new information.

Because no two people ever see exactly alike, we are all bound to live in somewhat different worlds. It is this difference that makes for both horse races and human growth, for there is always a somewhat ragged fit between what we and others consider real. This misfit can be especially apparent during times of change— our own, the environment's, or both—and it is at such times that we may lean especially hard into the wind to restore meaning, to make sense of what seems to be shredded by the gale. This leaning outward has been labeled "cognitive dissonance," the gap between what we believe should be the case and what appears "in reality" to be true (Festinger, 1957). As with a vacuum, we abhor it and are drawn into the effort to close the gap, to restore coherence. Fortunately for most of us, the gaps are relatively minor parts of our total world. Most days the sun rises as we expect, and we are able to keep our balance in the breeze. But some people live in stormier spots, while others are more sensitive to change. Every gardener knows that the climate has everything to do with what can and cannot grow. Should it be any different with human beings?

The Holding Environment

In a book with the unlikely title *Maturational Processes and the Facilitating Environment,* D. W. Winnicott, a British child psychologist whose work is particularly germane to family systems theory, describes what he calls the *holding environment.* Deriving the term from the physical activity of holding an infant, he uses it to refer to the parents' psychological presence within which the child can gain a sense of the "continuity of being" necessary for successful separation from the mother (1965).

Since one important part of being a baby is to move, however haltingly, toward a new kind of independence, the environment must be neither so supportive that there is no motivation to leave it nor so harsh that if the child does she wishes she hadn't. To provide a "good enough" environment, Winnicott says, parents must be neither negligent nor perfect. For a child to develop a sense of self, she must be able to make some sort of association between what she does and what she gets, between action and consequences. If, as in the case of poor parenting, her actions are met with random punishment, she learns that she is no good; if met with indifference, that she is unimportant. In either case she feels powerless. Conversely, if all of her needs are met before she even knows she has them, she fails to learn that her actions make a difference: that wailing with hunger brings food. The value of hunger is that if both she and her environment respond appropriately, she learns that she can make a difference in the world. In crying, she takes a first tiny step to defining who "she" is. She begins to trace a boundary between herself and her environment. Identity is born—and is born again and again with every new tracing for the rest of her life.

A good-enough holding environment helps us carve that boundary in a way that allows us to consolidate each new sense of self so that we can maintain meaning and coherence in the world and yet remain open to a lifetime of fresh wonders. As any parent who has held a crying child knows, it's all in the balance. There is a time to hold and a time to let go. In that knowing, says Winnicott, in our sensitivity to our children's needs for being held and being free, lies our gift to their growth.

Kegan has extended Winnicott's insights across the whole life span. In *The Evolving Self,* he describes how we move through a procession of holding environments, or "cultures of embeddedness." Each holds us for a time in equilibrium, supporting and releasing as we grow. Although he describes these cultures as discrete entities, it is probably more accurate to think of each as blending almost imperceptibly into the next, like the view through a microscope as we change focus. With each new turn of the knob, a fresh perspective emerges even though the object under examination remains the same.

The first environment, which Kegan calls the "mothering culture," is in harmony with the earliest developmental stage, the "incorporative" self. It is characterized by both physical holding and a certain failure to meet the child's every need. (Most parents know how easy it is to "fail" that way; it's nice to know that perfect parents aren't perfect.)

The next, or "impulsive," stage is accompanied by the "parenting culture," in which the child's needs for fantasy and intense attachments are met but the child is encouraged to leave the immediate warmth of the family for brief periods, encouraged to be responsible for his or her own feelings and to experience qualified independence.

As the child moves into the school years, a third environment, the "role recognizing culture," swims into focus, supporting emergence of the "imperial" self. Here, the child's budding independence and self-sufficiency are encouraged more actively, yet at the same time the culture demands that the child acknowledge mutuality in his or her relationships, emphasizing the importance of trust among friends.

With the onset of the teen years, the importance of interpersonal relationships intensifies in the "culture of mutuality," which ushers in, and is enhanced by, the growth of the "interpersonal" self. Subjective feelings are more fully acknowledged, and collaborative self-sacrifice takes on a greater value. Although supportive of these qualities, the culture demands that the adolescent assume individual responsibility amidst the wash of mutual friendships, asserting the concurrent importance of independence from the group.

If conditions are right, this environment yields yet again in later years to the "culture of self-authorship" as the "institutional" self emerges. Authority becomes something we possess rather than defer to; a career rather than simply a job, a life partner rather than a helpmate fill our sights. We find ourselves among friends who value our uniqueness, and we lean toward those who see beyond our external, social masks. Institutions that emphasize competence and achievement hold for us more appeal than those offering simply a sense of belonging or status.

Yet for some, this is not enough. As with all holding environments, this culture too hosts the worm of its own destruction. We begin to question the value of so separate a self; we yearn for work that offers a deeper meaning, friends who speak to our vulnerability, a spirituality that asks new and more profound questions. We are propelled toward the "interindividual" balance in which a "culture of intimacy" holds us as we grow in our capacity for mature love, interdependence, and a new kind of self-surrender.

Kegan's sense of the evolving interplay of self and environment is exquisite. We both create and are created by our environment as we move along, and if our movement is relatively smooth, we remain always open to that critical discontinuity that makes an environment neither too harsh nor too perfect but just good enough. As Winnicott first suggested, always the good-enough environment both meets and contradicts our needs for growth and in so doing calls forth an essential developmental dialogue, an internal conversation through which we struggle to make sense of the conflicting messages coming from a changing world (Basseches, 1985).

It is this evolving set of contraries within successive holding environments that gives Kegan a framework for suggesting a common form for each culture of embeddedness. Environments, he tells us, provide three things: *confirmation, contradiction,* and *continuity*.

When we look at the confirming aspects of an environment, we see those parts that essentially conform to the shape of the individual. When a father holds a crying child, he holds him close until the sobbing begins to subside. In that act, he communicates that he can acknowledge his son's pain and yet not be drawn into it. As teachers, when we confirm we let our students know that we understand their ideas though we may not agree, their fears though we are not afraid, their pain though we are not hurt.

Environments contradict by raising questions about the adequacy of confirmation. Contradiction is the antithesis to confirmation in the developmental dialogue; it is the gap between person and world, things as they might be and things as they are. As the child's sobbing slows, the father can release his son to reenter an uncertain world. The time for holding has passed. Good mentors let their students know that authority has its uses but is limited, and the task of reentering the world includes taking one's own authority along.

In the idea of continuity lies the synthesis, the bridge from one developmental balance to the next. The adequate environment, says Kegan, "sticks around," like good parents when their twelve-year-old decides to "run away." Such bridging between old and new worlds allows broad movement to take place and helps those in transition to know that there is some meaning and coherence in what can seem fragmented and senseless. Just knowing there is a connection between worlds, that there will be someone ahead when we arrive yet still there should we turn back, can be the extra encouragement we need to swing out over the brink. This is why mentors are ambivalent figures; they must represent both old and new worlds at once. Not only by being there and listening but also by their mere existence as experienced travelers, mentors provide continuity. Beyond that, by offering a map (by including discussions of personal evolution in literature, history, or art courses, for instance), a teacher can oftentimes make the sense of continuity still more concrete for her student.

In a subsequent elaboration of this scheme (1994), Kegan places the later three "balances" (which he now calls "orders of consciousness" to emphasize their extension to the social realm) in dialogue with such "demands of modern life" as parenting, work, diversity, healing, and learning. The chapter on learning is of particular value to adult educators who seek a fuller understanding of the role that transformative learning can play in modern life.[2]

With all of this in mind, let us turn now to meet Anne, a thirty-five-year-old student in an external degree program that links term-long correspondence study with two-week periods of campus residence. Her purpose in returning to college is "to become educated." Listening in on our conversation, consider how Anne is moving; note her attitude toward authority, her view of knowledge, her sense of a growing edge. But consider also the forces in her life: her friends, relatives, and culture, her goals, aspirations, economic situation, and values. How does each contribute to the swirl of support and challenge—the ecology—that holds and releases her as she grows?

Seeing the Connections Among Things

Two years ago, at the encouragement of her husband, Anne decided to return to college. It was an enormous step, for not only did she have two children in school but her family was stationed in Saudi Arabia, half a world away from where she was to spend her two-week "residencies" twice a year.

The first residency was particularly difficult. She had married directly out of high school and never been separated from her family for more than a few days. She was homesick and found many of the other students difficult. The strong feminist orientation of the program disturbed her. "I just wasn't ready for it," she explained. But she managed to stick it out, completing a study in women's literature with an outspoken feminist mentor—a study about which she is curiously silent.

The second time around might have gone more smoothly as she studied art, a field in which she felt more confident. In this case, however, her male adviser "came too close. He didn't seem to care whether I was married or not." When she rejected his advances, she felt he took it out on her artwork, calling it conventional and too inhibited.

But again she prevailed and returned for a third term. This time, she wanted to study philosophy to sharpen her "critical thinking." "I feel all the time put down by men," she told me. "And I guess I want to learn how to argue back, how to think like them," she added. "But it's difficult for me to be critical. I really get excited by new ideas, but every time I learn something that I think sounds right, I hear another idea and then I think that one is right, and then they just all sound right so I find it hard to pick any of them apart."

We talked a while longer about her experiences thus far in the program, and it became increasingly apparent that she felt adrift. "I came into this program pretty sure I knew what I believed, but now, with all these different ideas, I'm not so sure anymore.... I just don't know what I believe in."

I agreed to work with her, and we put together a study around the idea of virtue: How do you know something is good? Since she wanted to work with "philosophical ideas," we made up a lengthy reading list of Greek philosophers, adding a world history text, books on critical thinking and problem solving, and materials to help her apply all of this to the Saudi and American cultures of which she was a part. She was to write a sequence of papers, first describing Greek ideas of virtue, next exploring the genesis of Christian definitions, and finally reflecting in light of her reading upon the values she grew up with and those surrounding her in the Middle East. Then, off she went.

Now, six months later, she returns a week early to discuss an extension for the study. It has not gone well. Although the quality of what I received was fine, there was little of it. Her few letters spoke darkly of "difficulties with my family." We find a quiet corner of the student lounge, and I ask her about it. Outside, the late April sun has thawed winter to a few scabs of snow tucked in the shadows. The grass is a tentative green.

"Well, what's been most important about the study hasn't been the actual learning," she begins, flashing me an apologetic comic pout. "It's been overcoming my feelings about the study itself. It was a study where my mind would seem to turn off; it turned against me. I'd get distracted."

That was obvious. Since shortly after she left in October I kicked myself for having apparently miscalculated her capacity. Yet it didn't make sense. From all I could tell six months earlier, she certainly had the brains to handle the material. Needing something concrete, I ask her if she can think of a time when she felt particularly "distracted."

"Yes," she replies. "It was in December. I was overwhelmed with getting ready for the holidays, and on top of that I wasn't feeling very good about myself anyway." She pauses a moment, looks around the room as if for an escape, and then plunges on.

> Well, my father-in-law came to spend the month with us. He's a Christian minister with a really good education, and so naturally he was interested in what I was studying. I told him philosophy. Well, the first thing he said, even before we even tried to talk about Socrates or any of the other philosophers, was the fact that he wanted to make sure I knew that . . . that . . . he wanted to make sure that I didn't get led astray by philosophy because unless I had someone to lead me correctly, I would jump to conclusions that weren't valid. And I think he was also afraid—and I think that I

probably reinforced his fear—that I would come to some
conclusions that were not necessarily biblical.

She adds the footnote with a mischievous wince. The theme is
growing familiar, but I'm not yet sure how central it is to her tale.
As she goes on, I begin to get nervous.

So we started to talk about it. And for every point I tried to bring
up, he had another point. And for every point, he had questions,
things I hadn't thought about. I can't even recall right now because
I got so intimidated. And the fact that whenever I would say
something, or would express an opinion, he'd say, "Well, you know,
I've studied at Harvard, and I've taken four years of Latin," and he
just gave me the impression that I didn't know what I was talking
about. And because I didn't have enough knowledge to back it up, I
became very frustrated.

As she speaks, my disquietude gives way to dismay. Frustrated?
Is that all? What has this man been doing to her? I lean forward,
watching every word.

At one point, we were talking about philosophy, and he said, "Well,
I have a friend who studied every imaginable philosophy and after
years of work, he came to the conclusion that the Bible is the only
book in which forty different authors came to the same
conclusion." And I said, "Well, if I had the time, I could find forty
different people who could come to the same conclusion as
Socrates did and some of the other people having one perspective,
and that's to find the ultimate truth. I mean Christians aren't the
only ones seeking the truth!" And he was really upset with me for
that. Besides, just because forty people agree doesn't make it true!

I'm not sure where she is taking us, but her defiance is clear
enough. I nod visibly and smile my approval. She goes on.

And later, I was telling him about certain diaries I had read in which
a woman described her perceptions of the Civil War that were quite
different from the usual descriptions, and he said, "You really
should be careful about what you read because I can see it is
leading you in the wrong direction, because if you want to learn
about history, read authentic history books where men are scholars

and have studied this." And I said, "Well, everybody's perception is different. This is just their view, what's in *their* hearts." And he said, "You can't believe that stuff." And I said, "Why not? The books are just somebody's perception of what happened." And he said, "No. Men who are scholarly and did research are the people that you should listen to." And I said, "Do you mean that you're telling me that what these women have written is not valid?" And he said, "Yes."

At that point I said, "That's absolutely ridiculous! People can have different perceptions of the same thing. For instance, there can be one problem and one person can come around from the right and be able to solve it, and one person can come around from the left and approach it in this way. And they both come to the same solution to the problem in different ways. Are you trying to say there's only one way?" And he said, "Yes."

And then my husband came in and asked him to go out for a walk. And as he was leaving, I said, "Yes, and white bread is always better than brown bread!" But the whole thing made me feel very uncomfortable, because in times like that you don't have enough knowledge to back it up, and so I feel very intimidated.

By this time, I'm a jumble of emotions—appalled and angry at the self-centered destructiveness of this fatuous Polonius, pained at Anne's understated anguish, and intrigued too by the potential in her tale, with her sheer guts in standing up to his pomposity. But for some reason, in the search for an appropriate response, the detached analyst in me gets the upper hand. I decide to bring the event into the present and see what we can learn from it.

"What would you need in order to be able to battle more successfully?" I ask her, trying to give her a weapon.

"Probably to know more about the subject matter itself and to understand it in a better way. And probably just practice in learning how to debate that kind of thing."

From our previous work together and from several things she has just said, it is clear that she sees knowledge as cumulative. Her father-in-law derives his power from *the amount* of knowledge he possesses. Her shortcoming is that she doesn't have *enough* of the stuff. At the same time, she has significantly added a qualitative dimension. I decide to pick up on this leading edge in her thinking.

"How might you understand it in a better way?"

"Well, maybe like to see how it's connected to other things. Maybe to see how one perspective has evidence that supports it better from other parts of life, I guess. I'm not sure." She shakes her head slowly. "But I don't know." She looks down at her hands and pauses a long moment. "I don't know. Maybe it just isn't worth the fight. I mean with people like that."

She has picked up the battle metaphor, and I am left with several choices. I can continue with that, I can go with her leading edge about making connections, or I can respond to her obvious emotional distress. The despair in her voice leads me to the last. As it turns out, the decision to go with her feelings takes us into a whole new area.

"Yes," I say softly. "But it doesn't do your ego any good."

She laughs, brushing away the emotion. "Well, you know, as they were leaving, he came to me and he said, 'Mom and I have been talking, and we seriously think you should take up interior decorating.'"

"Oh my God," I think, the anger rising again. But I let it go and begin to look for supports. "Where is your husband in all this?"

"Well," she replies, "he's kind of in the middle. He tries to explain to me that I have to consider the source and that Dad's from a different generation and... I guess I can sort of see that, but it doesn't make me feel much better. And I think my husband feels that I'm making him choose in a situation like that. And he doesn't think I should even discuss it. But I can't put my books away. I can't get further behind!"

Her voice is tinged with desperation, but this time I decide to continue to work with her strength.

"How did you end up handling it?"

Her face and voice brighten again. Despite her fragile appearance, she possesses an awesome resilience.

Well, I felt pretty good after I made that comment about white bread. And just after, I was talking with my daughter, who had been having real trouble while Grandpa was here, and she just wanted to stay away from the house as much as she could. And my mother-in-law came in and said she had heard part of the conversation. It was interesting because we were talking about different ways of seeing, and she hadn't heard the part about how there was "only one truth." So we were talking about it and we got into some of the things she had read. Well, she's really been growing a lot. She's seventy, and it's really neat. So we were having a conversation and I was talking about two ways of seeing things, and she said, "Isn't that just wonderful? You should ask Dad about that." And I said, "I *did*." And she said, "What did he say?" And I said, "He said there was only one way." But you know, he had put himself in a corner by saying there was only one way. And he's in education and we know there's more than one way.

By this time I have cooled off again, and my fascination with this whole extraordinary tale bubbles forth. I decide to share it with her.

"Well, one of the things that intrigues and pains me as well is that as people are beginning to grow, they get out of whack with their environment. And here's Anne, struggling to find her own truth in this environment in which she is growing, and here comes Grandpa who really threatens to hold her back."

Still steaming along, she breaks in:

I feel I have a lot of forces working against me. In that situation I felt like I won one battle, but I feel like that it left me feeling very inferior because I was struggling at that time to read this book, working so hard to try to figure out how to pronounce some of these words, and I'd ask my husband, and Grandpa would come along and pronounce the word, and it just seemed like he knew everything. I'd feel so stupid that I couldn't figure it out for myself. It was so easy for him and so hard for me, and in this environment, your ego is being damaged on a daily basis. You're constantly being reminded that you're only a woman, that you're inferior.

I ask her what she means about "this environment," and she talks at length about the difficulty of being a woman, not only in the Saudi culture but in the American compound as well. She is allowed to make no business transactions without her husband's approval, she can never venture out alone or with other women, and even among Americans she rarely feels understood. Being a student sets her apart. Though a few women support her, when she tells people what she is studying most are indifferent. Men challenge her, and she feels she's being tested. "It's scary to me," she says. "So I find myself not saying what I'm doing. Or just letting them take over the conversation."

As our talk winds down, we turn, rather unsuccessfully, to a discussion of how she can set up a network at home of people who might be supportive. "They're all wrapped up in their own worlds," she says. "I feel pretty much alone."

Clearly, woven through this vignette there are conversations within conversations within conversations. At one level we hear the authoritarian, dualistic voice of Grandpa thundering its certainty against Anne's quavering but courageous multiplicity as she struggles to affirm her own different voice, not simply to oppose his but to legitimize her own. She argues not that she is right but that her way of seeing is more adequate. Yet because her balance is still unsure, she feels helpless, drawn back by assumptions she has still to reject.

At another level, there is the conversation between Anne and me. It is not a carefully constructed clinical interview; it's simply one of a number of meetings I hold with her in the course of our work together. I am not trying to push her anywhere, to "make her develop." Yet powerful developmental forces are at work, and I seek to help her understand those forces in a way that she may feel less overwhelmed by them.

At this point, however, I want us to consider what Anne's story has to say about the ecology of adult learning. She herself picks up on the language of systems when she says, "I feel I have a lot of forces working against me." Just what are those forces? How do they work against her? What is the interplay of other, more positive forces in her life?

In thinking about these questions, we must first establish what systems we are talking about. Consider the Anne whom she views as her "self" and the Anne I see to be one system. This "Anne system" is embedded in another system we might call Anne's world: what both she and I consider her outside world of people, information, and significant events. For purposes of the exercise, these are our main two systems, one a subpart of the other. In defining them this way, it should be emphasized that we are constructing our problem from our perceptions, not from any objective reality. All of our data come from what Anne told me on tape in response to my questions about her interpretation of an event. We are not seeking the facts in Sergeant Friday's sense. Rather, it is *how Anne makes meaning* of all of this that we are after.

A second task is to decide what the goal of the system is. Although both individuals and environments are in motion and could thus be said to have goals, to keep things in bounds let's consider only Anne's goals for now. Her purpose in returning to school is to become educated.

When I ask Anne what education means for her, she replies that it helps her to "feel I am doing something with my life," and she goes on to explain that she wants to learn more so that she can feel more equal to other people, "especially men who are always putting me down." How can she do that? By learning more and arguing better. When she compares herself with those in her home environment, she tends to describe them as "having so much knowledge," whereas what she admires about her fellow students is that they seem to be so worldly and "critical." Thus, she sees home through the eyes of an earlier developmental stage, school through a later one; she looks to her study with me to move her from the first way of seeing (represented by home) to the second (being in the world).

Not surprisingly, my own goals for Anne are informed by much of the developmental thinking we have discussed previously. While I generally find it difficult to peg a person in any single stage, it is apparent to me that Anne is working with a view of knowledge and authority that Perry terms multiplistic. That is, she sees knowledge as concrete but quite diverse; she clearly agrees with the classic multiplistic assertion that "everyone has a right to his or her own opinion"; conversely, she feels quite isolated in her quest for truth. After all, if there is no ultimate truth, if the world is entirely subjective, then we are hopelessly sentenced, as Tennessee Williams had it, to "solitary confinement inside our own skins."

Part of this sense of isolation derives from Anne's stance toward authority: fiercely opposed to Grandpa's effort to exercise it over her, but still strongly swayed by it. Authority still rests in lots of knowledge and a Harvard education. She seems caught between a thesis that "truth is objective and supported by sheer weight of facts" and an antithesis that it is personal and subjective. Since the thesis seems still to hold more weight, she looks there for an escape. Knowledge, for her, is still "out there," found rather than constructed, and to become her own authority she needs more facts. Yet another part of her believes that this way leads toward becoming more critical—toward seeing how things are connected, how to support assertions with evidence, how to argue more effectively. This, after all, is the style she sees around her when she is on campus.

It was in an effort to address these two parts of her that we designed her study around both Greek philosophy and critical thinking skills. I hoped that by acknowledging and building around her desire to accumulate knowledge, I could help her see that her strength lay in its use rather than its quantity.

But Anne's growth was more than just intellectual. She was struggling to transform her role from "only wife and mother" to include responsibility to herself and to those beyond her immediate world. In Kegan's terms, Anne seemed on her way from an interpersonal orientation toward an institutional stance. Her ambivalence toward the feminism of her fellow students attested to her dilemma: how to remain a good wife and mother on the one hand yet acknowledge the view of herself that was materializing with increasing clarity as she emerged from the protection of the earlier stage. Still firmly connected to an interpersonal self—a self in which loyalty is primarily to those we know face-to-face—she was hearing ever more loudly the call of women she did not know but whose plight moved her as she grew increasingly willing to acknowledge and care for her own pain. Again, the way through the dilemma, the transformative questions, still lay ahead: "How can I have both my family and my self?" "How am I connected with women I don't know face-to-face?" Those were questions demanding formation of, and trust in, an abstraction for which she was not quite ready. Her movement was clear enough, though. Desperately in search of her own voice from among the cacophony of male voices around her, she felt the pain sharply as her voice was drowned out again and again and again.

Given the systems we have defined and the goals we have seen, what are the forces working against Anne? In this particular drama, Grandpa clearly moves downstage center. It is quite plain to Anne, without knowing a thing about Perry's research, that her father-in-law is "against" her—not because he disagrees, but because he sees the world in a way that she thinks is too simple. (Remember that we are talking about a Grandpa whom Anne has constructed. It is impossible, and probably irrelevant, to know whether he is "in fact" dualistic.)

But she is caught in a bind because she also gives him considerable authority. She is not yet able to dismiss his perspective and thus defuse his power—or perhaps more accurately, she is too emotionally embroiled to separate the way he thinks from who he is for her, a stance her husband is urging on her. In effect, she *gives* him his power by virtue of her own worldview, not yet sufficiently distanced from his to free her from its power. So when he makes that crack about interior decorating, he strikes at the very heart of her aspiration to grow out of her interpersonal world, for interior decorators are seen by neither Anne nor Grandpa as career professionals with an integrity of their own. Rather, for both of them interior decoration is a way to keep her in her place, a glorified housewife.

One can scarcely imagine a society less supportive of Anne's aspirations than the Saudi one where she finds herself. Yet her own culture is small comfort. She sees few others who understand her or who can share with her the experience of returning to school. The highly conventional world of an overseas compound can brook little deviance from what it views as propriety. The men, especially, seem to be career-oriented expatriates with little of the sort of caring sensibilities that Anne needs, especially from those to whom she still gives too much power. Caught as he is between his concern for her and his obligations as son and businessman, her husband plays a mediating role. But he seems unable to give her the emotional support she wants, to acknowledge to her that he knows how important the conflict with his father is. Rather, he chooses to separate the two and downplay the entire scene.

In addition to her relatives and the surrounding cultures, Anne's role as wife and mother—as she construes them—come constantly into conflict with her job as student. The holiday preparations were only a glimpse of the dozens of daily demands from her family that would drift like some oblivious, indifferent iceberg between Anne and her study. The desperation she feels ("I *can't* put my books away; I *can't* get further behind!") is endemic to women like Anne, trying to be mother, wife, and student, struggling to resolve the conflicting demands of the old and the new selves.

The material of her study also seemed to get in the way as much as it helped. Some of it was difficult, the words unpronounceable. Because of her view of the nature of knowledge, she felt she had to read each book, cover to cover, understanding each page before going on. To skim for important ideas (which ideas were more important, anyway?) seemed like cheating to her. She carried an almost moralistic set of convictions about "proper" study that is characteristic of many students in her position: one must read and understand all assignments and not speak until the right answer is known; papers should be complete and perfect before they are read (soliciting help on drafts is dishonest); to use an index to locate relevant material without reading the entire work is cheating. "I never feel I can talk about a subject until I know it well," she tells me. "I can't talk about it in bits and pieces." And authors? People who write books always know what they're talking about. If you can't understand them, it's your fault, never theirs.

Undergirding all these inhibiting forces is her own limited worldview Because we are talking always about a *perceived* environment, the problem ultimately circles back to how Anne sees the world and makes meaning of her experience. None of the forces that seem so inimical need be so intrinsically. But the particular set of lenses she is wearing mandate that it be so. Helping Anne change those lenses, enabling her to see all her emperors in the flesh, is at the heart of her educational transformation. But before we get to that, let's consider some other forces in Anne's environment. Which ones can help her through? What factors support her growing edge?

Despite feeling at times a misfit among her fellow students, Anne made close friends and listened earnestly to their "more radical" views. Although she thought them often too critical, she felt the power of their thinking and was drawn toward the people around her who seemed so much more self-contained than she. Somehow they knew something that she needed to learn. What was it?

Anne's husband seems at different times both helpful and unhelpful. It was he, after all, who encouraged her to get into all of this in the first place. That it may cost him his wife must have occurred to him, but she still sees him as generally supportive. "He does more of the housework now than he used to," she says approvingly. And his mediation in family conflict is more than a neutral activity, for it relieves her of at least some of the guilt for her part in the initial stress.

It is noteworthy that immediately following the argument with Grandpa, Anne turns to her daughter to share their mutual feelings toward him. As women, they have in common the experience of subordination, and Anne is increasingly finding a voice in which to express her mixed feelings about men. Next, enter mother-in-law. All three women continue the discussion, this time in a much more mutual and caring way. Later in our own conversation, discussing differences between men and women, Anne said this:

> If a woman finds out [about my study], she's either not interested or says "that sounds terrific!" And then she'll start saying something like, "Isn't it hard? Don't you have trouble?" Real personal questions about it. They kind of make you feel better because you start saying, "Oh," and you start remembering things you have read. She comes on to you as a . . . almost an "I wish I could do that. Tell me about it." And you start saying, "Oh, you could do it." And then I start remembering things when I'm in that situation . . . with a woman it always comes out on a personal level, about how we deal with a subject. . . . It stimulates a lot of personal feelings.

It is clear that in other women Anne finds the support she needs—not simply to heal wounds but to make herself still more vulnerable, to talk about what she is learning, to hear herself speaking at last in her own voice. Unlike most of the male world around her, she knows that in her vulnerability lies her strength. The tragedy is that there seem to be so few women to whom she can turn.

Although some of her assignments turned out to be more inhibiting than helpful, this was not always true. Anne found the several problem-solving books to be quite enjoyable. They answered her own need for practice in an area where she felt weak, and they were calibrated in a way that allowed her to grasp most of the problems and feel a much-needed sense of accomplishment. Further, through them she could learn how to approach problems more effectively; they helped her toward constructing a methodology for making sense out of former confusion and thus for pulling the pieces of her multiplistic world into new coherence—an essential step in her expansion toward contextual thinking.

She found much of the reading in philosophy difficult, but our correspondence helped, she said, to clarify much of what was going on in *Symposium* or the *Crito*. More important was her feeling of accomplishment at having worked her way through some of these texts. This was full-fledged adult literature, and in knowing that she had read and understood them she was able to make a very important statement to herself about her role in the larger world outside of her home. Finally, because the history text we used was arranged thematically rather than chronologically, Anne was able in her writing to draw effectively on both historical and cultural data to support her speculations about what finally emerged as our culminating question: "What makes a virtuous woman—in the eyes of the Greeks, the early Christians, contemporary American culture, and Anne Guildhall?" In writing her final paper, she was able to view a common topic (of obvious personal concern to her) from several perspectives while at the same time drawing on these perspectives to begin formulating a statement of her own personal philosophy. In this act, she also spoke for the new self she was becoming.

But beyond these factors, it seems to me that the most important aid in Anne's odyssey was her own courage. It allowed her to stand her ground against her father-in-law's pomposity and come out with a victory, however Pyrrhic. It gave her what she needed to remain in her residencies despite feeling a misfit, and thus to make friends, converse long hours, and absorb bits of powerful and transformative knowledge. Ultimately, Anne's courage enabled her to open her eyes just that extra crack, letting her see what previously she dared not. Once inside, such information inevitably does its work, for it demands a place. Thus we create for ourselves each new world.

Perhaps because she lived in so isolated an environment, the conversation with Anne allowed me to see more clearly than ever before the wonderful intricacy of our work. Neither Anne nor I nor anyone else in the drama was untouched by the others. Grandpa was responding to a study that Anne had developed with my help, yet his response affected Anne, who in turn provoked a new response from me. And that was only one interchange among three characters! Clearly we were all moving in a *complex, interactive dance with the environment*.

Then, too, I began to see more clearly how that environment would in some ways *confirm,* in some ways *contradict,* and in some ways *provide continuity* for Anne's movement. I could see how valuable it could be for us to see the whole lives of our students as much as possible so that we could better know when to move ourselves. Part of the job, it seemed, was to acknowledge my part as one of the forces in Anne's life and to work in the ways suggested in the previous chapter.

But another part was to help Anne see the forces impinging on her life, myself being one of them. *For mentors are both a part of and "meta" to the environment.* Viewed from one stance, they are simply another of a number of forces working for or against the traveler's evolution. But from a different angle, they seem to hover above the flood, sending down messages to the beleaguered voyagers, helping them to see what they cannot, warning them of looming gales or lurking shoals. From there, they can help their charges understand from a greater perspective the forces affecting them, enabling them to change direction. For this reason, it is valuable for mentors to carry a map with them that they can share from time to time. If it is done with appropriate care and right timing, then offering some aspects of developmental theory to students can enable them to take their development into their own hands.[3]

Thus, mentors can do more than simply add to the environmental forces at work on the learner. They also help the traveler see more clearly the environment itself—where she is headed so that if she can't avoid the pitfalls, at least she can know better how to take fuller advantage of the unique opportunities that most pitfalls offer. It is because of this special quality that I want to discuss separately what mentors do. It seems that the time has now arrived.

Chapter Eight

The Yoda Factor
Guiding Adults Through Difficult Transitions

> *I must only warn you of one thing. You have become*
> *a different person in the course of these years. For this*
> *is what the art of archery means: a profound and*
> *far-reaching contest of the archer with himself. Perhaps*
> *you have hardly noticed it yet, but you will feel it very*
> *strongly when you meet your friends and acquaintances*
> *again in your own country: things will no longer*
> *harmonize as before. You will see with other eyes and*
> *measure with other measures. It has happened to me too,*
> *and it happens to all who are touched by the spirit of*
> *this art.*
> —EUGEN HERRIGEL, *ZEN IN THE ART OF ARCHERY*

> *Unlearn, unlearn!*
> —YODA, IN *STAR WARS: THE EMPIRE STRIKES BACK*

A green, gnomelike creature small in stature and great in wisdom, Yoda appears midway through the *Star Wars* trilogy to provide Luke, the hero, with the knowledge he needs to save the galaxy from the lowering power of Evil. For the last eight hundred of his nine hundred years, Yoda has been training the Jedi knighthood to serve as agents of virtue in the struggle between the light and the dark side of the Force. He is a mentor's mentor. Along with his former protégé, Obi-Wan Kenobi, he guides Luke through his transition into adulthood, confirming his value, challenging his ability, and reminding him of his destiny: to meet and resolve his conflict with his father, avatar of darkness.

The primary theme of the trilogy is that of a young man coming of age, making his own place in the galaxy while acknowledging his debt to his father. Some twenty-eight hundred years ago, *The Odyssey* told a similar tale about Telemakhos. Mentors figure prominently in both, for as long as young people are faced with growing up into the world, mentors are needed to help them.

But although mentors are surely stars in the drama, the part they play varies importantly according to the particular transition faced by the protagonist. Since most of us make a number of changes throughout our lives, it is not surprising that on reflection we may recall a number of mentors. Some remain for years, some for only a few months; sometimes the relationship is intense, sometimes purely instrumental; and though mentors may seem more plentiful in our earlier years, they often appear in less conventional form later on. Yet always, if we are to call them mentor, they helped us through a transition of some sort. And if the relationship was positive, we have grown from it in some way, for the idea of growth is inextricable from the idea of mentor.

Recall that Levinson suggests that mentors are characteristically a half-generation older than protégés—just the right age to mediate between parents and children. This makes good sense and is a useful guideline for calling someone a mentor rather than friend, or even teacher. Yet it seems too restrictive to account for the numerous mentorlike relationships that people report when they begin talking about their lives. Perhaps it would be more useful to let the quality and power of particular relationships help us define mentor rather than this arbitrary (though clearly helpful) age criterion. If we simply think of a mentor as someone we feel drawn to who seems to know things about life that we need to learn, it may help us to recognize that mentors can appear throughout our lives, whenever we encounter a new transition.

As the nature of the transitional task changes, so do our mentors. It seems more than coincidental, for instance, that as a young man seeking validation of my own dream I found most of my mentors in men who seemed the personification of what I wanted to believe possible for myself—especially in the world of work. Yet at midlife, my mentors were more often women, some older but some younger than myself; what I was then to learn had less to do with becoming a functioning part of the working world or with resolving parental issues than with the kind of inner realignment that Levinson describes—a redressing of earlier imbalances between masculine and feminine, attachment and separateness, young and old.

But mentors are more than simply isolated individuals who enter our lives, intervene, and depart. Rather, they are creations that emerge out of particular demands our lives make on us. When they do their work well, they help us see not only the tasks before us but also the broader context that gives those tasks meaning. With Yoda, they remind us of our destiny.

In Anne's case, just the act of listening to her story, of giving her an opportunity to speak about her struggle and to name it, helped her bring it under a new kind of control. Listening, as a friend once observed, is a powerful intervention, perhaps the most powerful we have as mentors. It is not a passive process, for the good listener is always alert for things of special significance in a tale and acts, however subtly, on what he hears. Thus, when Anne began her story, she knew by my interest that here was something important. I leaned forward; I nodded at certain times and not others; I cheered some acts, ignored others; I asked questions, focusing attention on particular people in her drama, asking how she felt about this or what she meant by that. And at one point, I sketched a model of how I was interpreting the story, one that gave her some new language and a more detached way of understanding her dilemma. Throughout, I was attempting to let her know that her inner life was important—but that reflection upon it was important too. Thus, I was *selecting* particular elements of her story, reinforcing some, letting others slide unnoticed. In this way, I became a mirror in which to see herself anew. How much credence she gave to the new image was a reflection of the power she chose to give me as a part of her transformation.

In the remainder of this chapter, we look more closely at how mentors tilt the mirror they hold up to their students. I suggest that mentors seem to do three fairly distinct things: they *support*, they *challenge*, and they *provide vision*. As through much of this book, I use the term *mentor* and focus on the role primarily because this is the work I do. But I hope it is fully apparent that the functions and activities described in the following pages are by no means restricted to that particular work. They are drawn from a wide range of sources—experiential, literary, and theoretical. At bottom they are principles offered to anyone concerned with guiding development, be they teachers, physicians, advisers, administrators, counselors, civic leaders, pastors, rabbis, or other mentors.

Similar to what Winnicott means by holding, the notion of *support* refers to those acts through which the mentor affirms the validity of the student's present experience. She lets him know through her empathy with his feelings or her comprehension of his words that he is understood. In systems language, she attempts to bring her boundaries into congruence with his. The analogy to physical holding is a good one, for as Erikson has eloquently reminded us the capacity to trust flows at the source of the entire developmental process, and we first learn to trust by being held well as infants. Trust is the well from which we draw the courage to let go of what we no longer need and to receive what we do. Without a reasonably well-established sense of basic trust, it is difficult to move ahead. Courage and trust are sister and brother.

The function of support is to bring boundaries together; *challenge* peels them apart. The mentor may assign mysterious tasks, introduce contradictory ideas, question tacit assumptions, or even risk damage to the relationship by refusing to answer questions. The function of challenge is to open a gap between learner and environment, a gap that creates tension in the learner, calling out for closure. The work of closing that gap strengthens our sense of agency, of power in the world. Thus, the twin elements of support and challenge lead to developing the twin capacities for trust and agency.

But there is a larger context. Simply to provide support and challenge leaves unanswered the question "toward what?" And although ultimately the leap must always be made into the dark (Shunryu Suzuki notes that to attain enlightenment we must know it is impossible; Tillich says the same in a Christian context), mentors do offer a kind of light. This third function I call *providing vision*. It is similar to Kegan's idea of the "confirming" function. Mentors hang around through transitions, a foot on either side of the gulf; they offer a hand to help us swing across. By their very existence, mentors provide proof that the journey can be made, the leap taken. In helping their charges look ahead, form a dream, sketch their own maps, mentors offer "a fair chance of winning through," as the Old Man said to Telemakhos. Always this is done in the service of what Sanford calls self-reflection. That is, unless we are able at some level to name the change, to see it explicitly in a new way, the transformation is not complete; as a generation of psychoanalysis would confirm, it is only by bringing our changes into conscious awareness that we can be assured that they will stay put. "No amount of situation or behavior changing will lead to personality development in adults," says Sanford, "unless accompanied by self-reflection" (1980, p. 65). Mentors can help us do that. "Welcome," they say in a thousand languages, "to the new world." This is the kind of critical reflection that is central to transformative learning (Mezirow, 1991; Brookfield, 1987; Cranton, 1994).

It should be apparent that any interchange with a student involves a mix of support and challenge, both going on at once. Though useful, to separate these two functions is arbitrary, since what is support for one person may be challenge to another. In a fascinating experiment some years ago, researchers delineated those supports and challenges that were most appropriate for "dualistic" students on the one hand and "relativistic" students on the other. Dualistic students felt support in a high degree of structure and were challenged by diversity. Relativistic students, on the other hand, found support in diversity and challenge in the necessity to make commitments amid uncertainty (Knefelkamp, Widick, and Parker, 1978). The researchers then designed classes to fit developmental needs with appropriate environment. Subsequently, a wide array of researchers and teachers have described such efforts (Schlossberg, Lynch, and Chickering, 1989; Mezirow and Associates, 1990; Brookfield, 1990; Merriam and Caffarella, 1991; Merriam, 1993).

Here is one way to visualize the effects of support and challenge on development:

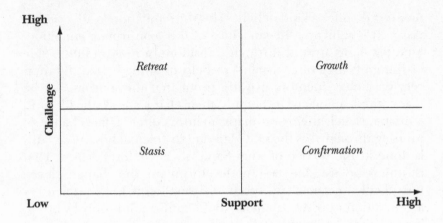

If both support and challenge are low, little is likely to happen. Things stay pretty much as they are. If support is enhanced, however, the potential for some sort of growth increases, but it is likely to emerge from the inner needs of the learner rather than from any stress imposed by the environment. The learner is confirmed and may feel good about himself but may also lack the capacity to engage productively with the outside world as well as he might if he were encouraged to communicate more actively with it. The risk that some highly student-centered college programs run is that in encouraging primarily self-expression, they fail to help their students acknowledge the legitimacy of a world different from their own and thus miss the crucial leap into contextualism.

Too much challenge in the absence of appropriate support, on the other hand, can drive the insecure student into retreat, forcing a rigid epistemology to replace the promise of a more fluid and complex worldview. It is no coincidence that many of the converts to new radical religious groups have dropped out of college after a year or so. Overstrained by the diversity they encounter there and undersupported in what can be a tragically cold and uncaring environment, they fall back to a more secure adolescent conformity, safely embraced by authoritarian simplicities. It is reassuring to know that in time most recover enough to leave their sanctuaries, but the costs in the meantime can be considerable (Levine, 1984).

Finally, in an appropriate mix development can occur. Just what that is, of course, depends on the particular needs of the student and style of the mentor. Clearly, not every teacher works for every student. But if we are to believe that good mentorship can be learned, then it is in our interest to expand our capacities and deepen our sensitivity. To that end, let's look at some of the things that effective mentors seem to do.[1]

Support

Support is the activity of holding, of providing a *safe space* where the student can contact her need for fundamental trust, the basis of growth. It means moving to confirm the student's sense of worth and helping her see that she is both OK where she is and capable of moving ahead whenever she chooses. In the next several pages, we consider several supportive functions. The list is not exhaustive, yet perhaps it identifies the primary elements of mentorship.

Listening. It is obvious that mentors must literally hear what their students are saying, but the term *listening* goes beyond merely hearing. It means actively engaging with the student's world and attempting to experience it from the inside. What does it *feel* like to be this person? How does she see the world, make sense of diversity and complexity? What are the forces holding and propelling her life?

It is remarkable to listen to a good mentor talk about her students. Joanna, who interviewed Martin back in Chapter Four, can tell you the ages and names of her students' children, how things are with their spouses, how they are feeling about their work, and what they want from their educations—usually on the basis of a single conversation! It is not that she pries into their lives so much as that she simply evokes the kind of trust that calls her students' stories out. And as they tell, she listens.

Mentors often have a good sense of their charges' inner lives as well. Again, this knowledge seems to arise less from probing than simply staying alert to what their people are telling them both explicitly and implicitly. They tend to accept the concerns and fears of their students rather than hastening to assure them they shouldn't get so upset or that what concerns them is inconsequential. Describing first impressions of mentors, protégés often say such things as "I felt that he *saw* me more clearly than anyone had before" or "It was so powerful to have someone you respect

see you so well, know you so well." The sense of being seen clear
through comes from the willingness of the mentor to accept where
the student is and to acknowledge the legitimacy of that stance
rather than to see the student as someone in need of modifica-
tion. In many cases it also comes from the student's need to be
seen this way. Particularly at early stages, we *want* our teachers to be
omniscient.

This is not always easy to handle. For some mentors, to be
given the kind of power that many students proffer at the outset of
the journey can be disconcerting. That is probably just as well, for
students' need to give authority to their mentors is best understood
as a transitional need, one we ought to help them outgrow. Yet to
reject that need outright can be injurious to the potential learning.
Part of the art of the job is to accept without clinging to the
authority we are given; the other part is to let it go when it no
longer serves its purpose.

An important way in which some mentors establish a trusting
bond is through mirroring the language and even the movements
of their students. Close analysis of the dialogues in this book reveals
a number of such cases. Bandler and Grinder (1975) developed
their entire theory of neurolinguistic programming (NLP) out of
such uses of language in its many forms. In most cases, mirroring is
intuitive on the part of the mentor. Yet intuitions can be sharpened,
and even though there is a clear danger of manipulation inherent
in NLP increased awareness of how we listen and respond on many
levels can improve both advising and teaching.

Providing Structure

Some years ago I helped to develop a "learner-centered" curriculum for adults. Most of the prospective students had no more than
a high school education completed years before. They were anxious about returning to school, and their study skills were rusty.
Yet still aflame with our own countercultural ideology, we rejected
such traditional trappings as clear course sequences, class syllabi,
and even reading lists. Indeed, the very word *curriculum* carried
for us a smarmy connotation. Why should we lay such a heavy
trip on our students? They were adults, weren't they? They could
make up their own curriculum as they went along. Needless to say,

we learned—slowly I must admit—that our students needed more than that.

Although it makes sense intuitively, there is also ample evidence supporting the contention that anxious students need considerable structure and guidance, especially when they have been away from study for years. For such students, close personal attention, clear expectations, specific assignments, short and achievable tasks, and predigested material (textbooks rather than source material) are important. Summarizing research on the effects of anxiety on learning, Peterson and Snow conclude that high-anxiety students who are low in ability do very poorly without close guidance (McKeachie, 1980). This does not necessarily mean, however, that they need a teacher hovering over their shoulder. Related research suggests that such students do well with programmed instruction materials, and certain computer applications may have promise. Lectures, often considered anathema for adults, may in fact be quite appropriate in their time if they are carefully designed.

Paradoxically, close support can often provide the best setting for the kind of creative play that results in effective problem solving. As long as the support is open-ended, allowing a sense of safety for the student without at the same time constricting, it can be an effective setting for the sort of "loose qualitative analysis" that seems to be an important first step for skilled problem solvers (McKeachie, 1980; Rybach, Hoyer, and Roodin, 1986).

The important point here is that for the majority of adult students just easing their way back into higher education, a high degree of structure may be supportive at first. Those who have left their need for dualistic thinking behind quickly enough make it clear that they have minds of their own. As teachers and mentors, we ought to resist the quite understandable temptation to thrust all students into the cold at once simply because some have profited from that treatment. On the contrary, we would do better to start inside until it is clear they are ready. Then we need only open the door.

Expressing Positive Expectations

In a detailed and practical study of the skills possessed by effective teachers and mentors in adult programs, Carol Schneider and her colleagues found that having positive expectations of students is one of the most important aspects of effective advising. Good mentors and teachers believe that average students are competent, they identify and affirm others' capabilities, they express the view that students are capable of change, and they accept student suggestions for changes in learning plans if they are "consistent with the student's learning objectives" (Schneider, Klemp, and Kastendiek, 1981).

Describing what their mentors did that was most helpful, students in my own research replied that they "gave me confidence in myself," "kept pushing me and telling me I could do it," and "had faith in me even when I didn't." Effective mentors seem to wield much of their power through the vision of the possible they hold for their students. Thus, they balance both a present sense of where their students are and a dream of what they can become—without allowing either to eclipse the other. It is almost as though they hold both present and future, actuality and possibility in tension, offering it for their students to accept.

But the stunt is not always easy. As teachers we are bound to be confronted at times when a student's work falls short. Balancing the imperative of providing honest feedback with the equally compelling need to let them know that they can do it is enough to strain the best of us. Those who manage it often do so by nesting their criticisms within a positive frame. Said one mentor, "I can always find something good to say, and I usually lead with that." He went on to describe how he tries to help his students see the problem in terms of their own best performance and highest expectations (standards he helps them construct) so that they are measuring themselves in their own terms rather than his. "I reminded her about an excellent paper she had written before," he said, describing a student in a sociology class. "I said, 'I know you can do it because you did it then,' and she had to agree." Thus, by holding her to her own terms, he was able to reflect back a clear image—one she could recognize but with which she was not wholly familiar. She had to stretch to accommodate it. In his recent detailed and very practical study of the activities of mentoring, Norman Cohen (1995) writes with sensitivity and wisdom of this aspect of "the art of mentoring."

Piaget's concept of *décalage* is useful here. Recall that no one is ever wholly in one stage or another. Thus, although we function most of the time in a given stance, we carry both past and future capacities as well. Under stress, we tend to slip back; we tighten our grip on what feels most secure. When we feel safe, on the other hand, we can relax and reach out. That's why a supportive tone to the relationship is so important. It lets the student move to her leading edge. Knowing this, mentors sometimes reinforce the growing fringe of a student's thought by listening for it and naming it, as I did when Monique toyed tentatively with the word *tolerance*. By giving it my blessing, I endowed the term with special power—a power that apparently endured for some time. I met her on the street two years later, and one of the first stories she told was about how much more tolerant she was than her coworkers. Some years after that, she received a master's degree in human services and is now working in administration.

Serving as Advocate

Campbell reminds us that mentors are often seen as powerful allies on the journey. They intercede with the powers, they translate arcane runes, they protect the pilgrim from assault. This aspect of concrete, instrumental help is one of the most frequently cited functions of mentors studied in the business world. They literally give their charges a boost up the corporate ladder, putting in a good word for them at key meetings, suggesting their names for promotion. Similarly, academic mentors sometimes sit on committees reviewing their students' work and as such may be called on to explain or defend it.

Knowing this, students understandably feel anxious, for the system itself grants mentors considerable power. As students would hand me their study plans, I often needed to reassure them against feared decimation at the hands of a faceless and distant review board. The fear was real and legitimate. For some, any show of uncertainty on my part would trigger escalations of anxiety. The power they gave me seemed to grow in direct proportion to the threat they felt.

Similarly, as guides we often provide support simply because we have been there before and appear to know where the journey leads—be it through the tangled mysteries of distribution requirements or the terrors and delights of multiple truths. Whether conducting an independent study or a full class, the mentor is seen to possess knowledge, skills, or wisdom that lies ahead for the student. Given such power, it is not surprising that our support can be so delicious, our criticism so devastating.

Sharing Ourselves

"I wish I could just know him better as a *person*" *is* a common sentiment among protégés. As long as the relationship is relatively complementary in form, the student is bound to feel the more vulnerable. Initially, especially for students at fairly early developmental positions, the distance is usually acceptable. Indeed, so strong is the need for authority in early positions that one would be unlikely to hear such a student wishing to see his mentor's clay feet. As things progress, however, the pressure increases for the teacher to reveal himself as human, not god.

Conversely, as he does so, the protégé finds it increasingly easy to project himself into the mind and spirit of the mentor, thus speeding the breakdown of a constructed ideal and inappropriate authority. How and when this occurs varies greatly, but a healthy relationship, like a healthy individual, needs to grow in the capacity to share inner concerns more freely. Timing, as usual, is paramount. Given too soon, the receiver may ignore it or perhaps actively reject it. Given too late, it may simply be scorned. But with proper care, the gift of self-disclosure can lead to a valuable deepening of the relationship for both partners.

Making It Special

One of the most compelling qualities of the relationship is that it feels so special. The student feels uniquely *seen* by the mentor, and if the mentor is endowed with particularly desirable qualities or unusual power in the world, the effect can be a potent tonic. Here, a protégé speaks of his first encounter with his mentor:

> It was like I was so awed by him, I was so impressed with his brilliance, with his history, with his personableness, with his profound sense of me. It was like he saw *me* in ways that I couldn't even see me. Like he valued me in ways that I did not value me. It felt like he loved me in ways that I did not love me. And I was so awed by that [Zucker, 1982, p. 120].

This sense of specialness can be both a support and a challenge, of course, for however much one might try to remove expectations, they are inevitably a part of the gift. The question is not whether they exist but how they affect one and how powerfully they are mediated by a sense of one's own given value. To the extent that the mentor knows and values the student as a unique person—and that the student senses this—the relationship maintains a reasonable balance.

Additionally, this specialness creates a kind of two-person hothouse. Within its walls, the student can reveal herself in ways that she would not to others, for there is an understood quality of trust about it. The relationship becomes a special culture in which certain kinds of growth are encouraged and others discouraged. To an extent, the outside world is sealed off, as it must be if this inside world is to offer special opportunities not available under ordinary circumstances. Because the experience of being closely listened to is so rare for many people, it can also be just the needed catalyst for cautious emergence of a new sense of self. By listening, the mentor can give the new self an audience, often for the first time, an ear to hear the first tentative affirmations of a position the student knows to be on her leading edge, ideas too risky to entertain outside the safety of this space, a still tender voice speaking itself into being.[2]

Mentors do a lot of supporting, and it should come as no surprise that this particular activity seems to come more easily to female than male mentors. If mentoring is an androgynous act, then support is to challenge what female is to male. Indeed, the male conditioning in me shies away from the whole idea of support as somehow "soft" and indulgent, whereas many female mentors seem reluctant to challenge, impose their own values, or otherwise do what they feel would be violence to the integrity of their students. Rather, they tend, like Grace and Dolores, to provide a less intrusive environment—one that leaves the student more freedom for exploration.

They seem as well to draw the line less sharply between themselves and their students. Perhaps this grows out of a conviction that the quality of the relationship is fundamental to effective mentoring, and out of a fear that to separate themselves too much from their students would endanger the relationship. It is noteworthy that when I asked the mentors and students what their most important duty was to each other, the women overwhelmingly named honesty and openness as central. Asked why, they explained—sometimes with a hint of exasperation—that obviously you can't have a nurturant relationship in which there is no trust. Dolores put it this way:

> Without honesty there is no relationship . . . there could be no trust without honesty. [And why is trust important?] I don't feel that I would follow anyone down any path if I didn't trust them, and I would not trust somebody if I did not feel that they, within their conscious effort, were being honest. And I would not expect anybody else to follow me if I was not honest with them and they could not trust me.

The men placed less value on honesty, more on activities like providing guidance and fostering independence. It was as though they focused primarily on themselves or the student while the women were looking at the space in between. It is a fascinating distinction and seems to bear out the speculation about the female need for connection, the male's for separation. But for now perhaps it is enough to note it and observe that some of us are better at providing support and others at offering challenge. Both, finally, must be given a voice in the developmental dialogue between self and other, separation and attachment, letting go and reaching out.

Challenge

Just as support calls the mentor to conform his boundaries to those of the student, challenge peels them apart. It means opening a distance in the relationship, drawing the student outward to fill the gap, straining him to move, to accommodate his inner structures to the new environment created by his mentor's distancing. In social science language, it means creating a cognitive dissonance, a gap between one's perceptions and expectations ("I think I should be *there,* but I see myself *here*").

Leon Festinger (1957), who invented the term *cognitive dissonance,* maintains that there is an intrinsic human need to close such a dissonance, to harmonize it again with our own inner selves. That, he says, is what learning is about. We move to close gaps.

Likewise, it seems that teaching is at least in part about opening gaps. Mentors toss little bits of disturbing information in their students' paths, little facts and observations, insights and perceptions, theories and interpretations—cow plops on the road to truth—that raise questions about their students' current worldviews and invite them to entertain alternatives to close the dissonance, accommodate their structures, *think* afresh. Indeed, more than any other adult educator, Brookfield (1987, 1990, 1995) has argued this point: that transformation demands a deep rethinking of our fundamental assumptions and that the role of the "skillful teacher" is to enable that to happen.

Here are some of the ways they do it.

Setting Tasks

Most commonly, and most visibly, mentors set tasks for their charges. The tasks may be obvious—memorizing sacred texts, doing homework, writing papers—or they may appear nonsensical. Herrigel's archery master told him he must stop trying to hit the target. Hank told Richard to argue against himself, and Virgil directed Dante downward on his upward journey. Sometimes the tasks are incomprehensible because the teacher is holding a perspective the student has yet to develop. Still living in a tacit world, Richard found it difficult to suspend judgment. Virgil knew Dante could never see the light until he had plumbed the darkness. And sometimes, as Mr. Miyagi, the teacher in *The Karate Kid,* knew, a "mindless task" is just what we need to teach us about our minds.

The frequently overblown fascination with behavioral objectives was often garnished with claims that students ought always to know where they're going before they set out. Although the competency-based movement did right a good many educational wrongs in its time, we do well to remember that sometimes our minds can be our own worst enemy, that a good dose of confusion is exactly what a student may need. There are places on the map that disappear when we look at them, and sometimes the only way to get there is to go somewhere else.

In addition to setting the exercises, mentors often ask for some kind of analysis of the tasks, reflection on the meaning of the job. This may come in conversation, or it may come in a more formal assignment such as a paper, a project, or a test. The value of this is, of course, that it encourages the student to create a context for the activity and see more broadly than just as the task alone. In addition, it allows for generalizing the principles so that the student can apply the learning in settings other than the immediate one. In a larger sense, it encourages the student to think about her own thought, a skill essential to strengthening formal reasoning.

Throughout, the mentor is there, encouraging, cajoling, threatening, but always selectively reinforcing this behavior over that, casting light on one aspect of accomplishment rather than another, and thus bringing the learner to see a different world than she might otherwise see. Through this close interaction in which the student's energies are bent toward accomplishing the task, the teacher's standards and expectations become internalized in the student. In effect, the student comes to incorporate the mentor within herself. This growth of an inner teacher can effectively complement the other dimensions of internal enrichment as the "self-authorship" of which Kegan (1982) speaks. Ultimately, the student becomes her own guide—a blend of her own shape with that of her mentor.

Thus, the mentor's challenge to reflection encourages the protégé to speak out increasingly in her own voice. This often comes slowly, especially when the student is struggling with the straps of dualistic authoritarianism. ("Who, me?" says Betty. "I don't know anything worth talking about." Surrounded by an overwhelming world of authorities, she feels quite incapable of peering over the wall for herself.) Several students in an educational philosophy class I once taught were perplexed when I asked them to criticize some of the readings. "Why would you assign us to read these experts," asked one student, "and then turn around and ask us to criticize them?" It simply did not make sense given what she believed to be the purpose of education.

This is the time when plagiarism can be less a crime than a sad misunderstanding. "Why should I put it in my own words when the textbook puts it so much better?" "Who knows the facts better than the author?" That the teacher might prefer a student's own thought to an expert's knowledge seems barely conceivable. Education, after all, is about getting knowledge from authority. That one might use one's own capacity to ask questions and organize thought while still using the ideas of others has not yet come clear. The synthesis between self and other that allows each its legitimate function still lies ahead. But calling the student's voice to emerge is of central importance, for clearly we do not learn to speak unless encouraged to do so, nor to think without practice.

Engaging in Discussion

Summarizing prevailing research findings of value to college teachers, McKeachie emphasizes that college learning involves constructing new frames of meaning. To help our students in that endeavor, he notes, "we need to carry on discussions in which students have an opportunity to express their problems and progress" (1980, p. 90). As must be apparent by now, one of the most enjoyable aspects of the mentor's work is the sort of developmental dialogue that appears in the vignettes. Absolutely fundamental to all human development (Fogel, 1993), dialogue is central to the mentor's role. A primary purpose of a developmental dialogue (or what Mezirow [1991] refers to as "discourse") is to help the student engage different perspectives, different ways of viewing a problem or a phenomenon. In the trusting and privileged relationship between a caring teacher and a student, the risk of exploring new ideas is minimized, and the student is encouraged to experiment in ways she might not otherwise try. Such discussions, it should be emphasized, are most effective if the mentor considers her task not to instruct but rather to understand her student's thought and perhaps to raise questions about it. Jane Vella (1994, 1995) has written persuasively and practically of the power of this approach.

In a classroom, for instance, it can be effective to ask an outspoken student if he has understood a position just expressed by another student. Indeed, for discussions of controversial matters, an instructor may insist that speakers not express an opinion until they outline the previous speaker's point of view satisfactorily. Even where the subject under discussion is not overtly controversial—describing how a Native American saw the coming Europeans or how a wealthy suburbanite views the world—it can be important to encourage students to take perspectives that differ from their own. In his slim and elegant treatise on "a spirituality of education," Parker Palmer suggests that "to teach is to create a space in

which obedience to truth is practiced." Such a space, he says, is one
in which differing views are given respect, yet in which each person comes to hear his or her own voice more clearly and honestly
(Palmer, 1983, p. 69).

If class discussion is not possible, written papers or well-
wrought examination questions may accomplish the purpose. But
the act of getting outside of one's own world and seeing it through
the eyes of another is of profound developmental significance. It
demands that in some small way we cross the boundary between
ourselves and the other person or idea or sensation; in so doing,
the boundary becomes just a bit more permeable to new ideas and
fresh views. In time, we come to recognize that those we may once
have viewed as "them" have become part of a larger "us." In the
study that grounds our book *Common Fire* (1996), it is this transformation, achieved in dozens of tiny increments, that powerfully
contributes to the formation of commitment to a *common* good
rather than to defense of one's own private welfare.

Heating Up Dichotomies

One effect of this encouragement to take differing or opposite
perspectives is that the exercise heats up the dichotomies and
creates greater pressure for resolution. The process can be painful
at times as we hem and haw between the pro and con of a political
debate, our inner or outer selves, or the demands of our family
members. Yet the inner dialogue is important, for it is through
this back-and-forth movement that we slowly build a platform on
which to stand and from which we can look down to construct a
synthesis that holds both parts.

It is important, at the same time, that the student be helped to
recognize the *legitimacy* of the other stance. It is common enough
for students after a while to acknowledge that theirs is not the only
way, yet it takes time for them to recognize and know in their bones
that those other ways are in some sense equally legitimate to their
own. "If I could only get them to see that the Kulungi Rai are *full
human beings* struggling to make sense of their world as we do of
ours," said a colleague, "instead of just thinking they were quaint."
That's a deeper understanding, calling on the development of
contextual thought. And it takes time. It's a long journey from

"Our ways are right, theirs are wrong" through "Our ways are sensible, theirs are quaint" to "Our ways make sense to us, theirs to them; we differ because our worlds differ." Yet it is only on the basis of this last viewpoint that we can begin to construct a reasonably compassionate world in which to resolve our differences without violence. The mentor can help that come about by challenging us to consider each side, to give each its due before we take a stand.

Constructing Hypotheses

A particularly interesting part of the shift from a conventional, culture-bound stance into contextual thinking is the development of what Piaget called hypothetico-deductive reasoning. This is the ability to spin off a chain of reasoned implications from a consciously constructed hypothesis. While this can be accomplished by precontextual thinkers, it becomes a regular mode of operating when we shift from seeing the possible as simply a subset of reality to recognizing the real as only a portion of the possible. At this point, thinking takes off and we begin to develop the capacity to imagine a world better (or worse) than the one in which we now live. With the development of self-conscious, assumptive thought, we can give this utopia its own legitimacy, a *real possibility*. A variation is the as-if game. "Let's assume . . . ," it begins, and goes on to construct an elaborate argument based on a hypothetical assumption. One imagines that the hugely popular computer simulation games must offer opportunities to help students develop this capacity, since they allow elaboration of any number of theoretical possibilities based on explicit premises.

Thus, the ability to let air under our assumptions seems a necessary precursor to contextual thought. That is, to see how ideas different from ours exist in their own legitimate framework, it is necessary to leap out from our shell of absolute certainty and construct a whole new world based on some other person's ideas of reality, other assumptions of truth. People practicing this form of reasoning may begin sentences with "Given . . . ," "Assuming . . . ," or "What if . . . ?" It is this sort of reasoning, this ability to cast a net of possibility out ahead of one's footsteps, that finally enables us to cross over the yawning gap that separates belief from faith and to leave behind our need for the bedrock certainty of absolutes.

Once we finally realize that even our former absolutes are relative to some context and rest on some assumptions, we are at least free to risk movement out of the cave. This is why Plato's allegory of the cave makes such a marvelous teaching device for raising questions about students' givens. It forces them to consider, sometimes for the first time in their lives, that what they take for reality may be an illusion. Can there be any question why it is so important for people of all ages to exercise their imaginations? Only if we have practiced soaring above reality and living in imaginary worlds can we risk the flight over the existential abyss when its time comes.

The ability to reason rests paradoxically on willingness to suspend it. So it should come as no surprise that certain highly authoritarian groups and cultures struggle to limit their children's opportunities for fantasy. At some level, they seem to realize that in our imagination is the power to transcend our need for absolutes, that in our dreams rest the seeds of freedom.

Setting High Standards

One of the most persistent findings in studies of teacher effectiveness is that good teachers set high expectations for their students (National Institute of Education, 1984; Light, 1992). They help their students construct positive, self-fulfilling prophesies for themselves. Speaking of his goals for Emily at a time when she seemed still wandering in a forest of specifics, Bob hoped she would come to see how things are intertwined: "instead of having separate notes in a melody, she will have a whole piece of music that makes sense." He encouraged her to study in ways that would help her do that. When Hank challenged the adequacy of Richard's second paper, he made it clear that he expected serious thought, but he went on to describe for his student what he meant by that. The expectations were high but not incomprehensible; he took pains to couch them in terms that Richard would understand. Indeed, Hank routinely required students to rewrite their work regardless of how good it was. It taught them, he said, to reflect on their thinking, to see themselves through others' eyes—a central developmental accomplishment.

One of the dilemmas in teaching is that teachers generally both give tests and grade them. They thus retain dictatorial power.

The paradox is that the ultimate goal is to free students from this power—in Ken's terms, to "help them fly." Thus, though good teachers set high standards, they work at the same time to help their students construct their own inner teachers, their own sets of expectations for themselves. They do this in part by making explicit both their expectations and their reasons for them.

Good teaching ought to help students learn not simply to answer questions but to ask better ones themselves. Students' growth ultimately depends on their developing the ability to look dispassionately at their own performance, their own answers to their own questions, and decide for themselves how they've done. What teachers need to teach above all is how to learn, not how to be taught. A major task of the mentor in this regard, then, is to challenge students to challenge themselves.

Vision

In the Castaneda books, one of Don Juan's main purposes is to teach Carlos to "see." By this, he means not simply the ability to perceive a different world but actually to apprehend reality more fully and comprehensively. The mentor is using vision as a metaphor for greater understanding.

Vision, in its broadest sense, is the field on which the dialectical game between the old self and the new can be played; it is the context that hosts both support and challenge in the service of transformation. By providing vision, mentors hang around while the protégé takes the leap. Athena appears as Mentor at the beginning and the end of *The Odyssey,* for instance, but takes other forms in between. The enduring quality of this sort of guidance is captured mythically in numerous tales as mentors reappear to their protégés after death in the form of spirit guides. Even in their absence, mentors set a climate of expectations and provide a sense of continuity.

Modeling

Mentors most obviously provide vision by modeling the person whom the protégé wants to become. The model may be quite literal at early stages of development. A child, for instance, thinking concretely, may express a wish to become a lawyer like Mom or a teacher like Dad. Later on, the attachment is likely to be around general attributes rather than to a particular role: a mentor is attractive because, like Ken for Betty, he was so "knowledgeable" and spoke so distinctly, or because, as Jean said of Dolores, "She's got it all together, and I definitely haven't." Later still, the appeal may be integrated with conscious awareness of what the student herself needs at that time. Alison, for instance, knew that she needed "a certain standard," yet she also sought someone who was both passionate about her field and willing to work with her on her own terms. She describes Robin's appeal in richly interpersonal terms, with a clear sense of how she needs to be held.

As with lovers, mentors and protégés seem most strongly drawn together when each seems to fill a need in the other. But as with lovers also, if one partner grows while the other remains the same, the affair may fall apart. Students who return to higher education in quest of more job opportunities or higher social status, for example, may look to their mentor initially as one who has what they want for themselves. Henry Higgins and Eliza Doolittle are the classic case here. He would teach her how to speak "correctly" and how to appear in public. The phenomenon is common in programs for adults, especially since so many adult students are the first of their family to complete college. For them, a college education may represent a sharp shift in social class. As the film *Educating Rita* poignantly demonstrates, however, if the education seeps in, such appearances are soon enough seen for what they are, and if the mentor is unable to transcend superficialities, the relationship is likely to crash. As the protégé changes, so also will her need for a model. This may be quite appropriate, of course. Unlike romantic love, there is no imperative that the pair remain eternally intertwined. The mentor's task may very well be completed when the student leaves for good.

In other cases, the attraction may come from a protégé's desire to master a subject or develop a particular skill. This form of attraction is particularly common in the arts and among sports figures: Degas for Mary Cassatt, Haydn for Mozart, or Michael Jordan for Scott Pippin. But though we may be drawn to mentors for such immediate purposes, as we grow we come to realize that their gift is not the opportunity to become *like* them but the challenge to become more fully ourselves *through* them. They call forth the best we have. They invite us to transcend ourselves. They embody our deep aspirations.

Keeping Tradition

Yoda was nine hundred years old. Part of the reason for portraying mentors as aged is that as guarantors of continuity they pass on tradition to the next generation, what Schachter-Shalomi (1995) calls "intergenerational bestowal." Regardless of our ideological stripes, teaching, as Neil Postman points out, is a conserving activity (1979). We have a stake in fostering, if not such values as free inquiry, responsible scholarship, and moral decision making, then at least a committed iconoclasm. We may not be interested in watering the ivy on the walls, but most of us would agree that something goes on behind those walls that is of enduring value. Said one student, "The master may be wrong, but not the faith." To this we owe our allegiance, both as mentors and students; this is what we seek to help our students discover.

The danger in this case, of course, is that we confuse the dancer with the dance. Thus the Zen master urges aspirants to "kill the Buddha," and Sufis remind students that the master is the one who destroys the idol you make of him. The story goes that a novice once surprised Hildegard of Bingen in the kitchen devouring a huge plateful of pheasant. Dismayed, she wondered aloud if this was appropriately restrained behavior from her mentor. Replied Hildegard, "When I fast, I fast; when I pheasant, I pheasant!"[3]

Although our students may take a while to recognize it, what is important about our minds—or so our minds would have it—is not what is in them but how they operate. What we model for our students is less our knowledge than our curiosity—the journey, not the destination. As teachers, we recognize that we are channels through which information flows, configuring itself into certain patterns they may name knowledge. However, the tradition we keep is not so much the knowledge itself as the capacity to generate it. When the time comes, we must have the wisdom to release our hold on both the knowledge and our students.

Offering a Map

In a sense, just by being who she is, the mentor is a map for her student. But the process can be much more than this. One of the adviser's earliest pieces of business is to listen at some length to a new student's story—her travels and her dreams. The experience of being listened to closely, of being asked such questions as "Why are you coming back to school?" "What do you want for yourself?" or "What would you really like to learn?" can be of great importance in helping a person begin to formulate her own plans more clearly. The decision to make major changes in one's life is often made intuitively; but to think about the meaning of the decision in the larger context of one's life is crucial if one is to integrate such a decision well and construct of it a foundation for further growth. Mentors have an important part in making this happen through the interest they express in their questions about the whole lives of their students. Out of these questions students can then begin to construct their own maps in their own terms.

At the same time, I have found it useful to offer to students some of the developmental maps that appear here in earlier chapters. In one of my more successful seminars, I provided a core of common readings in developmental literature and then assigned special project reports on particular theorists in accord with what I felt to be key issues for each student: Levinson for a young man in transition, Fowler for a woman of deep religious commitment, Gilligan for a mother entangled in the demands of work and family. Because each knew I had selected the work for him or her, each took special interest in that particular map and drew unique value from it.

Naturally, it is not necessary to require such a course for all students. But familiarity with several developmental schemes offers the adviser valuable tools for helping students see their own journeys more clearly and thus take increased responsibility for their academic lives (Winston and others, 1984; Pascarella and Terenzini, 1991). As Cohen observes, ". . . the alert mentor will be aware of how far the mentee has already journeyed, what needs attention now to assist the mentee's development during the relationship, and why the mentee should address certain concerns in the present relevant to the future" (Cohen, 1995, p. 119).

Suggesting New Language

The words we use and the way we use them are powerful indicators of how we see, of our particular vision of reality. A glance at the scoring manual of any given developmental scheme makes this obvious. In Perry, for example, early dualistic writing is character- ized by short, simple sentence structures, frequent use of absolutes (*never, completely, right-wrong*) and little use of *I*. Later, multiplistic writers tend to use language in highly personal ways, frequently referring to themselves at considerable length. They tend to make long lists of attributes, linked poorly if at all. At more contextual levels, qualifiers proliferate; terms such as *it depends* or *assuming* set language up off the ground, sentence structure is more var- ied, and there are fewer clichés but more qualifiers. There may be a sense of motion in the language, as though the speaker sees ·herself in a fluid world, moving somewhere rather than frozen in some absolute syntactic soup. Mentors can learn much from the way their students use language.

According to Fowler, mentors' primary function is to "nurture us into new metaphors." They give us new ways to think about the world. The good teacher helps students not so much solve problems as see them anew. Mentors can give us new language, magic words in which are contained whole different frames of reference. Thus, language can be a catalyst for change as well as an indicator of it. Among some Hindu sects, for instance, the first act of the guru is to give the aspirant a sacred syllable or phrase to repeat during meditation. This mantra serves as a connection between the student and the source of "higher consciousness." In this way, language can *evoke* intimations of new meaning.

Teaching a course once, using the journey as a metaphor for growth, I found that students took readily to it and used it to see their lives' movement in a new way. I encouraged students to work with the metaphor both in journals and aloud, interviewing one another and sharing their stories. Many found that for the first time in their lives they had both a rich metaphor in which to frame the experience of their growth and attentive listeners for whom to construct it. The combination was memorable for all of us. In this light, Jung's comment that mentors are people who ask us *who we are* and *where we are going* shines for the crystal insight it is.

Providing a Mirror

One of the more important aspects of the special mirror that mentors hold up to their students is its capacity to extend the student's self-awareness. To see oneself anew, from a range of vantage points, is the chief way we distill what we are learning from the challenges and supports of our world. In an expanded view of the self, one might almost say, lies the definition of development itself, for it is only if we are able to place ourselves in the context we create for everyone else that we become fully relativistic in our own worldview.

One way of doing this is by providing feedback to students about their own learning styles. Citing research describing several styles, McKeachie suggests that teachers can help students "identify their own most effective learning strategies" and "use a larger repertoire of methods of learning" (1980, p. 89). Kolb (1984) offers a widely-used "learning style inventory" for self-diagnosis. Claxton and Murrell (1987) summarize a range of such models. In effect, the mirror can both show students their best side and suggest new ways to see the world.

Socrates used the mirror to bring his students to see more broadly the ramifications of their particular perspectives. Drawing out his victims on a string of if-thens, he would lead them inexorably to discover the logical implications of their givens and thus to see themselves in an expanded context. Teachers often find themselves doing this, working with students to help them comb their ideas, to see that if they are to be consistent with a given set of assumptions or beliefs, then logic may demand that they alter some of their conclusions. As a result, students come increasingly to see their own thought, to recognize it as a phenomenon in itself.

This works well, of course, if the student is engaged and willing to listen to a logical train of thought or entertain new information. In some cases, this may not be possible. Faced with conclusions she was unwilling to accept, for instance, Betty preferred to seal out the disturbing information her mentor offered. Richard, on the other hand, was drawn in by his own adulation for his mentor and evidently felt safe enough to risk realigning some of his assumptions and conclusions to make a more coherent and consistent whole. The result, of course, was a new level of self-awareness on Richard's part and a new capacity to see himself as capable of change. Hank's efforts to help his student form that new image seem, in part at least, to have been vindicated.

If there is trust in the relationship, the student feels it is safe to leave the epistemological home and enter another for a while. This is important not because this one is better but because in each departure comes the ability to release old knowledge, in each arrival the will to accept new information. It is the traveling that most we learn from travel.

| Chapter Nine |

The Art of the Mentor
Limits and Possibilities

Those having torches will pass them on to others.
—PLATO, *THE REPUBLIC*

The Great Depression still lingered and the war lay ahead when Gladys and her husband piled their old car with belongings and headed north from Connecticut to Vermont. They found a small farm high on a ridgetop and spent the next decades struggling to grow a living. To supplement their income, Gladys took in a few elderly boarders. Over the years, the number increased until she found herself the proprietor of a substantial nursing home. The family business flourished under her energetic hand, but in time, as she reached retirement age, her son took over and she moved out with her husband into a smaller, modern ranch house. Not long afterward, finding the walls closer than she expected, Gladys decided to go to college. She called me for an appointment.

We first met in the garret of a refurbished apartment house that served as office for the local community college. Sitting diagonally across the cluttered table from her, I marveled at the energy of this wiry, gray-blonde woman who had done so much with her life. She told me she wanted to be a teacher now that her work with old folks was over. I explained that it would require a stiff slate of classes and practice teaching to become certified. It could take her several years.

"Oh no, I haven't got that long!" she laughed with dismay. And although we shifted to more realistic goals—taking children into her home to teach, working as a teacher's aide, helping with the local Headstart program—it seemed to me that she had seized on work with children more out of a sense that such work would be convenient and socially acceptable than out of any deeply rooted inner calling.

Yet despite her diffidence, Gladys spoke with striking certainty about what she believed to be right and wrong. At one point she mentioned a neighbor who recently took her own life.

"It was so wrong," she said, shaking her head. "I just can't understand what would make a person want to do that." I agreed with her that it seems a shame to us but added, "Well, Gladys, sometimes it is hard to judge a person until we can see through their eyes."

She gave me a sidelong look, somewhere between disapproval and puzzlement.

"Well, that sort of thing is plain wrong. The Lord gives us our lives, and it is not ours to decide a thing like that!" she replied, fire in her eye. Gladys is a deeply religious Charismatic Christian. I backed off. Not a time to press, I thought. We passed on to more pleasant topics.

After considerable discussion, we decided not to set a firm goal for the time being. She needed to explore other possibilities, so I asked her what interested her, what she wanted to learn more about, practical considerations aside. She was silent a moment, then turned back to me with a touch of irritation.

"How do I know what I'm supposed to study?" she snorted. "You're the expert. You tell me." I winced, as I always did when someone gave me that kind of power. I explained the broad program requirements, and after further conversation she agreed to warm up by writing about her experiences with the nursing home. It would give her a chance to sharpen her writing skills and pull together her past.

Several days later I ran into her son. "Mom's all excited about her study with you," he told me. "But you know," he added confidentially, "I don't know what she's doing it for. She can't benefit from a college degree. We keep telling her, 'We love you the way you are.'"

I might have recognized at the time the significance of that event, but I did not. I was still sure that given her own need to change, the power of the subject matter, and my mentorship, Gladys would inevitably grow as she should. What difference would her son's passing remark make?

Two years and a number of diverse courses later, nearing graduation, she invites me for breakfast. It is an archetypal Vermont fall morning. The crackling maples, fanned in a fresh morning wind cold out of the north, flare against the blue sky. For years I have watched autumn come and go in these parts, and always it catches me off guard; always I am staggered by the outrageous gall of these trees, flouting the good taste of summer with such wild extravagance.

Gladys greets me warmly as my briefcase and I appear at the door.

"I'll have the muffins ready in just a moment," she says, setting a cup of coffee on the lace doily in front of me. I leaf through her file as I wait, recalling our long passage together. The first writing exercise about her life in the nursing home is blossoming into a full-fledged book now. Twice more, she has worked on it with different teachers, expanding, honing, tightening. The first draft was riddled with clichés and homilies, crudely organized, yet shot with moments of great clarity and power. Now, as we approach her final year, she is investigating how to get it printed.

The muffins arrive, fat and fluffy. Gladys joins me, and after commenting on the lovely morning, she gets right to business.

"I'm still mad about Arthur," she says. "I've never gotten a C before. All through school I always got good grades. I felt disgraced. I felt like quitting."

My stomach drops. I had hoped it would be forgotten. Last spring a local writer worked with her on the book and was less than generous. We spoke about it at the time and, although I was sympathetic, I agreed that the grade was probably appropriate. "I refuse to treat her as a special case just because she's on social security!" he fumed. "That's just the trouble with these programs. You bleeding hearts do no favors for these students by relaxing standards for them. Her writing is too personal; she's got to get some distance from it if she ever wants to be good." To my rather feeble rejoinder that good writing ought to be concrete, he replied, "Yes. But it must be *artful* detail. Good writers don't just blurt it out; they *think* about what they choose to blurt out. Gladys still needs to think about her work, and you can't do that until you can distance yourself from it."

Gladys is looking at me now, almost pleading, her eyes red. "I mean, what does he know about nursing homes? He's probably never even been in one; I've run one all my life! How can he give me a C about my life's work?" The tears come now and I reach over to touch her hand lightly. "I'm worth more than that!" she declares, tempering her discouragement with outrage.

"I know, Gladys," I answer. "Of course you are." I'm not good at these scenes, and as it often does, my mind clogs and then spins off. *She is so concrete,* I think. She's just not separating form from content; she thinks he is criticizing *her* when he is talking about her writing style. She still hasn't made that leap from *being* her ideas to *having* them; she is still embedded in her experience. He's absolutely right; she *is* her experience, she doesn't *have* it. No wonder she feels so hurt by criticism! Who wouldn't if they felt their whole being was under fire, rather than how they do a particular thing?

"Let's look at the paper, Gladys," I suggest. She rummages around in a file, pulls it out, and we go through it together. At my suggestion, the instructor asked her to write a section on the "ideal" way to care for the aged. We hoped to get her to think critically, to draw a set of concrete inferences from a purely hypothetical base.

It didn't work. She simply wrote about all the ways she would improve her existing home if she had unlimited money. For the most part, the improvements called for *more,* not *different.* Where she did call for qualitative changes, they seemed essentially random; there were no discernible principles underlying them. It was all very well for some people to be idealistic, she wrote, but she was too busy for that. To run a good nursing home, a person had to be practical. It appeared simply beyond her to imagine that nursing homes might not have to exist at all—that some *ideal* of care for the aged might have power beyond her present reality. To do that, she would have to uproot her most basic assumptions, question the premise on which she had built her entire life. Who among us can do that? It was too much, and the result was simply to make her feel like a failure. The power of authority was still immense, the master code still veiled.

In my frustration, I thrust the paper aside and launch into a sermon. She needs to loosen her ideas from everyday practical realities, I tell her. The way she has written about the experiences of some of her patients is lovely, and I explain to her how important it is to practice seeing things through the eyes of others without letting her own judgments intervene.

"Look, Gladys," I blurt, feeling defeated and righteous, "You're in the big leagues now. You are after a real education, not a damned degree. Part of that means that you need to get better at *thinking*—thinking critically, thinking abstractly, thinking imaginatively, thinking about what you do, not just acting! Among other things," verging on sarcasm now, "this means that you need to be willing to question your own beliefs about what is right and wrong—and just maybe be prepared to let *go* of some of them."

This tough, diminutive woman half again my age looks up at me, her eyes dry now, hardening, "Are you gonna teach me to do that?"

Knocked off kilter, I sputter petulantly, "Well I hope so!" Then, apologetically I add, "At least, I hope you'll learn to."

"Let me get you another blueberry muffin," she announces, pushing her chair back abruptly and heading for the kitchen. I stare stupidly at the plate. Clunk.

While she is out rummaging in the kitchen, her husband, Frank, appears. We exchange wisdom about the weather for a moment and then he blurts out, "I don't see what the hell she wants this damned degree for. It ain't going to do her a damned bit of good." But before I have a chance to reply, Gladys is back and he is gone. I forget the incident and try to pick up the mess I've made.

"I'm sorry about my lecture. I hope I didn't come down too hard."

"Oh, no. That's your job, isn't it?" she replies, mischief back in her eye.

"Yes," I acknowledge, "I suppose you're right in a way. But it's more than that, Gladys. I really care about how you're doing. I want you to do the best you can. It pains me to see you hurt like that, but I also want you to make the most of your education."

She pats my hand. Her recovery has also put me back in my place. At that moment I notice the small, brass crucifix on the wall. The words are out of my mouth before I have a chance to catch them.

"Now there was a real dreamer," I nod to the wall. "That man was the idealist of all idealists. It's a good thing for all of us that he was willing to go beyond 'practical concerns.'"

She glances at the wall, then back to her empty coffee cup. For a long while, she says nothing. Her face looks suddenly tired. Then, much more softly than before, she says, "Well, you know, you get out on this degree road and you travel and travel and travel and after a while you just want to get it over with."

"Sure, I know," I reply, thinking of my own long years on that road. "But where's the journey taking you? What's it all for, finally?"

"To be happy, I guess. Isn't that what life's about? So we can just be happy?"

"Maybe, in a way. But I don't think that's what Jesus wanted, what he died for. Don't you think he wanted more for us than that?"

To be happy, I repeat to myself, holding the frustration in this time. Look on the bright side. Be respectable. Put on a happy face. Fit in. Conform. See yourself through others' eyes, never your own. Deny your own needs, deny pain, deny darkness. I remember how she shied away from writing deeply about her own suffering during those years of struggle, how in an art class she refused to sketch a portrait of her aging husband. "Why would I want to do that?" she told her teacher. "He used to be such a handsome man." Always she wanted to draw what she *ought* to see, never what her eyes told her. "Gladys," I want to shout. "You are missing so much! Why do this to yourself?" But I let it go. There's no sermon left in me. Leave her alone, Larry. Just leave her be.

"Well, maybe," she murmurs softly, "maybe Jesus did want more...." At once she shunts it aside. "But that's just my personality, I guess. I just want to get this degree thing out of the way."

"And then what?"

"Well, for a little while I'd just take a rest. But then," without irony she chuckles, "I know I'd wish I was back in it again."

"It sounds a little like you're racing through the woods on a lovely spring day just so you can get to the other side," I offer. "You could just say, 'Wait a minute. There's no reason to get to the other side. I think I'll just enjoy it here. There's a nice flower; here's a nice tree. What a beautiful sky!'"

"Yes, I guess that's true," she sighs. "My daughter tries to tell me that; everybody tries to tell me, but I don't listen. I've always been like this since way back when."

I push back my chair, hook an arm over the back, and speak to the ceiling. "Gladys, what if you were to imagine that you were at the last day of your life—you know, the next day it's going to be all over—what would you like to be able to say? Is the point of living just so you can make it to the end of your life?"

The silence holds us both for a long moment. Then, softly, almost whispering, she says, "You're right. It isn't. You're right."

Leaning forward again, I tell her, "Gladys, this isn't something I'm saying just because of the stupid degree program. It's something we all need to remember, me included. Especially me." I stop, unable to hold her eye. She doesn't need this, I think. And I know I have some listening to do, myself.

We are silent a long time, each looking at the floor between us. Finally, she heaves a long sigh, looks up at me, and asks, "Well, Larry, how many credits will I have to take to finish?" And we're back to earth.

Some time later, as I drive back between the garish maple walls, I wonder what I'm doing, whether I have a right to intrude so deeply into this heroic woman's life. She is so richly embedded in her world of family, neighbors, work, so firmly held by the years of unquestioning struggle, so rewarded by the comfort of a neat and secure home. She will change no further; why should she? Hasn't she reached her dream?

But I know it's not so simple. Happiness, she says, is what life is all about, yet it continues to elude her. Why else would it be so important to her? Why else would she be running so hard? Why else would the tears come so readily when she speaks of those years? What's missing? Is it something she lost, or has yet to find? And where am I in all that? Wouldn't she be better off if I just let her alone, let her have the damned degree, forget about the education? The questions go unanswered. But the morning is delicious.

A few months later, Gladys completed her book. She asked her former art teacher to illustrate it and had it privately printed shortly after she graduated (Marcotte, 1984). It was reviewed in the local paper and was a great source of pride to her and her family. There, pictured on the back cover, she strides confidently toward us, graduation robes proudly flaring, diploma in hand, beaming with delight. She made it.

A year later her husband died. Three weeks later, Gladys followed him.[1]

Smoldering Questions

It has been years now since that blueberry muffin morning, and I am far from Vermont. Yet the questions struck in that encounter still smoulder. That frustration, for instance—I have felt it with other students as well, as have most teachers. To be sure, part of it comes simply from our own desire for our students to succeed. But I cannot help noticing the sarcasm, even the tinge of anger, in my reaction to what I saw as Gladys's complacent myopia, her determined conventionality, and it makes me uneasy. Some part of me felt betrayed by Gladys's "refusal to grow," and therein lies, I think, a caution for all of us. For all of its virtues, one of the great liabilities of strong conviction is a tendency to cast ourselves as heroes in our own stories and thus armor against the very openness that we are trying to awaken in our students. When does our zeal as teachers proceed more from our own needs to "teach" than theirs to learn?

But in addition to challenging our own hubris, the story asks something too, I think, about the social context of human development. Most adults are enmeshed in a rich network of relationships, in which we mentors play only one part. Our students also sport spouses, partners, children, aging parents, friends, a work world, reputations, habits, and deep convictions, each bringing a particular tug to the web. As we come to understand the larger context of development, our own inflation may snap into truer focus and we may become less vulnerable to feeling frustrated or betrayed. Moreover, we are in a better position to work with and encourage those naturally occurring "mentoring environments" (Parks, 1992; Kegan, 1994; Daloz, Keen, Keen, and Parks, 1996) from which they learn who they are and who they can become. The story of how these webs of belonging both enhance and inhibit the growth of adult learners is only beginning to come into view.[2]

Quite understandably, breakfast conversations like these may seem far removed from the proper terrain of education, and Gladys's story stirs a nest of questions, some practical, some philosophical. Each carries beneath its sting an important prompt to further reflection that, unwelcome as it may be, keeps the discussion alive and the journey fresh.

Most obviously, *how realistic is this kind of mentoring for most teachers?* Who has time for conversations like this when they have more than a hundred regular students, dozens of advisees, and endless committee meetings—not to mention the article they promised to complete a month ago? Right. None of us does, myself included. I interviewed Gladys with support from a research grant. Still, there must be something we can do.

Let's acknowledge that not everyone can become a Gladys or an Eric for us; we can afford to give precious few of our students that kind of time and energy. Yet if every teacher made a point of spending at least some real time with at least some students, our colleges and universities might be better places for genuine learning to occur. I recall a teacher once who must have been easily as busy as I am now, who consciously set aside office hours for appointments with each of his students "so I can get to know you." Simple as it was, he was the only professor I ever had who did that, and I have never forgotten.

Interestingly, in a study of 570 students across a range of ages, Harvard's Richard Light asked of his voluminous data the question, "Is there any common theme that faculty members can use to help students, and indeed that students can use to help themselves?" Here is what he found: "All the specific findings point to, and illustrate, one main idea. It is that students who get the most out of college, who grow the most academically, and who are happiest, organize their time to include interpersonal activities with faculty members, or with fellow students, built around substantive, academic work" (Light, 1992, p. 32).

In addition, we can set our minds to inventing ways of creating fuller mentoring environments on and off our campuses so that the burden does not fall so heavily on our shoulders alone but may be shared among students, faculty, and others as well. Surely one place to begin is by experimenting in our own classes, trying out new components to encourage development, or designing new courses with multiple disciplines and perspectives.

Another place to look is at the advising role itself. How might it be reframed to incorporate *and value* the principles of mentoring as well as simply allocating students and credit hours? Beyond that, we would do well to examine the structures of higher education itself that seem to make it so difficult for us to engage our students in the kind of dialogue that we long for and know lies at the heart of our work.

For some, conversations like mine with Gladys may always seem little more than hand-holding. *What is the place of subject matter in all of this?* It may be fine for, say, an English course, but how does this apply to a concrete subject like bookkeeping?

Indeed, subject matter is enormously important. To emphasize development is in no way to deny the importance of content. But there is no such thing as content apart from how it is understood; given the clear evidence that modes of understanding evolve in human beings, it is valuable to recognize how our students are understanding our subject matter.

Nor does teaching from a developmental stance require radical individualization of the curriculum. It is richly textured rather than finely tuned teaching that allows the most room for growth and learning. Perhaps some subjects appear to lend themselves more readily to serving intellectual development than others, but all knowledge exists in some context. The developmentally conscious teacher strives to make the context explicit for students to recognize that even the most mundane facts take their meaning from some setting. As a wise financial officer once observed, "even a bookkeeper must make decisions about what story she wants the figures to tell." Some of the best work with Perry's developmental model has been conducted by mathematics professors (Knefelkamp, 1998).

Others fear that paying attention to our students' development verges too much on psychotherapy. "What if we surface deep problems in our students—or ourselves? We are not trained for that." True. Anna Freud (1935) notwithstanding, teachers are not and probably should not be trained in psychotherapy; clearly we need to know when we are out of our depth. But simply listening with compassion and insight to the pain and struggles of our students is not psychotherapy. To share our common humanity with another person is a gift of birth, not of training, and the capacity to care for and about our students is available to all of us. Through the recognition that careful listening affords by creating a space where our students can name their struggles, mentors can help students heal. As Bill Perry used to say, "If my pain has not had a place to live, how can I let go and move on?" Is it too much to ask that we accompany our students in this way?

Over the years, I have come to believe that the line between learning and healing is finer than we might think. A disturbing number of adult students come to us with wounds that inhibit their ability to learn. Just as a physical injury might constrain our bodily flexibility, might not our capacity for further learning be limited by emotional wounding? Might not learning itself be a form of healing? Within the obvious limits, perhaps a deeper understanding of the dynamics of healing would inform our knowledge of learning.

Finally, in recent years serious questions have been raised about the fundamental assumptions underlying transformative learning and adult development theory.[3] "Isn't the very idea of development a linear, Western idea?" asks the postmodernist, charging that to claim universality for any definition of growth is illegitimate intellectual "hegemony." The developmentalist retorts that the postmodernist is simply an absolute relativist, taking delight in deconstructing everything in sight like a three-year-old with a meat cleaver.

But the discussion is considerably more profound than that (see Mezirow, Pietrykowski, and Inglis's exchange in *Adult Education Quarterly*, 1998), and whenever I have listened to the criticisms (Broughton, 1987; Pietrykowski, 1996; Merriam and Caffarella, 1999) I have learned much. Critical pedagogy, for instance, reminds us that the power ratios between ourselves and our students are a function of larger economic and social forces that shape both ourselves and our students. These forces themselves must be confronted if we are to see any socially significant transformation among our students. Were I to write this book again, there would be far more attention to the issues of poverty and oppression that surrounded me right there in Vermont.

Moreover, most developmental theory has focused largely on the individual removed from social context. To some extent, this book does that; the primary emphasis, for instance, is on the mentor-student pair rather than on the broader influence of mentoring environments. This is a limitation, as anyone would know who has seen a graduation ceremony of adult learners. All at once we see the extraordinary range of family and friends who make up the invisible webs of support and challenge that hold our students (Crowell, 1996). Anne's story in Chapter Seven attempts to recognize this phenomenon, and I hope the moral of Gladys's story is clear. In missing the significance of her son's and husband's comments, I failed to recognize that I was asking too much of her. She lacked support at the most fundamental levels. In the years since, as a result of the *Common Fire* study and a generalized critique of individualism (Bellah and others, 1985), not to mention my passing years and partnership with Sharon Parks, I have come increasingly to recognize the deep truth—and, frankly, the joy—of our human dependence on one another.

Early developmental and transformative learning theory have been criticized as well for placing too much emphasis on cognition rather than on the full spectrum of emotional, moral, spiritual, and sensory experiences that may accompany change. For the most part, I think this criticism misses the mark. Few of the approaches to development that I am aware of would question the importance of these factors. But most have taken pains to rest their theories not at the cognitive level but beneath that, at the level of meaning making itself. As Kegan (1982), Courtenay, Merriam, and Reeves (1998), and Mezirow (forthcoming) point out, it is our tacit epistemology that shapes what we feel about our experience.

At the bottom of all these questions is a healthy recognition that we all carry cultural baggage, perhaps most of all those who claim to have none. What matters is the willingness to acknowledge our own assumptions; listen for those of others; and continue working at more adequate, permeable, and inclusive ways of knowing. Appropriate educational growth, as Dewey put it long ago, must always create the conditions for further growth (1938).

In the final analysis, teaching is a moral act. We can no more escape from our values than from gravity. Like it or not, we teach what we believe. Although we need not teach *only* what we believe, when we do affirm our convictions we owe it to our students to do so in light of their right to differ as well as their responsibility to recognize their interdependence with others. Bronson Alcott had a point when he said that good teachers "have no disciples,"[4] but if our students cannot recognize where they learned this, then we may have failed them. It is time, then, as the journey winds to a close, for me to set forth my own convictions about the purpose of education and why mentoring matters.

Education as Care

The proper aim of education is to promote significant learning. Significant learning entails development. Development means successively asking broader and deeper questions of the relationship between oneself and the world. This is as true for first graders as graduate students, for fledgling artists as graying accountants.

A good education ought to help people become both more receptive to and more discriminating about the world: seeing, feeling, and understanding more, yet sorting the pertinent from the peripheral with ever finer touch, increasingly able to integrate what they see and to make meaning of it in ways that enhance their ability to go on growing. To imagine otherwise, to act as though learning were simply a matter of stacking facts on top of one another, makes as much sense as thinking one can learn a language by memorizing a dictionary. Ideas, as Whitehead observed years ago, only come to life when they root in the mind of a learner.

Why Mentors Matter

This book is dedicated to the proposition that enabling ideas to root in the minds of learners is an act of care and is not without risk. As we develop, we progressively take apart and put together the structures that give our lives meaning. And although the stage on which we are standing may grow daily less adequate, it can be frightening to think of dismantling it, for we imagine it to be all we have. To build fresh structures, we must reach out ahead of ourselves, and we fear the chasm below. Viewed thus, success at the educational venture is less a function of brains than of balance and courage. It means being willing to doubt when it would be safer to believe, and to believe when we would rather doubt. Like walking, it invokes a deliberate forward thrust, throwing us off center, demanding compensation. Each step in its own way threatens us with annihilation.

What allows us, ultimately, to take the risk is faith that we will survive. At the heart of development lies a delicate balance between trust and agency—a capacity to let go, to receive clear-eyed what the world has to offer, and also to assert our own power, to declare our right to be here. We simply do not learn these things in a vacuum. We need other people to show us, to accompany us, to hold the hope and steady our faith that we will make it. And we also need people with whom to practice: parents, friends, children, teachers. For in relationship, we both form and heal what we come again and again to name our self. This is why mentors and mentoring environments play such a key role. Without adequate support, many learners—like Gladys—may decide to stay where they are.

Thus, when we no longer consider learning to be primarily acquisition of knowledge, we can no longer view teaching as merely the bestowal of it. If learning is about growth and growth requires both trust and agency, then teaching is about recognizing and nourishing the conditions in which trust and agency can flourish (Palmer, 1998). Teaching is thus preeminently an act of care. We must be concerned not simply with how much knowledge our students may acquire but also with how they are making meaning of that knowledge and how it is affecting their capacity to go on learning. As mentors, we share responsibility for this process. Like guides, we walk at times ahead of our students, at times beside them; at times, we follow their lead. In sensing where to walk lies our art, for as we support our students in their struggle, challenge them toward their best, and cast light on the road ahead, we do so in the name of our respect for their potential and our care for their growth. As Dante's Virgil knew, to teach is to point the way through the fire.

But this is not enough. Virgil also called attention to "the singing from beyond." Effective mentors add value and moral content to the relationship. They inspire a sense of worthy purpose. For young adults in particular but also for older adults seeking a new direction, the mentor holds the promise of something greater, of a new, fuller, even *wiser* participation in the world.

If we are to realize our own potential as mentors, our work is to help our students see beyond the status quo and dare to imagine a more adequate world. We do this not merely by helping them gain critical purchase on the headlong rush of the culture, but more, by helping them form a moral center, a basis for commitment grounded in recognition of our shared interdependence with all of life. If they are to be more than simply happier ("Is that all it's about, Gladys, just to be happy?") but are to participate as agents in the transformation of the world, then we must offer them a constructive alternative by pointing to and living a more adequate possibility ourselves.

We are, says Erikson, "the teaching species." The drive toward generativity is an essential antidote to the threat of stagnation in the adult years. Without the affirmation born of extending ourselves beyond self-preservation, without the impulse to further this wisp of life in a dark universe, the questions that might enable us to move on toward something like wisdom would go unasked. We need our students as much as they need us.

So, finally, we come around to ourselves again. We too are in movement. If we are to teach with life and vigor and hope, then we must recognize that we teach not just for our students and not just for the world, but for ourselves as well. It has always felt a bit trite to me when teachers declare that they learn as much from their students as their students do from them. And yet when we encourage students to learn about the things that truly matter to them, they are forever finding new material, recounting new experiences, introducing new content to our own understanding of our subject matter. It is no exaggeration to say that the bulk of my reading list comes from my students. Moreover, because each student has a different way of hearing what we have to say, we find ourselves reframing our words and our knowledge over and over. In that dialogue, the knowledge changes, and we change.

As I learned from Gladys, our students teach us about ourselves—sometimes more than we want to learn. The experience can be at once confirming and humbling, for not only do they teach us our strengths but also our limits. *Humility* shares its root with *humus,* or soil. Our feet, in the end, *are* of clay, and sometimes both partners need to recognize that this is good; clay is of the earth where our feet belong. And it is from the earth that new seeds grow.

On Painting Naturally

I recall that when I first began to think seriously of writing about Mentor's role in the drama of human development, I struggled to balance the intensity I felt from my own experience with the detachment necessary for a sense of perspective. I was aware of the shortcomings of too personal a pursuit of knowledge; yet I knew also that my greatest source of strength lay within me, in my own insight and passion. I remembered Robert Pirsig's remark that if you want to paint a perfect picture, you must first "make yourself perfect and then just paint naturally" (1974, pp. 324–325). It seemed to me that my path led that way. "Best concentrate on the work," I told myself, "then write about it."

For the most part I have tried to do that. It should be obvious that I am a good distance yet from perfection, and I have long since rejected this as an attainable or even desirable goal. But still there is a lesson here. Good teaching rests neither in accumulating a shelfful of knowledge nor in developing a repertoire of skills. In the end, good teaching lies in willingness to care for what happens in our students, ourselves, and the space between us. Good teaching is a certain kind of stance, I think—a stance of both receptivity and presence.

But receptive presence is hard, active work. We are not *simply* nodding and smiling, holding and comforting. We *do* demand. As educators, we do have a responsibility to maintain standards and hold high expectations for our students. Education is legitimately a social as well as a personal affair; fairness is fully a part of our work. Yet fairness is not all there is to the game. There are times when justice for all must be tempered by compassion for one. Human *being* is both hard and soft. Care is both just and loving.

Because neither students nor teachers are inert objects, because we are reflective and growing beings responsive to our own ontology, because for all of us the world is emergent, teaching and learning are finally about relationship. In the dialogue between mentor and student lie most of the educational questions worth asking. "Give me a log hut, with only a simple bench; Mark

Hopkins on one end and I on the other," said President James Garfield of his former mentor, "and you may have all the buildings, apparatus, and libraries without him" (Rudolph, 1962). Most of us might trade the hut and bench for a book or two, but there is a certain truth in this wistful rhetoric. For more than any other factor, it is the partnership of teacher and student that finally determines the value of an education. In the nurture of that partnership lies the mentor's art.

Afterword

Mentorship and the Cultivation of Wisdom: An Invocation to Athena

> FOOL: *If thou wert my fool, nuncle, I'd have thee beaten for being old before thy time.*
>
> LEAR: *How's that?*
>
> FOOL: *Thou shouldst not have been old before thou hadst been wise.*
>
> —WILLIAM SHAKESPEARE, *KING LEAR*, 1.5.35–37

I began writing this book toward the end of my fourth decade; I am now in my eighth. In a real sense the book and I have grown older together. It began as a quest to understand better how my students were growing and what difference, if any, we mentors were making in their lives. The quest concludes with a question: *At this time in history, when our world is in such a fragile place, how might we best cultivate in our students and ourselves the wisdom to match the times?*

In Chapter Nine, I wrote that teaching is a moral act, "preeminently an act of care." The proper aim of education, I suggested, is to promote development, and such development ought to be toward discriminating more finely yet growing increasingly able to integrate our experience and to make meaning of it in ways that enhance our ability to go on developing. Almost thirty years later, that still makes sense to me: education ought to infuse us with the desire and ability to make increasingly comprehensive meaning of an ever more complex world. But what does that mean for us as mentors? *What is the telos of mentorship?* It's a big question, and I want to suggest a big answer. I propose that our work as mentors is ultimately nothing less than *the cultivation of wisdom*—in our students, of course, but necessarily in ourselves as well. For in the end, if we are to serve well as mentors, we are going to have to become wise ourselves—or at least to risk the journey toward wisdom. In this Afterword, I invite you to accompany me on an exploration of what such a journey might look like. What does it mean to become a wise mentor?

As Mentor is the embodiment of Athena, goddess of wisdom, we expect him to be wise. At the outset of *The Odyssey*, he sends young Telemakhos off on a quest to find his father and discover his purpose in life. "Reason and heart will give you words," Mentor tells him, "and a spirit will counsel others. I should say the gods were never indifferent in your life." Let me begin, then, by casting myself as Telemakhos.

I count three classic mentors in my life. All, as I knew them, were wise men, though wise in different ways. And each was flawed in his own way as well. None was perfect, but at least as I have constructed them, they stand as men to emulate. Like Mentor, they bore some essence of wisdom, some gift of that clear-eyed goddess herself, that they made available to me. And I cannot help noticing that the gifts they gave me were exactly those that I needed at that particular time in my life. Fred Rudolph, a college professor, ignited my '60s idealism, sending me off to the Peace Corps and a lifelong commitment to the common good; Harry Barnes, a master diplomat and peacemaker, brought reason and heart to that idealism with a personal and respectful regard that I still cherish today. And Adam Curle, an internationally esteemed pacifist and mediator, lived within an imagination of spiritually informed wisdom that continues to inspire me beyond his death several years ago. The gods have not been indifferent in my life.

I am quite certain that these men thought of themselves as ordinary people; it was I who dubbed them "mentor." Did I just conjure them up? I think the answer is yes and no. "If mentors did not exist, we would have to invent them," I wrote in these pages, and from this end of my life it appears that, sure enough, at least in part, we do. Now finding myself well beyond where my mentors were when they blessed my life with their wisdom, I want to try to get some language around that gift, harness some of its qualities, imagine how wisdom actually becomes embodied as words, gestures, silences, a certain kind of *presence*.

Imagining Wisdom

For almost as long as I can remember, I have been drawn to images of wisdom. As a boy reading *Captain Marvel* comics, I was fascinated by the wise old man, Shazam, whose name when spoken could turn the chubby and feckless Billy Batson into mighty Captain Marvel. The idea that I might have such power inside me was intoxicating; it's no surprise that I was later so enchanted by Athena's magic. For those of us who respond to the call of mentorship, the archetype of wisdom can exercise a powerful tug.

Wisdom. We hear the word often. It is used almost as an incantation and sometime accolade: "she radiates a kind of wisdom," "he is one of the wisest people I know," "thank you for sharing your wisdom." We speak of the wisdom of the ages, of wise leaders, of Nature's wisdom, even of the wisdom of a child. And some of us long for it ourselves. What would it mean, we wonder, to be wise—to possess such wisdom? Is it something we can acquire like a gemstone—some bauble for the mind? Can we get it from books? Do we learn it from others? From experience? Or is it, as Piet Hein wryly observed, "the booby prize given when you've been unwise"? Does it ripen from within, or do we slip it on like some hooded robe? Or perhaps it's a matter of sheer grace—a gift outright that may or may not descend on us, something beyond our choice.

We feel we can recognize it when we see it, but it can be maddeningly difficult to define. Curious, I began asking friends to describe a wise person they knew. "She has a way of being able to touch the heart of things," thought one. "He's never impulsive," said another; "he always takes a long view." "It's not a performance," speculated a third. "The people I think of are *real;* they see things the rest of us don't." Another recalled, "He had such a big heart, such compassion and commitment to justice." Said yet another, "It's an uncommon grasp of some deep truth. She connects the dots; she is mindfully present; she's amazingly accepting, but also savvy, not naive."

That all felt true enough, and useful, but then I decided to ask people who were not quite so much like me. "He takes no guff; he knows what's right and acts decisively," snapped one. Another purred, "She lives according to Scripture; she is the purest person I know, and she always has a wise saying to share." Or another: "He is a truly self-made man who did it his way without depending on anyone else." And another: "He would give me advice that I could apply to my life, for everyday living, that was *practical*. He can understand those fancy words, but he doesn't use them on me." Others added "they can tell right from wrong," "they speak common sense," or "they are loyal and respect tradition." For these folks, wisdom had quite different qualities.

Like beauty, wisdom is in the eye of the beholder, and what to some may be a staggering insight, to others may be patently obvious, and to still others may be incomprehensible nonsense. My little experiment probably yielded more information about my informants than about the topic. Wisdom, it seems, does not glisten from the fixed turrets of the Celestial City; it is a shape-shifter, taking myriad forms in a variety of circumstances.

Still, as I thought more about these responses, I realized that we most often call people wise who have opened a new possibility, some larger way of seeing, inviting a more spacious consciousness. They seem able to name a reality that we recognize to be true but for which we have somehow lacked the language.

It's a chestnut of cognitive-developmental theory that we seem able to recognize, but not articulate, a way of knowing just ahead of where we are. That's why, I suspect, wisdom seems to shimmer a bit and why when someone illuminates the territory just ahead for us, we call the person wise. This helps explain why people's descriptions of wisdom can seem so diverse. If you are in the right place, you get it. If not, you frown and look around for someone who is *really* wise.

What's more, most of us agree that no single person is totally wise or compassionate all the time. Gandhi, for example, was unkind to his wife. Wisdom seems to show up in differing people in differing amounts as though in some sense it can be separated from its purveyor. But if you can separate it, is it only in the mind? And in whose mind anyway?

"Well, you know it's all projection," I said to my spouse and colleague, Sharon Parks, as we were discussing Abraham Lincoln's particular form of wisdom—his compassion, his humor, his staggering resilience. "I mean, no one ever actually measures up to whatever wisdom is projected onto them. Lincoln had his shadow too."

"Of course," she answered, "but what's significant is that we have such hunger for wisdom." And that's the point, I think. We have such hunger for wisdom, for some way to make worthy meaning of the variously excruciating ugliness, dazzling wonder, or sheer bedevilment that presents itself to us daily. Understandably we cast about for some evidence that the capacity to grasp it all might exist on this plane, that someone living and accessible might manifest this elusive quality of profound understanding so we can know that it's finally possible to make sense of all this mess. That's what Emerald was seeking when we met in that roadhouse back in Chapter One. "It seems everything is in chaos," she said over coffee. As her mentor, I had not created the chaos, but I had surely stirred it up, and she rightly looked to me to help her "find out what the hinge is, what the chaos hinges on."

That's the mentor's job, I think. We know full well that not all who seek mentors seek wisdom, nor need they do so. But if we have done our work, we have accompanied our students into the wilderness, wondered with them about what they see, and perhaps asked questions to help them find their way around in it. Over time they might even construct their own maps and make a path through. And yet we mentors live in the same wilderness as our students; we just hope that we understand its ways better, that Emerald's chaos has become our complexity, that we have become perhaps a bit wiser. So it helps if we recognize the time we have spent there ourselves and retain the insight that led us, if not out, then at least to a clearing.

Wisdom as Meaning-Making

"Organisms organize," Bill Perry used to say, "and what humans organize is meaning." At some point we realize that the more we make meaning of what is around us, the more chaos we recognize beyond us. We evolve ways of knowing to handle complexity, and then these same epistemologies reveal yet more complexity. There is no end to it. Perhaps wisdom is a word for a particularly elegant way of organizing meaning—a dawning recognition that we all live somewhere amid what we believe to be true, what we imagine might be true, and chaos.

Among the chief contributors to that chaos these days are the tectonic changes wrought by electronic technology over the past several decades. The participatory nature of the Internet has meant that the old controllers of information—newspapers, television networks, book publishers, motion picture studios—have lost their monopolies to a deluge of chatter from blogs, e-zines, social network sites, and whatever Google turns up next. While this has democratized information, it has also inevitably given us a new challenge: how to distinguish the treasure from the trash.

Inundated by a tsunami of information and the unharnessed relativism that accompanies it, we should not be surprised that in a desperate scramble for a tree trunk to grasp or a height to climb, many people turn to an array of religious, economic, social, judicial, and political fundamentalisms—anything solid that promises to make sense of things. Under such conditions, the immediate respite of an ideological foothold is understandably preferable to the flood beneath us. It matters less that it be true or applicable to a changed world than that it make us feel safe. Sweet reason yields to willful ignorance—a fear-born determination not to see what is right before our eyes.

As mentors, our task is to give our Emeralds the insight and courage to resist the retreat to such oversimplifications, to lean into their particular chaos, even as we continue to lean into ours. There is plenty of chaos to go around, and in the midst of great change and intensified complexity, we need the capacity to hold steady. This is precisely *not* the time to fall into easy ideologies or revert to simple answers. More than ever, we are enjoined to face the complexity clear-eyed, to invoke forms of wisdom equal to the bewildering challenge before us. If we are to convey to our students the wisdom they need in times like these, we must, ourselves, develop that wisdom—a larger consciousness, we might say, for the new commons. So let me begin speculating about what that consciousness might look like with an image from a land where, as a young man, I was sent by Mentor.

Our Shared Humanity

One morning, after several days of trekking alone in the back-country of Nepal, I slogged up out of a steamy valley, thirsty and famished, before finally coming upon a house where I might reasonably find nourishment. I called out at the gate, and after a time an ancient figure emerged from the shadows, her wrinkled face wreathed in a scarf held in a leathery hand. Might I buy something to eat? I asked. Her face broke into a toothless smile, and she gestured toward a mat. "*Au, Nani,*" she said. "*Bas, ta.*" Come in, sit down. Resting against my pack as she rummaged about inside the house, I realized that instead of calling me "Sahib," as was the universal custom, she had addressed me as *Nani*, "Little One," as if I were simply one of the family. To be acknowledged in such a familiar way was something I had rarely felt in Nepal even in the village where I had lived for two years. Handing me a wooden crock of millet beer, she asked me about my family. Did I have brothers and sisters? Was I married? Did I have children? Where was my country? I left some time later refreshed but also touched in some way that has remained with me for almost fifty years: What did this old woman have that empowered her to look upon a complete and perhaps frightening stranger as simply a fellow human being in need of nourishment? Was it naiveté or a kind of wisdom?

Many of the people we studied in *Common Fire* (Daloz, Keen, Keen, and Parks, 1996) seemed to have this capacity to see through superficial differences to a shared humanity. In such people, the capacity for empathy was richly developed, often through forms of personal suffering that, rather than hardening, had opened their hearts to the pain of others. We now know that humans are endowed with "mirror neurons," special receptors that enable us actually to experience the feelings of others vicariously. And we also know that our life experiences powerfully affect the degree to which we enable or shut off those neurons. Most of us have the potential for deep compassion, but we vary greatly in how we develop and exercise it. What habits of the heart and mind had enabled this old woman to move through a lifetime of harsh poverty, of relentless struggle, of children born and lost before their time, and yet retain such tenderness?

As I replayed this scene in my memory, I realized that wisdom is more readily conferred than claimed. Many people we call wise seem to embody a deep humility, and it is others who declare them wise; in fact, to claim the mantle for oneself generally betrays our hubris. Humility, as Socrates famously knew, is the first step toward true wisdom. This is not a false modesty but the result of a life-time of *positive disillusionment,* of noticing when one's illusions fail to conform with one's experience, and adjusting accordingly—a kind of fierce commitment to the truth of one's own experience. In the wise, I think, what we call humility is simply the grounded knowing that we are all human, ultimately finite. It is out of that groundedness, a radical knowing of our common humanity, that we are able to connect deeply with those different from ourselves. Such generosity of spirit is often accompanied by a kind of for-bearance, not in a flabby sense, but a recognition that none of us is without fault; people generally deserve more forgiveness than we offer them, and they are mostly doing the best they can for who they are. Says a Muslim parable, "Do not judge a man until you know why he weeps alone in his tent." Yet much as I might romanticize that moment in the village, I suspect that my wise old woman that day would be at a loss in today's kaleidoscopic com-mons. It takes more than conventional compassion alone, or even humility, to be wise in today's world.

Postconventional Thought

The cognitive-developmental theory that has shaped so much of my thought tells us that like any living organism, humans can adapt. That is, faced with a more complex environment, we may evolve a more complex way of making meaning to match it. This may happen a number of times in our lives, depending on the quality of the worlds we move through. In today's world, where we are surrounded by the relics of failed ideologies and inade-quate imaginations, what forms of wisdom can we cultivate that will be equal to the task?

The people we studied in *Common Fire* were able to sustain their commitment to the common good in the face of significant complexity, challenging diversity, and moral ambiguity. What they revealed was a kind of practical wisdom sometimes called postconventional thought. They were able to think critically—that is, they could stand back from a given worldview, including their own, and question it—yet they could also think systemically, connect the dots, recognize larger, interrelated patterns. They were adept at understanding and even taking many different perspectives without losing their own point of view. Thus they could retain their values while respecting the values of those who thought differently. And among some, we saw "paradoxical-dialectical thought," the ability to hold two or more conflicting ideas at once, maintaining the tension without rushing to judgment. This is often reflected in our common speech in the phrase "both-and" rather than "either-or" thinking. As we are able to hold apparent opposites and reflect on them, it often turns out that a third way will emerge that grasps the essence of both, unifying them in a larger light—a way of knowing that can yield wisdom.

The application of these capacities for perspective-taking and paradoxical thought to adult education have been creatively explored in Tisdell and Swartz's *Adult Education and the Pursuit of Wisdom* (2011), but they also turn out to be valuable in the business world (believed by some to be the "real world"). In an intriguing article in the *Harvard Business Review*, Nonaka and Takeuchi (2011)—significantly, a mentor and his protégé)—argue for the necessity of this sort of wisdom among corporate CEOs. And key among the elements they identify is a capacity for and commitment to mentorship. Even in the "real" world, mentorship and wisdom are intimately related.

Ethical Intent

But, I found myself wondering, if these components of wisdom are so practical, what's to keep them from falling into the hands of the wicked? Surely those who might be described as evil are smart enough to think this way. Yet when I tried to think of someone reprehensible whom I also considered wise, I kept coming up empty. It seemed that wisdom is rarely accorded to those we consider villains. They can be crafty, cunning, and even quite astute, but wise? Not that I could see. Wisdom seems to carry an implicit ethical quality. It calls us to our better selves. Even so, the wise are not simply tolerant. "Whatever" is not in their vocabulary. They know there is a time to exercise judgment as surely as there is a time to withhold it. Their wisdom lies in knowing when to do which. Wisdom seems to rest in the lap of some larger, unseen context that places our everyday thinking in perspective. And that context bends to the good.

Yet while this practical wisdom seems able to function well in the "real world," what did I mean, I wondered, by "some larger, unseen context"? I began to realize that at the end of the day, to see beyond wisdom as just "practical" or the world as only "real," you have to stand somewhere else. Maybe that's the secret power behind what we call wisdom—the wondrous capacity of the human imagination to compose ever larger, unseen contexts to stand in. Maybe that's what the Quaker mystic Douglas Steere (1997) meant when he said, "God is always revising our boundaries outward." Or just maybe inward as well.

Swamp Territory

For the past several years we at the Whidbey Institute have been taking leadership retreatants on a walk through a nearby swamp. Noting that leaders commonly prefer to stay on the high, hard ground, we then point to the obvious: most of our work takes place in the swamp of human relationships and unpredictable events, a land of ambiguity without clear boundaries, where there are no paths and where uncertainty thrives. We remind them that Thoreau, pant legs rolled up, used to stand barefoot in the swamp for hours, motionless. "When I would recreate myself," he wrote, "I seek the darkest wood, the thickest and most interminable and, to the citizen, most dismal swamp. I enter a swamp as a sacred place, a *sanctum sanctorum*" (1862, para. 45). We then invite them to speculate on the swamps in their lives, the places where it seems there is no way through. We speak of impasse and the dark night of the soul.

Conversations like this require a kind of hospitality to intimations of some larger orchestration of the "real world," both darker and more luminous. The deep etymology of the word *wisdom* rests in roots for the words *underworld* and *invisible*. Thoreau was not being merely contrary. He knew that swamps are places of both peril and promise, where life is constantly undergoing death and transfiguration. The paradox is that wisdom cannot grow without the nourishment of doubt, uncertainty, and sometimes sheer terror. It takes a certain courage to move into that darkness, through that swamp, to know it as a pathway to grasping the wonder, awe, and radical mystery of the life that holds us. We don't need to discard the "real world"; we need only redefine it with the realization that reality is ultimately nested in mystery, not the other way around. The universe may continue to reveal its secrets to us for all eternity and yet will remain intrinsically enigmatic.

Interdependence

A few years ago I began to notice that something curious was going on. The old ideologies that had helped me build and maintain a strong and rational sense of self through middle adulthood no longer held me in so firm a grip. Something in me seemed to be going soft. It was as if my armor had become more permeable, and I was able to allow into my inner world points of view and feelings that I had earlier sealed out: an insistence on personal self-reliance yielded to a fuller understanding of my vulnerability and the reality of human interdependence; a determined liberalism came to include a greater respect for the legitimate claims of conservatism and the pragmatic choices demanded in a democratic society; a spiritual longing for transcendence and light was countered by a pull toward the earth, darkness, immanence; and an earlier feminist ideology grew enriched by a more compassionate understanding of men's suffering. And I thought of Eric, the hunter back in Chapter Two who found himself unwilling to shoot that deer. I even found myself welcoming this apparent dissolution of a self I once thought so solidly established. What was going on?

I think I first began to wonder about the meaning of the term *interdependence* when I encountered it years ago in Sharon's book *The Critical Years,* her initial study of young adult faith development (Parks, 1986). We grow, she suggested, from dependence to independence to interdependence. That caught my attention because much of the thinking about the trajectory of development at the time led directly from dependence to independence: full stop. A mature person was autonomous, self-reliant, independent. What was this about yet another transformation? She didn't elaborate a lot on this last stage, but as electronic communication has laced the world together in recent years and as science has shown us a dazzlingly interdependent universe, her insight seems prescient, particularly in the West. To grasp this new reality in our bones requires a new consciousness, a developmental transformation.

Later, in a long conversation not long before he died, my mentor Adam Curle described Indra's Net, a mythic image from Hindu cosmology. The net extends invisibly throughout the universe. At each intersection, he said, glistens a jewel that represents a human life. Each jewel reflects every other, affects and is affected by the others. Little can be foretold but unpredictability and endless change. The boundaries between us are illusions; we are all members of one another, containing each other like the jewels. This was Adam's last gift, and its wisdom still shimmers before me.

We don't learn this in a cave. By definition, a rich apprehension of interdependence can only be grasped *in relation*. It is emergent by nature and must be cocreated in the transaction itself. But this recognition of the intersubjectivity of life, our radical contingency, our fundamental connectedness with all things marks, I think, a highly developed consciousness and seems essential to the evolution of the kind of wisdom I am reaching for here. That is, *this kind of wisdom is not so much about solving problems as it is about achieving right relationship*—a relationship not merely with other people but with existence itself.

That quality of relationship requires what one might call a "participatory consciousness." That is, it is grounded in the deep knowledge that we are all active participants in the construction and ongoing evolution not merely of our own lives but ultimately of life itself. It is a recognition that we now live not beneath but among the stars; that as Thomas Berry (1999) has said, the universe is not a collection of objects but a communion of subjects (p. 82).

Recall the Fool's plaintive observation to King Lear: "Thou shouldst not have been old before thou hadst been wise." We all face Lear's challenge. Age comes to us unbidden, but about wisdom we have a choice. Lear's tragedy was that somehow along the way he had failed to detect the opportunities that life offered him to transform his experience into learning and his learning into wisdom. Instead, his arrogance blinded him, and he slipped inexorably into madness. How do we learn to hear the thrumming possibilities within our experience, to choreograph that dance between age and wisdom so that our wisdom may be enriched by age and our age by wisdom?

For me mentorship is not simply an attempt to understand a role or get good at a job. Over the years it has become something much more profound. It has become a reminder that I, too, am called to continue to evolve—to grow not so much up as *down* and *in*—deeper and more grounded. It is a charge to squeeze hope out of the stones around us, a calling to inspire the next generation and the next and the next, for as my daughter Kate insists, "We live in the future now!" and my son Todd reminds me, "*¡Si, se puede!*": Yes, we can! As elders and mentors, it is our job individually and collectively to cultivate and nourish that claim and that confidence. But it must be a realistic confidence, as free as possible of delusion or cant. This will take a fierce commitment to truth, a disciplined capacity to evolve and teach our best wisdom, and an embodied knowing of the radical interdependence of all life. In the end, our charge is deeply moral.

If those who call us mentor have any right to expect from us something like wisdom, then we are called to live the transformation that we hope for in our protégés. And for that, may this book serve as a worthy guide.

Notes

Chapter Two

1. Some of the richest work that I know of in this area has been carried out by Michael Fagan (a former editor of *Mentoring International* journal), who has explored the wisdom archetype underlying the mentor. He presented a paper (unpublished) entitled "A Jungian Analysis of Mentoring" at the annual convention of the American Psychological Association in Boston in 1990. He is an administrator and chair of the psychology department at Kentucky Wesleyan College.

2. Despite its somewhat argumentative title, Margo Murray's book *Beyond the Myths and Magic of Mentoring* (1991) still stands as one of the most directly practical guides available on how to establish mentoring programs in institutions. We only hope that she recognizes that "beyond" myths lie more myths.

3. A search of the Web turns up a thick bed of references. Among them is a bibliography of studies of mentoring among women in scientific fields. See www.mentornet.net/html/bibliography.htm.

4. Sharon Parks (1992) has raised a wonderful question about the assumption that mentorship is necessarily about a one-to-one relationship, suggesting that for profound transformation to occur a "mentoring community" may be necessary. This insight is further enriched in Daloz, Keen, Keen, and Parks (1996) as well as in Mullen (1997).

5. From Albert Speer's Hitler to the sergeant in the film *Platoon,* the annals of mentoring are replete with tales of shadow mentors who lead their protégés down false pathways, believing themselves, rather than the vision they hold in common, to be

worthy of worship. Freud's biographer, Ernest Jones, refers to this as "the God complex" in *Essays in Applied Psychoanalysis* (1951). Perhaps the most complete treatment of this phenomenon appears in Anthony Storr's book, *Feet of Clay* (1996).

Chapter Three

1.   Despite the best efforts of most stage theorists to address the criticism, the charge that these theories are elitist and too linear tends to stick. Most subsequent work in this area has softened the starkness of the early models. See especially Kegan's latest book, *In Over Our Heads* (1994), in which he refers to the evolutionary stages as "orders of consciousness." At the same time, Kegan does not back down from a clear value position. His analysis of the postmodernist debate in chapter nine of that work is by all odds the clearest and most persuasive discussion of the issue that I have read anywhere.

2.   See my review in *Adult Education Quarterly,* 1996, *46*(2).

3.   A relatively informal support group for people around the country interested in both research and practice related to the Perry Scheme, the network has been operating for almost twenty years and has filled a cornucopia with bibliographies, resources, newsletters, and relevant articles elaborating on the original research. At the present time, it serves primarily as a central clearinghouse for Perry-related work and writing (particularly obscure and hard-to-find work in the area) through a regularly updated bibliography. Plans are under way to develop a Web page and listserv to provide a medium for regular exchange of ideas within this community. For more information, contact William S. Moore, 1505 Farwell Ct. N.W., Olympia, WA 98502; (360) 786-5094; wsmoore51@home.com.

Chapter Four

1.   Many are the connections, it seems to me, between learning and healing. A territory still largely unexplored is populated by a large number of adult learners who return to higher education carrying the scars of early wounding. Gina Higgins (1994) has estimated the number to be as high as 60 percent. Some of the most interesting work in this area is being done by Jane Adelizzi,

Diane Goss, and their colleagues at Curry College. See their edited volume, *A Closer Look* (1995).

2.   Indeed, I nearly made this mistake in my initial analysis of these stories. It was apparent to me that the two women, who did not leave home, could not have "developed," for every male knows that one must leave home in order to grow up. Fortunately, I was saved from this fate by the woman who was to become my spouse, Sharon Parks; she helped me see that the twin metaphors of home and pilgrimage carry considerable gender baggage. One may, after all, stay right at home and still grow. Her article (Parks, 1989) elaborating this point is a classic.

Chapter Five

1.   In fact, the very separation of spirit and intellect could be the culprit. What if we were to recognize that the two are intimately intertwined—that developing one depends profoundly on developing the other? Indeed, for most of human history, the proposition was never in doubt.

2.   It's a good thing I didn't try. After this was written, an avalanche of criticism was unleashed at this whole family of theory, both from deconstructionist critics and from exponents of critical theory. In responding to the criticism, Bob Kegan (1994) builds on a "lively division" of postmodern thought between deconstructive and reconstructive thought. The former, he suggests, tends counterdependently to make an absolute out of its own relativism, while the latter offers a way to view the world as having a certain coherence and predictability without at once reverting to a defense of modernist assumptions about reality.

Chapter Six

1.   In a brief but powerful essay, Arthur Wilson (1993) argues that adult cognition and learning are "inherently situated." The *particular* context in which learning does or does not occur, to say nothing of the content of the learning itself, he suggests, is more important than we usually acknowledge. This deeply grounded approach to understanding the nature of learning has profound implications.

2. The reference is to the acupuncturist Su Wen (mentioned in Chapter Two). In our subsequent study of the role of mentors in forming commitment to the common good, we heard any number of stories about the appearance of mentors at just the right time—just as young adults were seeking concrete evidence that their longings could be lived out across the years. See *Common Fire* (Daloz, Keen, Keen, and Parks, 1996).

Chapter Seven

1. Although the idea has been around in explicit form for some seventy years, the past decade has seen a quantum increase in public recognition of the power of systems thinking. Organizational consultants to the private and nonprofit sectors have been primary carriers of the idea, but it is less richly embedded in our educational curricula. We would hope to see the idea of *interdependence* taught more broadly in our schools, colleges, and universities in the coming years since it is a construct central to more adequate understanding of the world. One of the leading exponents of systems thinking, Pegasus Communications of Cambridge, Massachusetts, produces sets of excellent instructional materials.

2. Readers who require still more convincing might want to glance at my review of the book in the *Adult Education Quarterly* (Daloz, 1996).

3. This must be done with care, however, for students at relatively early developmental positions are vulnerable to taking a theory as gospel—a prescription for how to do it right rather than a helpful framework within which to understand their lives more adequately.

Chapter Eight

1. In his recent book, *Mentoring Adult Learners*, Norman Cohen (1995) has elaborated on the notions of support, challenge, and vision to develop a "principles of adult mentoring scale" that enables one to examine in rich detail the particulars of mentoring activities. The accompanying text contains a good deal of practical advice to aspiring mentors.

2. Interestingly, one of the early titles that the authors of *Women's Ways of Knowing* (Belenky, Clinchy, Goldberger, and Tarule, 1986) briefly considered was "A Still, Small Voice."

3. I am indebted to my colleague Vivienne Hull for this story.

Chapter Nine

1. This story appeared in a somewhat different form in *Lifelong Learning* (see Daloz, 1988).

2. Indeed, I have begged graduate students and colleagues for years (to limited avail) to undertake a study of what happens at home, around the kitchen table, when adult learners try to study—and in a broader sense, to change. We have yet to see a rich "thick description" of how the attitudes of family members, friends, and other elements of the holding environment conspire to enhance or inhibit the kind of transformational learning that we say we value. As this edition was in the copyediting phase, however, I received in the mail a completed Ph.D. dissertation from New Brunswick. Entitled "A Look Beyond the University's Walls," this excellent work, by Seth Crowell (1996), examines a number of specific supports and challenges from significant others in the students' worlds. It concludes that "this study affirms the position that development at its essence is a matter of relationship."

3. An excellent overview of the range of criticism of adult development theory may be found in Chapter Fifteen, "Critical Theory, Postmodern, and Feminist Perspectives," of Merriam and Caffarella's *Learning in Adulthood* (second edition, 1999).

4. It is a poignant irony that Alcott's close friend, Henry David Thoreau, features in one of the saddest stories we know about mentors. At the age of forty-three, entering his own generative years, Thoreau traveled to Minnesota in search of a cure for the tuberculosis that was to take his life two years later. He was accompanied by seventeen-year-old Horace Mann Jr., son of the educator. While the trip failed to cure Thoreau, it changed young Mann's life. Deeply influenced by Thoreau's intense curiosity about natural ecology, he majored in botany at Harvard, became curator of the plant museum there, and was headed for a successful academic career when, at the age of only twenty-four, he

died of tuberculosis that some say he contracted from his mentor
(Harding, 1962).

References

Adelizzi, J., and Goss, D. (eds). *A Closer Look: Perspectives and Reflections on College Students with Learning Disabilities.* Milton, Mass.: Curry College, 1995.

Adorno, T. W., and others. *The Authoritarian Personality.* New York: HarperCollins, 1950.

Albom, M. *Tuesdays with Morrie.* New York: Doubleday, 1997.

Allen, T. D., and Eby, L. T. *Blackwell Handbook of Mentoring.* Hoboken, N. J., Wiley, 2010.

Aslanian, C. B., and Brickell, H. M. *Americans in Transition: Life Changes as Reasons for Adult Learning.* New York: Future Directions for a Learning Society, College Board, 1980.

Bakan, D. *The Duality of Human Existence.* Boston: Beacon Press, 1966.

Baker-Miller, J. *Toward a New Psychology of Women.* Boston: Beacon Press, 1976.

Bandler, R., and Grinder, J. *The Structure of Magic.* Palo Alto, Calif.: Science and Behavior Books, 1975.

Baruch, G., Barnett, R., and Rivers, C. *Lifeprints: New Patterns of Love and Work for Today's Women.* New York: McGraw-Hill, 1983.

Basseches, M. *Dialectical Thinking and Adult Development.* Norwood, N.J.: Ablex, 1985.

Bateson, S. *Steps to an Ecology of Mind.* New York: Ballantine, 1972.

Belenky, M., Bond, L., and Weinstock, J. *A Tradition That Has No Name: Nurturing the Development of People, Families, and Communities.* New York: Basic Books, 1997.

Belenky, M., Clinchy, B., Goldberger, N., and Tarule, J. *Women's Ways of Knowing: The Development of Self, Mind, and Voice.* New York: Basic Books, 1986.

Bellah, R., and others. *Habits of the Heart: Individualism and Commitment in American Life.* Berkeley: University of California Press, 1985.

Benjamin, J. *The Bonds of Love: Psychoanalysis, Feminism, and the Problem of Domination.* New York: Pantheon Books, 1988.

Bernard, J. "Women's Educational Needs." In A. W. Chickering and Associates, *The Modern American College: Responding to the New Realities of Diverse Students and a Changing Society.* San Francisco: Jossey-Bass, 1981.

Berry, T. *The Great Work: Our Way into the Future.* New York: Bell Tower, 1999.

Bey, T. M., and Holmes, C. T. *Mentoring: Contemporary Principles and Issues.* Reston, Va.: Association of Teacher Educators, 1992.

Bridges, W. *Transitions.* Reading, Mass.: Addison-Wesley, 1980.

Bridges, W. *Managing Transitions: Making the Most of Change.* Reading, Mass.: Addison-Wesley, 1991.

Brookfield, S. D. *Developing Critical Thinkers: Challenging Adults to Explore Alternative Ways of Thinking and Acting.* San Francisco: Jossey-Bass, 1987.

Brookfield, S. D. *The Skillful Teacher.* San Francisco: Jossey-Bass, 1990.

Brookfield, S. D. *Becoming a Critically Reflective Teacher.* San Francisco: Jossey-Bass, 1995.

Broughton, J. (ed.). *Critical Theories of Psychological Development.* New York: Plenum Press, 1987.

Brown, R. D., and DeCoster, D. A. (eds.). *Mentoring-Transcript Systems for Promoting Student Growth.* New Directions for Student Services, no. 19. San Francisco: Jossey-Bass, 1982.

Campbell, J. *The Hero with a Thousand Faces.* Princeton, N.J.: Princeton University Press, 1949.

Chickering, A. *Education and Identity.* San Francisco: Jossey-Bass, 1969.

Chickering, A. W., and Associates. *The Modern American College: Responding to the New Realities of Diverse Students and a Changing Society.* San Francisco: Jossey-Bass, 1981.

Choderow, N. *The Reproduction of Mothering.* Berkeley: University of California Press, 1978.

Christ, C. P. *Diving Deep and Surfacing: Women Writers on Spiritual Quest.* Boston: Beacon Press, 1980.

Clark, M. C. "Transformational Learning." In S. B. Merriam, *An Update on Adult Learning Theory.* San Francisco: Jossey-Bass, 1993.

Claxton, C., and Murrell, P. *Learning Styles: Implications for Improving Educational Practices.* ASHE-ERIC Higher Education Reports, No. 4. Washington, D.C.: Association for the Study of Higher Education, 1987.

Cohen, N. H. *Mentoring Adult Learners: A Guide for Educators and Trainers.* Malabar, Fla.: Krieger, 1995.

Collins, N. W. *Professional Women and Their Mentors.* Upper Saddle River, N.J.: Prentice-Hall, 1983.

Commons, M. L., Sinnott, J. D., Richards, F. A., and Armon, C. (eds.) *Adult Development.* Vol. I: *Comparisons and Applications of Developmental Models.* New York: Praeger, 1989.

Courtenay, B., Merriam, S., and Reeves, P. "The Centrality of Meaning-Making in Transformational Learning: How HIV-Positive Adults Make Sense of Their Lives." *Adult Education Quarterly,* 1998, *48*(2), 65–84.

Cranse, R. "More Basic Than Basic." Unpublished manuscript, Special Services Project, Community College of Vermont, 1982.

Cranton, P. *Understanding and Promoting Transformative Learning: A Guide for Educators of Adults.* San Francisco: Jossey-Bass, 1994.

Cross, K. P. *Beyond the Open Door: New Students to Higher Education.* San Francisco: Jossey-Bass, 1971.

Cross, K. P. *Adults as Learners: Increasing Participation and Facilitating Learning.* San Francisco: Jossey-Bass, 1981.

Crowell, S. W. "A Look Beyond the University's Walls: Assessing the Level of Support and the Resulting Impact Adult Learners' Significant Others Have on Their Lives as Students." Unpublished doctoral dissertation, Walden University, 1996.

Daloz, L. *When the Thunder Comes: A Developmental Study of Adult Learners in Vermont.* Final report to the Fund for the Improvement of Postsecondary Education. Montpelier, Vt.: Office of External Programs of the Vermont State Colleges, 1981.

Daloz, L. "The Story of Gladys Who Refused to Grow: A Morality Tale for Mentors." *Lifelong Learning,* 1988, *11*(4), 4–7.

Daloz, L. "The Evolving Kegan." Review of Robert Kegan's *In Over Our Heads. Adult Education Quarterly,* 1996, *46*(2).

Daloz, L., Keen, C., Keen, J., and Parks, S. *Common Fire: Lives of Commitment in a Complex World.* Boston: Beacon Press, 1996.

Dante (Alighieri). *The Divine Comedy.* (J. D. Sinclair, trans.). New York: Oxford University Press, 1961.

Dewey, J. *Democracy and Education.* New York: Macmillan, 1916.

Dewey, J. *Experience and Education.* New York: Macmillan, 1938.

Dinnerstein, D. *The Mermaid and the Minotaur: Sexual Arrangements and Human Malaise.* New York: HarperCollins, 1976.

Elias, D. "It's Time to Change Our Minds: An Introduction to Transformative Learning." *Revision: A Journal of Consciousness and Transformation,* 1997, *20*(1), 2–6.

Erikson, E. H. *Childhood and Society.* New York: Norton, 1950.

Erkut, S., and Mokros, J. "Professors as Models and Mentors for College Students." Working Paper no. 65. Wellesley, Mass.: Center for Research on Women, Wellesley College, 1981.

Evans, N. J. (ed.). *Facilitating the Development of Women.* New Directions for Student Services, no. 29. San Francisco: Jossey-Bass, 1985.

Festinger, L. *A Theory of Cognitive Dissonance.* Stanford, Calif.: Stanford University Press, 1957.

Fogel, A. *Developing Through Relationships: Origins of Communication, Self, and Culture.* Chicago: University of Chicago Press, 1993.

Fowler, J. W. *Stages of Faith: The Psychology of Human Development and the Quest for Meaning.* New York: HarperCollins, 1981.

Fowler, J. W. *Becoming Adult, Becoming Christian: Adult Development and Christian Faith.* New York: HarperCollins, 1984.

Fowler, J. W., and Keen, S. *Life Maps: Conversations on the Journey of Faith.* Waco, Tex.: Word Books, 1978.

Frankl, V. *Man's Search for Meaning.* New York: Washington Square Press, 1959.

Freedman, M. *The Kindness of Strangers: Adult Mentors, Urban Youth, and the New Volunteerism.* San Francisco: Jossey-Bass, 1993.

Freire, P. *Pedagogy of the Oppressed.* New York: Herder & Herder, 1970.

Freud, A. *Psychoanalysis for Teachers and Parents.* New York: Emerson Books, 1935.

Frost, R. *Complete Poems of Robert Frost.* New York: Henry Holt, 1949.

Galbraith, M. (ed.). *Adult Learning Methods: A Guide to Effective Instruction.* (2nd ed.). Malabar, Fla.: Krieger, 1998.

Galbraith, M., and Cohen, N. *Mentoring: New Strategies and Challenges.* San Francisco: Jossey-Bass, 1995.

Gamson, Z. *Liberating Education.* San Francisco: Jossey-Bass, 1984.

Gibbs, J. C., and Schnell, S. V. "Moral Development 'Versus' Socialization: A Critique." *American Psychologist,* Oct. 1985, pp. 1071–1080.

Gilligan, C. "In a Different Voice: Women's Conception of the Self and of Morality." *Harvard Educational Review,* 1977, *47,* 481–517.

Gilligan, C. *In a Different Voice: Psychological Theory and Women's Development.* Cambridge, Mass.: Harvard University Press, 1982.

Ginsberg, M. B., and Wlodkowski, R. J. *Diversity and Motivation.* San Francisco: Jossey-Bass, 2009.

Goldberger, N., Tarule, J., Clinchy, B., and Belenky, M. (eds). *Knowledge, Difference, and Power: Essays Inspired by Women's Ways of Knowing.* New York: Basic Books, 1996.

Gray, M. M. *Mentoring and Coaching: An Annotated Bibliography.* West Vancouver, B.C., Canada: Mentoring Institute, 1989.

Greene, M. "Realizing Literature's Emancipatory Potential." In J. Mezirow and Associates (eds.), *Fostering Critical Reflection in Adulthood: A Guide to Transformative and Emancipatory Learning.* San Francisco: Jossey-Bass, 1990.

Hall, R., and Sandler, B. "Academic Mentoring for Women Students and Faculty: A New Look at an Old Way to Get Ahead." Project on the Status of Women. Washington, D.C.: Association of American Colleges, 1983.

Harding, W. *The Days of Henry Thoreau.* Princeton, N.J.: Princeton University Press, 1962.

Harris, M. *Dance of the Spirit: The Seven Steps of Women's Spirituality.* New York: Doubleday, 1991.

Heath, D. *Fulfilling Lives: Paths to Maturity and Success.* San Francisco: Jossey-Bass, 1991.

Hennig, M., and Jardim, A. *The Managerial Woman.* New York: Doubleday, 1977.

Herrigel, E. *Zen in the Art of Archery.* New York: Pantheon, 1953.

Hiemstra, R., and Sisco, B. *Individualizing Instruction: Making Learning Personal, Empowering, and Successful.* San Francisco: Jossey-Bass, 1990.

Higgins, G. O. *Resilient Adults: Overcoming a Cruel Past.* San Francisco: Jossey-Bass, 1994.

Huang, C. A., and Lynch, J. *Mentoring: The Tao of Giving and Receiving Wisdom.* San Francisco: HarperCollins, 1995.

Hughes, K., and Wolf, L. *Daughters of the Moon, Sisters of the Sun: Young Women and Mentors on the Transition to Womanhood.* Gabriola Island, B.C., Canada: New Society Publishers, 1997.

Inhelder, B., and Piaget, J. *The Growth of Logical Thinking from Childhood to Adolescence.* New York: Basic Books, 1958.

Jones, E. *Essays in Applied Psychoanalysis.* London: Hogarth Press, 1951.

Josselson, R. *Finding Herself: Pathways to Identity Development in Women.* San Francisco: Jossey-Bass, 1987.

Jung, C. J. *Psyche and Symbol.* New York: Doubleday, 1958.

Kanter, R. M. *Men and Women of the Corporation.* New York: Basic Books, 1977.

Keen, S. *The Passionate Life: Stages of Loving.* New York: HarperCollins, 1983.

Kegan, R. *The Evolving Self: Problem and Process in Human Development.* Cambridge, Mass.: Harvard University Press, 1982.

Kegan, R. *In Over Our Heads: The Mental Demands of Modern Life.* Cambridge, Mass.: Harvard University Press, 1994.

Kierkegaard, S. *Fear and Trembling.* Garden City, N.J.: Doubleday, 1954.

Klein, C. *Mothers and Sons.* Boston: G. D. Hall, 1985.

Knefelkamp, L. "Foreword." In W. G. Perry, *Forms of Intellectual and Ethical Development in the College Years: A Scheme.* (Reissued.) San Francisco: Jossey-Bass, 1998.

Knefelkamp, L., Widick, C., and Parker, C. (eds.). *Applying New Developmental Findings*. New Directions for Student Services, no. 4. San Francisco: Jossey-Bass, 1978.

Knowles, M. S. *The Modern Practice of Adult Education: Andragogy Versus Pedagogy*. New York: Association Press, 1970.

Knox, A. B. *Adult Development and Learning: A Handbook on Individual Growth and Competence in the Adult Years for Education and the Helping Professions*. San Francisco: Jossey-Bass, 1977.

Kohlberg, L. "Stage and Sequence: The Cognitive-Developmental Approach to Socialization." In D. Goslin (ed.), *Handbook of Socialization Theory and Research*. Skokie, Ill.: Rand McNally, 1969.

Kohlberg, L. *The Philosophy of Moral Development*. New York: HarperCollins, 1981.

Kolb, D. *Experiential Learning: Experience as the Source of Learning and Development*. Upper Saddle River, N.J.: Prentice-Hall, 1984.

Kram, K. E. "Mentoring in the Workplace." In D. T. Hall and Associates, *Career Development in Organizations*. San Francisco: Jossey-Bass, 1986.

Kram, K. E. *Developmental Relationships in Organizational Life*. Lanham, Md.: University Press of America, 1988.

Kremer, J. W. (ed.). "Transformative Learning—Special Issue." *Revision: A Journal of Consciousness and Transformation*, 1997, *20*(1), 7–14.

Levine, S. V. *Radical Departures: Desperate Detours to Growing Up*. Orlando: Harcourt Brace, 1984.

Levinson, D. J., and others. *The Seasons of a Man's Life*. New York: Knopf, 1978.

Levinson, D. J., in collaboration with Levinson, J. D. *The Seasons of a Woman's Life*. New York: Knopf, 1996.

Light, R. *The Harvard Assessment Seminars: Explorations with Students and Faculty About Teaching, Learning, and Student Life. Second Report*. Cambridge, Mass.: Harvard Graduate School of Education and Kennedy School of Government, 1992.

Loevinger, J. *Ego Development: Conceptions and Theories*. San Francisco: Jossey-Bass, 1980.

Luna, G., and Cullen, D. *Empowering the Faculty: Mentoring Redirected and Renewed*. ASHE-ERIC Higher Education Report series 95-3. Washington, D.C.: George Washington University, 1997.

Maack, M. N., and Passet, J. *Aspirations and Mentoring in an Academic Environment*. Westport, Conn.: Greenwood Press, 1994.

Maher, F. A., and Tetrault, M. K. T. *The Feminist Classroom: An Inside Look at How Professors and Students Are Transforming Higher Education for a Diverse Society*. New York: Basic Books, 1994.

Marcotte, R. *Leaves Turn at Maple Lane.* Newport, Vt: privately printed, 1984.

Marienau, C. "In Their Own Voices: Women Learning About Their Own Development." In K. Taylor and C. Marienau (eds.), *Learning Environments for Women's Adult Development: Bridges Toward Change.* San Francisco: Jossey-Bass, 1995, pp. 37–44.

Marsick, V. (ed.) *Learning in the Workplace.* London: Croom Helm, 1987.

McKeachie, W. J. (ed.). *Learning, Cognition, and College Teaching.* New Directions for Teaching and Learning, no. 2. San Francisco: Jossey-Bass, 1980.

Merriam, S. B. "Mentors and Protégés: A Critical Review of the Literature." *Adult Education Quarterly,* Spring 1983, pp. 161–173.

Merriam, S. B. (ed.). *An Update on Adult Learning Theory.* San Francisco: Jossey-Bass, 1993.

Merriam, S. B., and Caffarella, R. *Learning in Adulthood: A Comprehensive Guide.* San Francisco: Jossey-Bass, 1991.

Merriam, S. B., and Caffarella, R. *Learning in Adulthood: A Comprehensive Guide.* (2nd ed.). San Francisco: Jossey-Bass, 1999.

Merriam, S. B., and Clark, M. C. *Lifelines: Patterns of Work, Love, and Learning in Adulthood.* San Francisco: Jossey-Bass, 1991.

Mezirow, J. "Perspective Transformation." *Adult Education,* Feb. 1978, pp. 100–110.

Mezirow, J. *Transformative Dimensions of Adult Learning.* San Francisco: Jossey-Bass, 1991.

Mezirow, J. "Learning to Think Like an Adult: An Update of Transformation Theory." In J. Mezirow (ed.), *Transformative Learning in Practice.* San Francisco: Jossey-Bass, forthcoming.

Mezirow, J., and Associates. *Fostering Critical Reflection in Adulthood: A Guide to Transformative and Emancipatory Learning.* San Francisco: Jossey-Bass, 1990.

Mezirow, J., Pietrykowski, B., and Inglis, T. "To the Editor." *Adult Education Quarterly,* 1998, *49*(1), 65–76.

Miller, J. *Toward a New Psychology of Women.* Boston: Beacon Press, 1976.

Missirian, A. K. *The Corporate Connection: Why Executive Women Need Mentors to Reach the Top.* Upper Saddle River, N.J.: Prentice-Hall, 1982.

Mullen, C. A. *Breaking the Circle of One: Redefining Mentorship in the Lives and Writings of Educators.* New York: Peter Lang, 1997.

Murray, M. *Beyond the Myths and Magic of Mentoring.* San Francisco: Jossey-Bass, 1991.

National Institute of Education. *Involvement in Learning: Realizing the Potential of American Higher Education.* Study Group on the

Conditions of Excellence in American Higher Education. Washington, D.C.: Author, 1984.

Nonaka, I., and Tekeuchi, H. "The Wise Leader." *Harvard Business Review*, May 2011, pp. 59–67.

Novak, M. *Ascent of the Mountain, Flight of the Dove: An Invitation to Religious Studies*. New York: HarperCollins, 1971.

Palloff, R. M., and Pratt, K. *Building Online Learning Communities*. San Francisco: Jossey-Bass, 2007.

Palmer, P. *To Know As We Are Known: A Spirituality of Education*. San Francisco: Harper San Francisco, 1983.

Palmer, P. *The Courage to Teach: Exploring the Inner Landscape of a Teacher's Life*. San Francisco: Jossey-Bass, 1998.

Parks, S. *The Critical Years: The Young Adult Search for a Faith to Live By*. San Francisco: Harper San Francisco, 1986.

Parks, S. "Home and Pilgrimage: Companion Metaphors for Personal and Social Transformation." *Soundings*, 1989, *72*(2–3), 297–315.

Parks, S. "The University as a Mentoring Environment." Indianapolis: Indiana Office for Campus Ministries, 1992.

Pascarella, E. T., and Terenzini, P. T. *How College Affects Students*. San Francisco: Jossey-Bass, 1991.

Perry, W. G. *Forms of Intellectual and Ethical Development in the College Years: A Scheme*. Austin, Tex.: Holt, Rinehart and Winston, 1968.

Perry, W. G. "Examsmanship and the Liberal Arts." In H. Hayford and H. P. Vincent, *Reader and Writer*. (3rd ed.) Boston: Houghton Mifflin, 1969.

Phillips-Jones, L. *Mentors and Protégés*. New York: Arbor House, 1982.

Pietrykowski, B. "Knowledge and Power in Adult Education: Beyond Freire and Habermas." *Adult Education Quarterly*, 1996, *46*(2), 82–97.

Pirsig, R. M. *Zen and the Art of Motorcycle Maintenance: An Inquiry into Values*. New York: Morrow, 1974.

Postman, N. *Teaching as a Conserving Activity*. New York: Delacorte, 1979.

Ragins, B. R., and Kram, K. E. *The Handbook of Mentoring at Work*. Thousand Oaks, Calif.: Sage, 2007.

Roche, G. "Much Ado About Mentors." *Harvard Business Review*, 1979, *20*, 14–28.

Rubin, L. B. *Intimate Strangers: Men and Women Together*. New York: HarperCollins, 1983.

Rudolph, F. *The American College and University: A History*. New York: Knopf, 1962.

Rybach, J., Hoyer, W., and Roodin, P. *Adult Cognition and Aging*. New York: Praeger, 1986.

Sanford, N. *Learning After College.* (C. Comstock, ed.) Orinda, Calif.: Montaigne, 1980.

Schachter-Shalomi, Z. *From Age-ing to Sage-ing.* New York: Warner Books, 1995.

Schlossberg, N., Lynch, A., and Chickering, A. *Improving Higher Education Environments for Adults.* San Francisco: Jossey-Bass, 1989.

Schneider, C., Klemp, G. O., and Kastendiek, S. *The Balancing Act: Competencies of Effective Teachers and Mentors in Degree Programs for Adults.* Chicago: Center for Continuing Education, University of Chicago, 1981.

Shea, F. G. *Mentoring: Helping Employees Reach Their Full Potential.* New York: AMACOM, 1994.

Sheehy, G. *Passages: Predictable Crises of Adult Life.* New York: Dutton, 1976.

Speizer, J. J. "Role Models, Mentors, and Sponsors: The Elusive Concepts." *Signs: Journal of Women in Culture and Society,* 1981, *6*, 4.

Steere, D. V. *Dimensions of Prayer: Cultivating a Relationship with God.* Nashville, Tenn.: Upper Room Books, 1997.

Storr, A. *Feet of Clay. Saints, Sinners, and Madmen: A Study of Gurus.* New York: Free Press, 1996.

Taylor, E. W. *The Theory and Practice of Transformative Learning: A Critical Review.* Columbus, Ohio: ERIC Clearing House on Adult, Career, and Vocational Education, 1998.

Taylor, K., and Marienau, C. (eds.). *Learning Environments for Women's Adult Development: Bridges Toward Change.* San Francisco: Jossey-Bass, 1995.

Tennant, M., and Pogson, P. *Learning and Change in the Adult Years: A Developmental Perspective.* San Francisco: Jossey-Bass, 1995.

Thomas, R., Murrell, P., and Chickering, A. "Theoretical Bases and Feasibility Issues for Mentoring and Developmental Transcripts." In R. D. Brown and D. A. DeCoster (eds.), *Mentoring-Transcript Systems for Promoting Student Growth.* New Directions for Student Services, no. 19. San Francisco: Jossey-Bass, 1982.

Thoreau, H. "Walking," 1862.

Tisdell, E., and Swartz, A. (eds.). *Adult Education and the Pursuit of Wisdom.* New Directions for Adult and Continuing Education, no. 131. San Francisco: Jossey-Bass, 2011.

Tolkien, J. R. R. *The Return of the King.* New York: Ballantine, 1965.

Vella, J. *Learning to Listen, Learning to Teach: The Power of Dialogue in Educating Adults.* San Francisco: Jossey-Bass, 1994.

Vella, J. *Training Through Dialogue: Promoting Effective Learning and Change with Adults.* San Francisco: Jossey-Bass, 1995.

Vogel, L. *Teaching and Learning in Communities of Faith: Empowering Adults Through Religious Education.* San Francisco: Jossey-Bass, 1991.

Waters, M. (ed.) *Mentor and Protégé.* Overland Park, Kans.: Great Mother, 1998.

Weathersby, R. P. "Ego Development." In A. W. Chickering and Associates, *The Modern American College: Responding to the New Realities of Diverse Students and a Changing Society.* San Francisco: Jossey-Bass, 1981.

Weiler, K. *Women Teaching for Change: Gender, Class, and Power.* New York: Bergin & Garvey, 1988.

Wilson, A. "The Promise of Situated Cognition." In S. B. Merriam (ed.), *An Update on Adult Learning Theory.* San Francisco: Jossey-Bass, 1993.

Winnicott, D. W. *The Maturational Processes and the Facilitating Environment.* New York: International University Press, 1965.

Winston, R. B., and others. *Developmental Academic Advising: Addressing Students' Educational, Career, and Personal Needs.* San Francisco: Jossey-Bass, 1984.

Wunsch, M. A. *Mentoring Revisited: Making an Impact on Individuals and Institutions.* San Francisco: Jossey-Bass, 1994.

Zachary, L. *The Mentor's Guide: Facilitating Effective Learning Relationships.* San Francisco: Jossey-Bass, 1999, 2011.

Zucker, D. S. "The Mentor/Protégé Relationship: A Phenomenological Inquiry." Unpublished doctoral dissertation, Professional School for Humanistic Studies, 1982.

Zweig, C., and Abrams, J. (eds.) *Meeting the Shadow: The Hidden Power of the Dark Side of Human Nature.* Los Angeles: Tarcher, 1990.

Appendix

Much of the work with adult learners described in this book was made possible by the Fund for Improvement of Postsecondary Education (FIPSE), a discretionary fund associated with the federal Department of Education.

My own experience with developmental research comes in three layers. The first involved my participation in a collaborative network to explore the applications of current developmental research to postsecondary adult education. Under the guidance of Rita Weathersby and Jill Mattuck Tarule, representatives from Mary Baldwin College, Clark University, Loretto Heights College, and the Vermont State Colleges shared insights, program components, materials, and research data over the course of two years. During this time we began interviewing incoming and departing students on a systematic basis, interpreting the data through Loevinger's Ego Development scale and the Perry Scheme. Results were published by FIPSE in a booklet entitled *Designing for Development: Four Programs for Adult Undergraduates*.

The second layer found me directing a study to learn how rural adult Vermonters were affected by their return to higher education. A part of FIPSE's National Project IV (reported in Gamson, 1984), we administered a range of developmental measures on a pre/post basis to a sample of sixty entering, continuing, and exiting students over a year-long period. In addition, we conducted detailed preinterviews and postinterviews with twelve students. These were analyzed by trained scorers to determine Perry scores and to isolate the degree and quality of change, the nature of prominent issues, and indications of significant developmental components. Chief findings were that students did develop, generally entering with a good deal of multiplicity and leaving with a greater degree of contextual thinking. We described the "model" adult learner as being in transition from conformity to awareness of self as a responsible agent, as increasingly viewing education as an asset to one's whole life, and as moving away from authoritarian views of "truth." Prominent themes included development as a journey, the mentor as guide, "breathing again" as a metaphor of women's rediscovery of self, and shifting friendship patterns as a context of development. Details are contained in the report *When the Thunder Comes: A Developmental Study of Adult Learners in Vermont* (Daloz, 1981).

Having begun to see some patterns, I applied for and received a Mina Shaughnessy fellowship from FIPSE to look more closely at how rural Vermonters were affected by their return to higher education, especially at the role mentors played in development. To do that, I interviewed six mentor-student pairs on a pre/post basis over the course of a year, following them informally throughout that time. In addition, I tape-recorded conversations with my own students. Most of the vignettes in the book are based on these interviews and conversations. With one exception, the names and some of the circumstances have been changed. As I hope the book makes clear, the results of the study were often mixed (not everyone changed the way I thought they ought to) and always fascinating. Out of the experience I have learned and relearned two things: listening and being heard are extraordinarily powerful and tragically rare events in most of our lives, and people are wonderfully, endlessly complex. Not bad for a federal grant.

Index

A

Abrams, J., 149
Adelizzi, J., 148, 250n1
Adorno, T. W., 94
Adult development. *See* Development
Adult education. *See* Education
Adult learners: differences among, 14; education's accommodations to, 13–14, 111; family obligations of, 105–113, 110, 198–199; importance of seeing whole life of, 110–111; instructional techniques for use with, 119–121
Advisers, 6–7; developmental theory's value to, 45; as mentors, 22, 32–33, 156–157, 240–242. *See also* Mentors
Advocates, mentors as, 213–214
Aiken, G., 6
Albom, M., 18, 141–142
Alcott, B., 243
Archetype, mentor as, 17–18, 249n1
Armon, C., 137
Ascent of the Mountain, Flight of the Dove (Novak), 25
Aslanian, C. B., 44, 90
Authority: Perry on, 77, 78, 81–82, 94; students' changing views on, 94–96

B

Bakan, D., 27, 65
Baker-Miller, J., 58
Bandler, R., 210
Barnett, R., 58
Baruch, G., 58
Basseches, M., 137, 187
Bateson, S., 97, 140–141, 183

Belenky, M., 27, 58, 94, 112, 131–132, 157, 181
Beliefs: Christian, 97–105; as inhibiting education, 83; rigidly dogmatic, 113–118; transformation of, 143–145
Bellah, R., 242
Benjamin, J., 58
Bernard, J., 58
Bey, T. M., 18
Beyond the Myths and Magic of Mentoring (Murray), 249n2
Bond, L., 181
Brickell, H. M., 44, 90
Bridges, W., 136
Brookfield, S. D., 34, 95, 134, 177, 207, 217
Broughton, J., 241
Brown, R. D., 22
Buber, M., 181
Bühler, C., 47
Business, mentors in, 21

C

Caffarella, R., 4, 44, 90, 207, 241
Campbell, J., 26–27, 32, 137, 147, 165
Caring: in education, 243, 244; in mentoring relationship, 165, 175; teaching as, 246–247
Challenge, 206, 216–223; development and, 207–209; dichotomies as, 220–221; discussion as, 219–220; hypotheses construction and, 221–222; setting tasks as, 217–219; standard setting as, 222–223
Chickering, A., 21, 44, 90, 120, 121, 207

Choderow, N., 27, 58

Christ, C. P., 136

Clark, M. C., 44, 58, 69, 95

Claxton, C., 228

Clinchy, B., 27, 58, 94, 112, 131–132, 157

Cognitive dissonance, 216

Cohen, N. H., 18, 21, 212, 226, 252n1

Collins, N. W., 33

Common Fire (Daloz, Keen, Keen, and Parks), 139, 220

Commons, M. L., 137

Conflict: introducing, 123, 177, 220–221. *See also* Challenge

Context: for development, 238–243; learning as situated in, 110–111, 153–154, 251n1. *See also* Environment

Cosmogonic cycle, 147

Courtenay, B., 120, 242

Cranse, R., 97

Cranton, P., 27, 95, 120, 134, 207

Crowell, S., 242, 253n2

Cullen, D., 18

Cultures of embeddedness, 185–188

D

Daloz, L., 21, 80, 139, 220, 238, 249n4

Dante (Alighieri), 28–34, 89

DeCoster, D. A., 22

Development, 4, 45; as consideration in teaching, 240–243; context for, 238–243; education for, 12; effects of support and challenge on, 207–209; learning as, 243, 244; leaving home and, 251n2; mentoring in seminar on, 36–41; as more than change, 23–24; trust and, 128, 206; voice as metaphor for, 112; by women, 46, 55, 57–58, 68, 69, 130–132. *See also* Developmental theories; Transformation

Developmental theories, 41–42; criticisms of, 241–242; educational value of, 44–45; of faith, 129–130;

as maps, 46, 226; phase (psychosocial) theories, 46–47; stage theories, 47–48, 63–64, 250n1. *See also* *specific theorists*

Dewey, J., 45, 242

Dialectical thinking: defined, 138; teaching and, 145–146; transformation and, 137–142

Dialogue, 219–220

Dinnerstein, D., 58

Divine Comedy (Dante), 28–34

E

Education: accommodation to adult learners by, 13–14, 111; adults' reasons for seeking, 3–4; development's relationship to, 243, 244; family and, 105–113, 189–202, 198–199; fear accompanying return to, 91–93, 213; mentors in, 21–22, 32–36; midlife transition and, 59–60; moral judgment and, 83; reasons for return to, 90–91, 129; as transformational, 168; value of developmental theories in, 44–45. *See also* Learning

Elias, D., 27

Environment: cultures of embeddedness as, 185–188; holding, 184–188; perceived, 184; systems theory and, 182–184. *See also* Context

Erikson, E. H., 64, 127–128, 130, 206, 245

Erkut, S., 33

Evans, N. J., 58, 110

Evolving Self, The (Kegan), 47, 64, 185

Expectations, 211–213, 222–223

F

Fagan, M., 249n1

Faith, developmental theories of, 129–130

Family: mixed support from, 189–202; responsibilities to, 105–113, 198–199

Fear, accompanying return to education, 91–93
Feminism, 68, 189, 197
Festinger, L., 184, 216
Finding Herself (Josselson), 68
Fogel, A., 181, 219
Fowler, J. W., 23, 129–130, 227
Fraiberg, S., 24
Frankl, V., 133
Freire, P., 141
Freud, A., 240
Friendship, after mentoring relationship, 35–36, 169–171
Frost, R., 139–140

G

Galbraith, M., 21, 90
Gamson, Z., 44, 160
Garfield, J., 247
General systems theory, 182–184, 252n1
Gibbs, J. C., 128–129
Gilligan, C., 27, 46, 47, 58, 69, 112, 130–131, 132, 158
Goldberger, N., 27, 58, 94, 112, 131–132, 157
Goss, D., 148, 250n1
Gould, R., 47
Gray, M. M., 18
Greene, M., 121
Grinder, J., 210
Growth. *See* Development; Transformation

H

Hall, R., 21
Harris, M., 58
Havighurst, R., 47
Healing, education and, 103, 148, 241, 250n1
Heath, D., 4
Heinz Dilemma, 128
Hennig, M., 21
Herrigel, E., 203
Hiemstra, R., 21

Higgins, G., 250n1
Holmes, C. T., 18
Horizontal décalage, 127
Hoyer, W., 137, 211
Huang, C. A., 97
Hughes, K., 21
Hypothetico-deductive reasoning, 221–222

I

Identity: of adults, 65–67, 185–188; of children, 184–185; new, 150
In a Different Voice (Gilligan), 131
In Over Our Heads (Kegan), 47, 250n1
Individuation, 56
Inglis, T., 241
Inhelder, B., 121
Intellectual development, Piaget's model of, 47, 48, 126–127

J

Jardim, A., 21
Jones, E., 249n5
Josselson, R., 58, 68, 110
Journey: as continuing beyond mentoring, 34–36; in Dante's *Divine Comedy*, 28–34; metaphor of, 4–5, 14–15, 149–150; principles for guiding, 122–124; stories of, 25–28. *See also* Development; Transformation
Judgment, moral, as inhibiting education, 83
Jung, C. J., 17–18, 47, 56, 227

K

Kanter, R. M., 21
Kastendiek, S., 210–211
Keen, C., 21, 139, 238, 249n4
Keen, J., 21, 139, 238, 249n4
Keen, S., 22–23
Kegan, R., 44, 47, 64, 121, 125, 181, 218, 238, 242, 250n1, 251n2; on adult identity, 65–67, 185–188; developmental theory of, 47–48, 64–67, 84–85, 142, 250n1

Kierkegaard, S., 3
Klein, C., 58
Klemp, G. O., 210–211
Knefelkamp, L., 120, 207, 240
Knowles, M. S., 67
Knox, A. B., 4, 47
Kohlberg, L., 47, 128–129, 130, 131
Kolb, D., 228
Kram, K. E., 21
Kremer, J. W., 27, 95

L
Language, 227
Learning: as development, 243, 244; healing and, 103, 148, 241, 250n1; as situated in context, 110–111, 153–154, 251n1. *See also* Adult learners; Education
Levine, S. V., 208
Levinson, D. J., 20, 34, 46, 47, 204; developmental theory of, 46–47, 53–58, 83–84, 142
Levinson, J. D., 20
Liberal arts: end product of studying, 159–160; reasons for taking, 7–11; transformative potential of, 146
Light, R., 222, 239
Listening, 114, 123, 205, 209
Literature: journey stories in, 25–28; mentors in, 17–18, 20, 30–34
Loevinger, J., 47, 85, 129, 149
Lord of the Rings, The (Tolkien), 28
Luna, G., 18
Lynch, A., 21, 44, 90, 207
Lynch, J., 97

M
Maack, M. N., 21
Maher, F. A., 58
Mann, H., Mr., 253n4
Man's Search for Meaning (Frankl), 133
Maps, developmental theories as, 46, 226
Marcotte, R., 237
Marienau, C., 68, 110, 112
Marsick, V., 21

Maturational Processes and the Facilitating Environment (Winnicott), 184
McKeachie, W. J., 211, 219, 228
McLuhan, M., 141
Meaning: developmental theories and, 44–45; search for, 4, 12
Men: challenge offered by, 215, 216; influence of mentors on, 20, 21; reason for return to education by, 91
Mentor (character in *The Odyssey*), 17, 20
Mentoring relationship: adulation in early, 93, 156, 214–215; care in, 165, 175; with close personal ties, 171–175; development as focus in, 239–243; end of, 34–36, 165, 174–175; environment for, 238–240; friendship after, 35–36, 169–171; guiding principles for, 122–124, 176–178; listening in, 114, 205, 209; monitoring, 124, 178
Mentors: advisers as, 22, 32–33, 156–157, 240–242; as archetype, 17–18, 249n1; art of, 246–247; challenge activities by, 206, 216–223; in education, 21–22, 32–36; as gatekeepers, 96; guide for establishing program of, 249n2; as guides, 18–19, 32, 157, 249n5; in literature, 17–18, 20, 30–34; studies of influence of, 20–21, 55, 249n3; support activities of, 206, 209–216; timing of, 176, 252n2; transitional tasks and, 204–205; value of, 243–246; vision provided by, 207, 223–229. *See also* Mentoring relationship
Merriam, S. B., 4, 18, 44, 58, 69, 90, 120, 181, 207, 241, 242
Merton, R., 77
Mezirow, J., 27, 95, 133–134, 177, 207, 219, 241, 242
Midlife transition, education and, 59–60
Miller, J., 69

Missirian, A. K., 21
Modeling, 223–225
Mokros, J., 33
Monomyths, 26
Moral development, Kohlberg's stages of, 128–129
Mullen, C. A., 21, 97, 249n4
Murray, M., 21, 249n2
Murrell, P., 21, 228
Myths, of journey, 25–28

N
National Institute of Education, 222
Neugarten, B., 47
Novak, M., 25, 184

O
Odyssey, The (Homer), 17, 20

P
Palmer, P., 219–220, 244
Parker, C., 120, 207
Parks, S., 18, 21, 27, 69, 118, 135, 238, 242, 249n4, 251n2
Pascarella, E. T., 226
Passet, J., 21
Perry, W. G., 43, 48, 94, 96, 135–136, 148–149, 227, 241; developmental theory of, 48, 74–83, 85–86, 137, 240, 250n3
Perspective transformation, 133–134
Phase theories of development, 46–47
Phillips-Jones, L., 21
Piaget, J., 47, 48, 121, 126–127, 130, 212, 221
Pietrykowski, B., 241
Pirsig, R. M., 246
Plato, 231
Pogson, P., 4, 47, 120
Postman, N., 225
Psychosocial theories of development, 46–47

R
Reeves, P., 120, 242
Relationships: adult learners' network

of, 238, 253n2; teacher-student, 5; teaching as, 15; women's emphasis on, 69, 130–132. *See also* Mentoring relationship
Richards, F. A., 137
Rivers, C., 58
Roche, G., 21
Rogers, C., 95–96
Roodin, P., 137, 211
Rubin, L. B., 58
Rudolph, F., 176, 247
Rybach, J., 137, 211

S
Sandler, B., 21
Sanford, N., 77, 207
Schachter-Shalomi, Z., 225
Schlossberg, N., 21, 44, 90, 207
Schneider, C., 210–211
Schnell, S. V., 130
Schwartz, M., 141–142
Seasons of a Man's Life, The (Levinson), 46, 53
Seasons of a Woman's Life (Levinson), 57–58
Sharing, 170, 214
Shea, F. G., 21
Sheehy, G., 18, 55
Sinnott, J. D., 137
Sisco, B., 21
Specialness, 214–215
Speizer, J. J., 18
Spirituality, teaching giving consideration to, 130, 251n1
Stage theories of development, 47–48, 63–64, 250n1
Stages of Faith (Fowler), 130
Stevens, W., 147
Stories, 23–25; of journey, 25–28
Storr, A., 183, 249n5
Structure, 210–211
Support, 206, 209–216; advocating as, 213–214; effect of, on development, 207–209; expectations as, 211–213; of family/friends of adult learners, 189–202, 238, 253n2;

Support (*continued*)
providing structure as, 210–211; sharing as, 214; specialness as, 214–215
Systems theory, 182–184, 252n1

T

Tarule, J., 27, 58, 94, 112, 131–132, 157
Taylor, E. W., 134
Taylor, K., 68, 110
Teaching: authority accompanying, 94–96; as caring, 246–247; development taken into consideration in, 240–243; dialectical thinking and, 145–146; as relationship, 15; spirituality and, 130, 251n1; suggestions for enriching, 119–121
Teaching and Learning in Communities of Faith (Vogel), 130
Temporizing, 148
Tennant, M., 4, 47, 120
Terenzini, P. T., 226
Tetrault, M. K. T., 58
Thomas, R., 21
Thoreau, H. D., 253n4
Thurman, H., 22–23
Tolkien, J.R.R., 28
Tradition, 225
Transference, 104
Transformation: dialectical thinking and, 137–142; experience of, 134–136; growth as, 125–134; perspective, 133–134; through education, 143–145, 168. *See also* Development
Transformative learning theory, 134, 241–242
Transitions, return to education due to, 90–91
Trust: development and, 128, 206; engendering, 122, 176, 206
Tuesdays with Morrie (Albom), 18, 141–142

V

Vella, J., 219

Vision, 207, 223–229; language for, 227; maps for, 226; modeling for, 223–225; providing mirror for, 228–229; tradition and, 225
Vogel, L., 130
Voice: given to students, 123, 177; as metaphor for growth, 112

W

Waters, M., 18
Weathersby, R. P., 129
Weiler, K., 58
Weinstock, J., 181
"West-Running Brook" (Frost), 139–140
Widick, C., 120, 207
Wilson, A., 251n1
Winnicott, D. W., 67, 184–185
Winston, R. B., 226
Wisdom: embodiment vs. source of, 32; stage theory and, 64
Wolf, L., 21
Women: development by, 46, 55, 57–58, 68, 69, 130–132; family responsibilities of, 105–113, 198–199; leaving home by, 251n2; mentors' influence on, 20–21, 55, 249n3; reason for return to education by, 90–91; recognizing whole life of, 110–112; support offered by, 200, 215–216
Women's Ways of Knowing (Belenky, Clinchy, Goldberger, and Tarule), 131–132
Wunsch, M. A., 21, 22, 33

Y

Yoda, 203–204

Z

Zachary, L., 21
Zucker, D. S., 20, 214
Zweig, C., 149